© 2022 Louisville Urban League
Text © 2022 Louisville Urban League
Artwork © Individual Artists
First Published in the United States of America in 2022 by the Louisville Urban League
1535 W Broadway
Louisville, KY 40203
Phone: (502) 585-4622
www.lul.org

ISBN   978-0-9998831-2-9

Digital edition published in 2022

Cover photo: Tyreson Lancaster, Ty Takingphoto 2021

Photography:
Individual Artists

Design:
Lyndon Pryor: pgdesigns@gmail.com

STATE OF BLACK LOUISVILLE

THE PANDEMIC REPORT

2020-2022

ACKNOWLEDGMENTS

We gratefully acknowledge the many contributors to this project. It would not have been possible without the continued support of our partners, colleagues and donors. We want to express our deepest appreciation to those who donated time and services.

EXECUTIVE EDITORS
Asha French, Ph.D.
Ashli Findley

ASSOCIATE EDITORS
Lyndon Pryor
Sadiqa Reynolds

COPY EDITORS
Asha French, Ph.D.
Ashli Findley
Sadiqa Reynolds, Esq.
Lyndon Pryor

CONTRIBUTORS
Ashli Findley, Lyndon Pryor, Lisa Thompson, Anthony Smith, Butch Mosby, Ricky L. Jones, Ph.D., Marc H. Morial, Kaila Aida Story, Ph.D., Chanelle Helm, Marc S. Murphy, Michael Aldridge, Rashaad Abdur-Rahman, MSSW, Shameka Parrish-Wright, Kevin Cosby, D.Min., Hannah L. Drake, Judge Brian Edwards, Timothy E. Findley, Jr., Representative Keturah Herron, Amber G. Duke, Darryl Young Jr, Dr. F. Bruce Williams, Sadiqa N. Reynolds, Esq., Kish Cumi Price, Ph.D., Marland Cole, Matt Berry, Shashray McCormack, John Marshall, Ed.D., Corrie Shull, Janikaa C. Sherrod, MPH, Dr. Billie Castle, Tony Parrott, Sharise Horne, Armon R. Perry, MSW, Ph.D, Bert Little, Ph.D., Craig Blakely, Ph.D., M.P.H., Brad Shuck, Ph.D., Matt Ruther, Ph.D., Vicki Hines-Martin Ph.D., RN, FAAN, Kevin Dunlap, Jeana Dunlap, Rev. Dr. Jamesetta Ferguson, Johnetta Roberts, Cassia Herron, Celine Mutuyemariya, Cathy Hinko

BOARD OF DIRECTORS
Lorri Lee--Board Chair; John Borders, Yvonne Austin-Cornish, Patricia Carver,Condrad Daniels, Judge Brian Edwards, Vanessa Garrett, Dwight Haygood, Jr., Hunt Helm, Demetrius Holloway, Luther Ingram, Earl Jones, Diane Laughlin, Terryl McCray, Diane Moffett, Brigitte Owens, Diane Porter, Alan Quinkert, Jimmy Ray, Stephen Reily, John Rippy, Kimberly Sisnett, Carolyn Tandy, Neal Thomas, Purna Veer

CONTENTS

115 HOUSING

PATH-1 A PATH FORWARD FOR LOUISVILLE

HISTORY

Louisville Urban League

THE LOUISVILLE URBAN LEAGUE is a nonprofit, nonpartisan, community service organization dedicated to eliminating racism and its adverse impacts on our community. Our mission is to assist African Americans and other marginalized populations in attaining social and economic equality through direct services and advocacy in the areas of education, employment, housing, family development, and community development.

In 1920, just 10 years after what would become the National Urban League, the Louisville Urban League was founded and became a member agency of the local Community Chest. Elwood Street, serving as temporary chairman, appointed a five-person committee to create the framework for the local Urban League. The agency started with $1,000 raised by community residents at a public dinner. Incorporated in August 1921, the Urban League

of Louisville for Social Service Among Negroes eventually became the Louisville Urban League.

The leadership of the Louisville Urban League developed a strategic plan to create and nurture enduring relationships between the League, community leaders, public officials, and the business sector. In fact, the Louisville Urban League is the oldest HUD-certified housing counseling agency in the Commonwealth of Kentucky.

For nearly 100 years, the Louisville Urban League has been a consistent voice and a liaison for the city's underserved and minority populations. It will continue to address current issues and challenges with steadfast and sustainable solutions through direct services and advocacy in the areas of Jobs, Justice, Education, Health and Housing.

EXECUTIVE SUMMARY

Asha French, Ph.D., Editor
Ashli Findley, Editor
Louisville Urban League

This year's State of Black Louisville is a project in recovery and revisioning. We have recovered the essays the pandemic prevented us from publishing in 2020. We have also joined our community members in revisioning a new Louisville in the wake of pandemic grief and redirection. Still, the more things change, the more things stay the same. After all, the essays in this collection provide commentary on many familiar themes discussed in the 2018 edition: health in west Louisville, fair housing and homeownership, Black fatherhood, youth education, mental health, and the role of the church, just to name a few. This year's theme reflects the justice claims that remain steadfast over the span of 2020-2022, from reparations to social distancing.

Why the shift? Because we believe Black Louisville – and Black America, for that matter – cannot face this new, post-pandemic reality without a paradigm shift that includes the recognition, admittance, and disbursement of reparations. Even with the gains we've won since the narrative shift that occurred during the summer of 2020, reparations are still key to bridging the social (and socioeconomic) distance that remains between this city's Black and white residents.

As our authors prove in this collection, the call for reparations is about more than waiting on a government to do for Black people what it has done for other wronged groups. It is also a call to collective action. As poet June Jordan wrote, "we are the ones we have been waiting for." We challenge you to read each essay and take a hard look at what you, as an individual, and your organization can help tackle to make Louisville truly a compassionate city for all of its residents.

INTRODUCTION

Lyndon Pryor, Chief Engagement Officer
Louisville Urban League

Generosity is not justice.

Louisville is a challenging place. On one hand, there is an open acknowledgment of racial disparities, historical oppression, and tough talk about change and equity. Additionally, this community has an abundance of resources — political and financial — at its disposal to make that change happen.

Louisville, after all, is home to several significant initiatives: the first Center for Health Equity in the country, which publishes the Health Equity Report — a seminal work of root causes; the redlining report; the Greater Louisville Project, a public and privately funded research collaboration; and the Anne Braden Institute for Social Justice, to name a few.

Louisville is also home to hundreds, yes hundreds, of multi-million-dollar corporations, headed by wealthy individuals who rest comfortably in this nation's top one percent and who will rest there for generations. It is home to philanthropic organizations with sizable endowments and city officials who largely seem to be of one accord.

Louisville is indeed unique because we know the

history. We have the data and have published the maps. We know the problems, and we have the resources and capacity to solve them.

But on the other hand, knowledge and resources are only two legs of the three-legged stool of true change.

The third is a commitment to justice.

Louisville's problem is that many of those with power, influence, and control of resources lack the will and fortitude to get it all the way done. Change, here, seems to only happen around the margins. We can release a comprehensive report on redlining, but make no substantive changes to housing and investment policies to propel the reversal of redlining's impact. We fund workforce development programs, but not in amounts enough to adequately cover the comprehensive wraparound services families need to truly get on their feet.

We will support investments in supplemental tutoring services for students who are struggling, but not invest in policies and reforms to eradicate the underlying issues of segregation, bias, and instability that make such programs necessary in the first place. We will host clothing drives, blanket drives, and support homeless shelters, but it takes a global pandemic for us to begin to take steps toward proven innovations and interventions for affordable housing.

Yes, Louisville is great at being generous — and in this pandemic that generosity has increased, but we still lack the stomach to be just.

Generosity is about the perceived benevolence of the giver. It is a statement of their kindness, care, and willingness to part with some portion of their wealth or power, even if it costs them nothing. We are conditioned to be grateful for the generous and, on some level, we should be. Truly. But generosity is not justice, and generosity alone will not change community outcomes, erase disparities, or eliminate institutional barriers.

Justice, can.

However, justice — and by extension, equity — requires sacrifice. Real sacrifice. Justice requires an understanding that all wealth and power in this country have been built and distributed on a network of systems designed to exclude and disenfranchise certain people, namely Black, brown, and poor people. In response to that fact, justice requires the giver to feel the impact of their gift in ways that generosity will not. Justice means parting from wealth in ways that will not be recovered. Justice means creating a seat at every table you sit, or perhaps giving up your own. Justice is ceding power to those from whom it has been withheld and being willing to accept the results.

For the 2022 State of Black Louisville report, we continue to look at the core focus areas of the Louisville Urban League: jobs, justice, education, health, and housing. But we do so with a keen reflective look at the past two years. We have asked our contributors to also connect their pieces to the larger conversations of reparations, gentrification, the role of philanthropy, and, in light of the release of "A Path Forward for Louisville", justice.

We discuss gentrification — specifically toxic gentrification — because as investment finally comes to the West End, we can already see concerted efforts being made to maliciously acquire property, displace residents, and subvert Black ownership at every level. We discuss reparations, because there are few modern examples as clear as Louisville that can illustrate the intentional harm done to Black people by various public and private systems in the name of racism. If there was ever a case for redress, it is here, and if there were ever a time, it is now. The role of philanthropy — individual and institutional — is the elephant in the room. Many of the most generous organizations and individuals in Louisville have amassed their wealth in service to, or at least as the beneficiaries of, the very policies and practices at the root of Black suffering. Yet, their giving is confined to the levels of their personal comfort, because generosity never truly costs one their comfort. Justice might. And justice, because there is no real progress without it.

Despite all we have seen and endured over the past two years, in spite of the trauma, pain, indignity suffered by many at the hands of those sworn to serve us all, there is still hope. There is still an opportunity to do what is right, to put this city on a true path towards justice. If only we can muster the courage to do the work.

Black people in Louisville appreciate your generosity, but we deserve justice.

NEW CAREER PATHWAYS TO PROSPERITY

Lisa Thompson, Chief Impact Officer
Louisville Urban League

Google "Kentucky" or "Louisville." Basketball pops up. Look deeper into our economic structures, racial justice heritage, or educational attainment and it's clear that Louisville must deliver disproportionately for Kentucky to keep pace with peer communities to retain talent, attract new business, and develop the great people who live here.

The Louisville Urban League (LUL) leads our city to higher aspirations and achievements through inclusive practice, respect for outcomes, and progress toward informed goals. High workforce participation is vital to strong families, neighborhoods, and the regional economy. Louisville — the city that opened the nation's first African American library — can build a new road to African American prosperity by illustrating that symmetrical and concurrent investments in people and places bring justice and equity. National media is watching.

The Gentrification Experiment is a multiple installment report on "Matter of Fact with Soledad O'Brien." The first installment featured the Heritage West property with O'Brien interviewing the League's President and CEO Sadiqa Reynolds.[1] National intermediaries in community development are focusing on gains being achieved in Louisville's tough environment against the aftermath of redlining, urban renewal, and deep-rooted racial divides.

People and places both need restorative investment. The LUL calibrates these parallel energies, moving capital to key sites while resourcing the potential of residents and stakeholders. It is a leader in integrated strategies. We deliver progress in jobs, justice,

---

1   Matter of Fact with Soledad O'Brien. (2019). Gentrification Experiment: Updating a city without pushing out local residents. Retrieved from https://matteroffact.tv/gentrification-experiment-updating-a-city-without-pushing-out-local-residents-3/

education, health, and housing with special emphasis on the West End.

Here are some new Kentucky outcomes that will have a generational impact. The League doubled its job placements from 251 in 2017 to 512 in 2019. Even more impressive is the increase in economic impact: annualized wage attainment jumped from $5 million in 2017 to $12.7 million in 2019.

Imagine $12.7 million going into neighborhood stores, children's clothing, and groceries — every year. Funding partners made that happen when they invested in the League.

The National Urban League noticed, too, awarding the LUL two of its coveted workforce achievement awards this year. Not only are we placing more people in jobs, but we are placing people in higher-paying jobs with educational and health care benefits almost unimaginable only two years ago.

The LUL provides an equity-driven hybrid with specialized training, national credentialing, and parallel coordination of financial knowledge sharing and holistic health navigation. Clients rebrand themselves through expungement and essential skills learning in tandem so that resumes are strong, truthful, and protect privacy as never before.

The LUL thinks out of the box. We reorganized workforce infrastructure, data collection, and operations. We've booked our first pay-for-placement employment contracts after adding specialized training offerings with new partners like TARC and The Ohio Valley Educational Cooperative. This dramatically changes the career potential for hundreds whose prospects before were minimum wage/part-time jobs.

The West End is changing, and its people can't wait for slow systems to catch up. In 2020 and 2021, as the Norton Healthcare Sports & Learning Center at the Heritage West site and other bold visions are becoming reality, workforce opportunities will continue to mushroom.

Residents must be ready for new businesses to open in proximity — maybe even their own businesses! Financial equity is coming to some of the nation's most entrenched poverty areas. Solutions will make Kentucky distinctive. The LUL's collective and collaborative strategies depend on families securing good incomes that ensure they will not be pushed out of much-loved neighborhoods.

Wealth building, this time, must be possible for all. Kentucky's image thrives or perishes on its motto of "United We Stand, Divided We Fall." Racism divides us, but the Louisville Urban League is uniquely and powerfully positioned to unite us by maximizing the talent and power of Kentucky's people.

We must not fail.

PREPARING THE NEXT GENERATION OF PUBLIC SERVANT LEADERS

Anthony Smith, Executive Director
Cities United

Most local governments' leadership lacks representation from the diverse populations reflective of the communities they serve. They also struggle to attract a diverse pool of candidates with the right skills to serve as the next generation of public servants, helping address some of our cities' most pressing challenges.

Cities United partnered with the mayors of Louisville and Lexington to roll out a bold new initiative combating this lack of representation: the Civic Engagement Fellowship, known as THRIVE in Louisville and COACH in Lexington.

The Cities United Civic Engagement Fellowship is a 24-month intensive engagement program designed to build a pathway for young Black men ages 22–26 to be prepared to serve as the next generation of public servant leaders in their cities and beyond. Fellows are immersed in real-world experiences focused on four key areas: leadership development, community building, narrative change, and policy development and advocacy.

Each Fellow will undergo a series of personal and professional development sessions. Fellows receive ongoing training throughout their fellowship, including the opportunity to earn up to nine college credits. The first 12 months of the program focuses on the Fellows, giving them a better understanding of what they will need to be successful as a public servant. They get to put these new and/or enhanced skills to work during the second half of the fellowship, when they are placed into full-time positions within key departments in city government. At the end of the program, Fellows will become full-time city employees, with the desire and skill set to move into a leadership role.

THRIVE and COACH show what's possible when we stop warehousing our talent in our jails and detention centers and, instead, give them the support, trainings, and opportunities they deserve. We can build a pipeline of civically engaged leaders who are ready to serve in leadership roles within local governments — who will have the needed talent, insight, and experience necessary to help us realize our vision of safe, healthy, and hopeful communities for everyone.

The Civic Engagement Fellowships will help cities address the following:

- **Diversity:** According to the Center for Economic Studies, Blacks were underrepresented in high-wage, local government employment and overrepresented in low-wage jobs in the early years of this study, particularly in the South, but have since become proportionally represented in high-wage jobs on a national level.[1]

- **Attracting and retaining talent**: According to Greater Louisville Inc., Louisville is losing its edge for attracting and retaining talent in an increasingly competitive and global world. Data shows that Louisville has a higher population in age groups 45–65, which means that more of the population will be retiring in the next 20 years than those coming into the workforce.[2]

- **Identifying emerging leaders:** Endowing the next generation of leaders with the skills needed to meet ever-changing personal, economic, and social challenges is every community's most important shared responsibility. The deep-seated "status quo" of how a government should operate is no longer a valid solution.[3]

By addressing the above concerns, you not only build a more inclusive workforce; you create space for those with lived experience to influence policies — policies that will have an impact on their families, other young Black men, and the communities they call home. Keep an eye out for these young leaders. One might be your mayor in the next few years!

1   U.S. Census Bureau. (2014). Center for Economic Studies and Research Data Centers research report: 2013. Retrieved from https://www2.census.gov/library/publications/2014/adrm/ces/2013-ces-research-report.pdf

2   Greater Louisville, Inc. (2016). GROW! Greater Louisville region optimizing workforce. Retrieved from https://www.greaterlouisville.com/wp-content/uploads/GLI-GROW-Talent-Initiative.pdf

3   Harvard Kennedy School. Emerging Leaders [course]. Retrieved from https://www.hks.harvard.edu/educational-programs/executive-education/emerging-leaders

WE ARE INSPIRED BY THE CHARACTER OF JOE HAMMOND

Butch Mosby, President
Sponsor 4 Success Inc.

Joe Hammond opened Joe's Palm Room in Louisville, Kentucky in 1954. This jazz bar grew to be one of the top communal hubs in the United States. Renowned musicians would repeatedly pass through to jam; locals obtained gainful devoted employment; and a colorful community from all walks of life convened. These relationships inspired a thriving life in Louisville and Joe was at the center. He was involved in everything that improved people's lives from the inner workings of the municipal water company, to the neighborhood corner cleaners, and running the governor's campaigns by registering people to vote. While doing so, he was a man of integrity, honesty, humility and generosity. A true gentleman until the end.

We are from the West End, we are Black, we are successful, and there are many of us. We were born in the 70s, grew up in the 80s, left to go to college in the 90s, climbed corporate America ladders in the 2000s, and grew our wealth in the 2010s. Going into the 2020s, we want our 40 acres. We are not really interested in the mule. Keep it!

In this race for building generational wealth, we are winning. We own property, are invested in the stock market, and have businesses, savings accounts, bonds, and life insurance. Some of us even have donor-advised funds, but you don't know us because we no longer reside in Louisville. White flight was followed by Black flight. Yes, we left and dispersed all over the globe because there were limited opportunities. At the time, we did not realize we were targets of redlining, predatory lending, and more. But by the grace of God, we managed to escape the wrath of systematic and deliberate destruction of the neighborhoods we loved.

We intentionally displaced ourselves only to enter a world that was unfamiliar. We found ourselves being the only one. We do admire and celebrate our forefathers for being the first Black something, but

Image: Joe Hammond. Couurtesy of joehammond.org

there is nothing comfortable about being the only Black anything.

However, we are resilient like Joe Hammond, the man who successfully survived urban renewal and became one of Louisville's most influential businessmen. Mr. Hammond was a selfless person whose core life principle centered around dignity for all and improving the lives of others.

While systems were created to purposely strip us of our worth, Joe worked tirelessly to show everyone he touched they were inherently valuable. He built companies to give people jobs and better pay. He guaranteed loans to help young entrepreneurs start businesses. Some of them are still alive. Joe knew if he helped individuals become successful, it would be good for the Black community and good for Louisville overall. That's the kind of man Joe was, and we have found in him the model that ties who we are to what our city, at its best, has been.

Now, we are back collectively to resurrect Joe's character. We are doctors, lawyers, engineers, and business professionals. We are corporate trained, skilled, and organized. We have our own money, and we know how to raise more. Most importantly, we have his playbook.

JUSTICE

BLACK LOUISVILLE'S POLITICAL FUTURE IS BOUND UP IN KENTUCKY LEARNING CRITICAL LESSONS

Ricky L. Jones, Ph.D., Professor and Chair, Department of Pan-African Studies
University of Louisville

Despite obvious cleavages, Black Louisville can never fully culturally and politically separate itself from the city of Louisville. Furthermore, the city of Louisville can never separate itself from the state of Kentucky. This fact presents challenges that profoundly impact the lives and possibilities for blacks.

Even though they lost every other race in the 2019 elections, Kentucky Democrats were understandably excited that Attorney General Andy Beshear was able to barely defeat much-maligned Governor Matthew Bevin. To be sure, Beshear's win was cause for celebration in that a state's executive wields awesome power. That said, there is also reason to caution against unbridled enthusiasm that the Bluegrass State has turned the proverbial corner.

Kentucky still prides itself on being a "blood red state." It is also woefully undereducated (ranking 45th in education nationally).[1] These and other factors create a witches' brew scenario in which a significant percentage of Kentuckians remain entrenched in the past. The "Mad Governor" exited office in December of 2019, but Kentucky will elect more Matt Bevins if it doesn't learn some critical lessons.

The state needs to learn that today's Republicans are lying when they argue they are the "Party of Lincoln." In reality, they are antithetical to the Free Soilers and abolitionists who founded the GOP in 1854. These new guys are more the "Party of Strom Thurmond" than anything else. If Lincoln were alive today, he would steer clear of them and they would demonize him. Support them if you wish, but be informed and truthful about what you're supporting.

On election night, veteran journalist Al Cross reflected that Kentucky experienced a pronounced

---

1   McCann, A. (2020, January 20). 2020's Most and least educated states in America. WalletHub. Retrieved from https://wallethub.com/edu/e/most-educated-states/31075/

political backlash after the election of Barack Obama in 2008. When pressed, he admitted this was clearly driven by a virulent strain of racism still present in Kentucky. Those clinging to that mindset need to learn that we are beyond 1857's Dred Scott decision. Blacks *do* have rights that whites are bound to respect now — and that's not going to change.

Kentucky's Neo-Confederates need to learn that it's not 1895 anymore. Confederate statues reaffirming white supremacy are no longer being erected. They're coming down.

Retrograde folks worried about genetic annihilation need to learn that we're well beyond Kentucky's 1904 "Day Law." Not only are Black, brown, and white kids attending school together, they are becoming friends, dating, marrying one another, and having beautiful little sun-kissed babies. There will be more!

Kentucky needs to learn that Donald Trump lied through his teeth when he bellowed he has saved your "clean, beautiful coal." It's not the 1880s when coal was thriving. Coal is dead and it's not coming back. Accept that and adjust.

Homophobes in Kentucky need to learn that we're beyond the 1960s. Frank Kameny and his compatriots don't have to picket the White House anymore. Bayard Rustin doesn't have to sneak in and out of the South to help Martin Luther King Jr. because of fear of homophobic vitriol — even from the Black community. Accept that LGBTQ brothers and sisters will never hide in the shadows again.

Kentuckians need to learn that we're beyond 1973 and women aren't going back to pre-Roe v Wade barbarism and male domination. Sure, there are some women in the caves and hills of the state who are comfortable with cabals of men stripping them of their right to choose again. However, most modern women do not belong to that poorly-socialized lot. You can't take their shoes away and keep them perennially pregnant and slaving over a hot stove anymore, either. And yes, we're beyond 1920 so women can actually vote to protect their rights now.

Yes, Kentucky has much and more to learn if it wants to truly move into the 21st century. The alternative is to stay its current course and watch the state become an even greater anachronistic laughing stock to which no one wants to move and in which talented natives do not wish to stay.

If Kentucky does not learn these things and more, the fall of Matt Bevin will only be a temporary reprieve for it will elect other politicians who approximate his ideological zealotry, but function with more rhetorical sophistication and social sanity.

When confronted with the question of violence plaguing their communities, Bevin once told suffering Black people in Louisville they should find some preachers, march from block to block, and pray about it. If Kentucky does not change course, Black Louisville and the state will need more than prayer.

"ONCE AGAIN, BLACK PEOPLE ARE FORCED TO BE THE ARCHITECTS OF THEIR OWN FREEDOM"

National Urban League

September 16, 2020, Louisville, KY--Marc H. Morial, President and CEO of the National Urban League, and Sadiqa N. Reynolds, Esq., President and CEO of the Louisville Urban League, issued the following joint statement in response to the unprecedented settlement agreement between Louisville Metro Government and the family of Breonna Taylor.

We have no actuarial to calculate the price of a child's life for a grieving mother, but the family's remarkable achievement could mean that no other Louisville mother must walk in the shoes of Tamika Palmer, Breonna Taylor's mother.

The reforms upon which the family insisted, while enveloped in their own suffering, could have saved Breonna's life had they been in place earlier.

It is not lost on us that once again, Black people — through the gritted teeth of our own trauma and pain — are yet again forced to be the architects and orchestrators of our own freedom. It is long past time for America to recognize that survivors like Mamie Till (Emmett Till), Letetra Widman (Jacob Blake), Michael Brown Sr. and Lesley McSpadden (Michael Brown, Jr.), Gwen Carr (Eric Garner), and Tamika Palmer have been forced to act as instruments of change against systems that simply refuse to see us as human or equal.

It must end.

It is not the responsibility of Black people to repair or dismantle the racist systems that seek to degrade and dehumanize us at every turn, but we will act when those in power will not. In June, National Urban Affiliate, the Louisville Urban League released A Path Forward for Louisville, a comprehensive blueprint for addressing the needs of the Black community. Breonna's family and counsel yesterday highlighted this plan as a model to be supported and followed.

We join the nation in anticipating the prompt decision of Kentucky Attorney General, Daniel Cameron. We join Breonna Taylor's family in demanding that Louisville Mayor Greg Fischer and other public and private sector leaders invest in the priorities outlined by a grieving mother and the community that stands with her. Now more than ever, our country must blaze a path forward.

STATEMENT ON KENTUCKY REDISTRICTING MAPS

Louisville Urban League

January 19, 2022. The recent redistricting proposals announced by the Republican State Legislature is just another example of efforts being made across the country by members of the GOP to undermine the principles of our democracy and silence the voices of our most disenfranchised communities.

While Kentucky House Republicans would lead you to believe their proposed legislative maps amplify the voices of Black voters in the Commonwealth, they in fact do the opposite. This Republican redistricting proposal replaces current Kentucky House districts with solid majority Black voting age populations with districts that only meet the threshold of so-called "Majority-Minority" districts by combining the Black and Hispanic voters who in most of the proposed district barely comprise a majority of the voters in the district. In addition, this redistricting plan in one case completely eliminates one majority Black district and replaces the majority of its voters with white voters and in another attempts to deceitfully fool the public by claiming a district has a significant minority population by counting the prisoners in a correctional facility. This redistricting bill is nothing more than an effort to ensure Republican victories that benefit the powerful at the expense of the powerless at the ballot box.

Similarly, in the Kentucky Senate legislative maps for state senate and congressional districts were devised in secrecy by its leaders without the input of the citizens of Kentucky and in some cases at their expense in favor of the selfish desires of others. For example, the First Congressional District, whose western most point touches the Mississippi River and runs along the Kentucky-Tennessee border, now curves around the Second Congressional District into Central Kentucky and includes Franklin County, where Frankfort is located. Drawing this congressional district in this manner disenfranchises the people of Franklin County and prevents them from being able to vote with others in their region for federal representation that will address their needs and concerns. As State Representative Derrick Graham of Frankfort said "What it does to Franklin County is wrong. Franklin County was and is and always will be a part of Central Kentucky, both geographically and in spirit...Franklin County shares a lot of bonds with Western Kentucky, but we should not share a congressman." In light of the way these maps were presented to the public, the Louisville Urban League along with our other partners in the search for justice, fairness, and equality are continuing to analyze the proposed legislation presented by the state Senate.

New electoral maps are drawn every 10 years as part of a redistricting process triggered by census data that determine the allocation of political power, representation, and resource access at every level of government across the country. According to the 2020 census data, Kentucky's predominantly Black, urban districts including Louisville, Lexington, Northern Kentucky, and Bowling Green all experienced population increases. And yet, at first glance, the proposed maps do not reflect that trend.

If these maps are approved as is, this would divide communities and weaken minority voters' power. We must ask ourselves, what purpose do Republicans have to create these new maps if not to manipulate the voting system and increase party seats?

We must ensure our district maps are drawn fairly and are truly reflective of population trends. The Urban League of Louisville denounces these efforts from state House and Senate Republicans and urges Governor Beshear to veto this plan and engage voters in the redistricting process. We are a nonpartisan organization focused not on political parties but political power.

STATEMENT ON THE BREONNA TAYLOR CASE DECISION

Board of Directors
Louisville Urban League

OCTOBER 4, 2020. The city of Louisville, our city, has been at the epicenter of the nation's historic reckoning on racism -- for four straight months. Citizens of Louisville have been protesting on the street all that time demanding Justice for Breonna Taylor.

We know that organized, peaceful protests for a righteous cause have a long history of bringing positive change in our democracy. And we know, too, that when police aggression or opportunistic vandals turn protests violent, the righteous moment and the righteous message are hijacked -- and our cities are convulsed.

Louisville has been boarded up for too many months. Our hearts have been boarded up for too many centuries. This is us. It is time to turn the page. On Tuesday, Sept. 15, Louisville Metro settled a wrongful death civil suit with Breonna Taylor's family – a settlement that includes important reforms to address police accountability and to start to heal the broken relationship between LMPD and the community. We commend Breonna Taylor's mother, Tamika Palmer, and the family's attorneys, for pushing to include these reforms. We commend our local government for embracing these reforms. These measures are a win for our city, paid for with Breonna's blood.

Then on September 23, Kentucky Attorney General Daniel Cameron announced that no one will be held responsible for the death of Breonna Taylor. Instead, one officer was indicted for firing wildly, thereby endangering her neighbors. Fifteen hours of audiotaped recordings of grand jury testimony confirm that no case involving her death was even presented.

This is not what we were expecting from the attorney general's protracted investigation, and at least one grand juror was disappointed as well. This does not feel like justice to us, or to many people in our city. Where do we go from here?
If we can't find justice in the criminal justice system, we must pursue a new direction for our

governmental policies and societal values. We must preserve and honor the life of Breonna Taylor, and also the life of David McAtee, in our collective memory. We must move our community forward, in her name and in his name, to a better future.

Now is the time for every Louisvillian -- and especially those with power and resources -- to address and atone for more than 400 years of hateful, exclusionary and violent policies and practices intentionally designed to exclude Blacks from society and from the economy. There is no denying that this is our history – and there is no denying that it reaches into our present reality still today.

The city of Louisville will never thrive if so many of our Black citizens experience trauma and fear and pain, every single day. The city of Louisville will never thrive if so many of our Black citizens remain excluded from the economy, left with unmet basic needs, and over-policed on top of it all. The anxiety and frustration are real -- and exhausting. The anger is valid. The rage has been righteous.

Fortunately, there is a positive path forward for the community we love. In June, the Louisville Urban League and more than 50 other local organizations issued a 20-page document that sets out immediate and specific actions to help dismantle systemic racism so that Louisville can become a city where everyone thrives, according to the hierarchy of needs.

The Path Forward document calls for a $50 million Black Community Fund to:

- Support existing and new small businesses in West Louisville;

- Transform vacant properties into affordable housing and create a path for Black ownership;

- Create significant educational support to close the achievement gap;

- Access mental health professionals to support those who are struggling with the stress, the trauma and the crushing demoralization of racism.

The Path Forward document calls for social workers to help police with societal issues that aren't, in fact, criminal. This was addressed in the settlement and we expect this work to grow.

The Path Forward also includes solutions for Jobs, Justice, Health, Housing and Education – areas in which the Louisville Urban League has proven expertise and an infrastructure of established programs and partnerships that get results for real human beings, with human hearts, human minds, human faces, and human souls.

You can read the entire Path Forward Document here. And we hope you will.

The Louisville Urban League calls on Louisville Metro to engage with this document, to reopen the budget to support the many organizations doing the good work in our city, and to move these initiatives forward.

Louisville needs a new narrative – and that narrative must tell the story of a city where everyone can flourish in our multiethnic, multiracial, multireligious community.

Our downtown, and our hearts, have been boarded up for too long. It is time now to reopen our city, our hearts and our minds. The dividing walls of hostility must now come down, so we can walk -- abreast -- into a better community that champions justice for all. Let us move forward together. We cannot let this moment pass.

Lorri Lee, Chair
Yvonne Austin-Cornish, Ph.D.
Neville Blakemore
John Borders, Esq.
Renee Buckingham
Yulonda Burris
Billie Castle, Ph.D.
Dr. Brigitte Owens
Condrad Daniels
Hood Harris
Dwight Haygood, Jr.
Hunt Helm, Ph.D.
Demetrius O. Holloway, Esq.
Earl Jones
Diane Laughlin, Esq.
Terryl McCray
Diane Porter
Alan Quinkert
Stephen Reily
John Rippy
Neal Thomas
Purna Veer

STATEMENT ON THE DEREK CHAUVIN VERDICT AND THE ARREST OF DENORVER GARRET BY LMPD

Sadiqa N. Reynolds, Esq., President and CEO
Louisville Urban League

April 20, 2021. Like many across the country, the Louisville Urban League was anxiously awaiting the verdict in the criminal case against Derek Chauvin for the murder of George Floyd. We were hopeful that we would see what should have been certain justice, but we were all too aware that we have been let down many times before. With the announcement of a guilty verdict, we are relieved that this is not one of those times. While we recognize the gravity of today's verdict, we also understand that there is a needed sea change in policing in America. We grieve with the families that have lost loved ones to police violence in Minneapolis, Louisville, and across this country.

There will be attempts to analyze the trial, praise the prosecution, and there will most certainly be calls for peace and reconciliation. But we must start with an acknowledgment of the compound traumas and grief that racist and oppressive systems inflict upon Black bodies and minds at every possible turn. George Floyd should not be dead. His murder was an act of trauma on our community and country. The time it took to fire, indict, and arrest Derek Chauvin

further inflicted trauma. This trial, in and of itself, while masterfully executed, has levied a level of trauma for those of us with the strength to endure it.

It is also important to recognize something critical that happened during this trial. We saw several law enforcement officers take the stand against one of their own and without equivocation or serious rebuttal, declared the actions of a fellow officer to be wrong, contrary to training, and unacceptable. In the presence of so many other examples of "good cops" turning a blind eye to bad behavior by their colleagues, this is but a small departure from the norm, but it is not insignificant. And we hope that it is a sign of what is possible and a new direction for our country.

Of course we know we have further to go. Like many of you, we were alarmed and disappointed by a video showing the arrest of Denorver "Dee" Garrett, who was brutalized by the Louisville Metro Police during an attempt to detain him for an alleged misdemeanor offense. After a year of social unrest and active response to the killings of Breonna Taylor and David McAtee, it is disheartening to see these types of brutal tactics still in use against members of our community. This type of misconduct only serves to erode what little public trust remains. Our system of policing and the incestuous nature of the relationships between judge, prosecutor, and police must be dismantled and redesigned anew. But that will not happen overnight. It will require real work and commitment to change.

In the meantime, we have always known that officers are capable of better. We see it in the treatment of other communities every day. And while the testimony of officers in the Chauvin trial and the statements by Louisville Police Chief Erica Shields are positive steps toward accountability, the reality remains that we must deal with the violent inequities of treatment before they happen and challenge a system of implicit bias that is prevalent in police, policy, and behavior.

If this city, or this country, is to ever know prolonged peace, every person, regardless of race, zip code, or alleged act must be met with humanity. And when those principles are breached; truth, transparency, and justice must swiftly follow.

As always, we remain hopeful and stand ready to serve. We encourage community members to use the mental health resources at their disposal or to email health@lul.org if you need referrals. We are experiencing compound trauma and we cannot ignore the impact it is having on our community.

POLICING IS GOING TO KILL ITSELF

Sadiqa N. Reynolds, Esq., President and CEO
Louisville Urban League

May 10, 2021. No officer should have fired a weapon because no officer should have been there! Breonna Taylor was not a suspect. It was a botched and unnecessary raid.

The same ego that sent police into Breonna Taylor's home is the ego that sent them to 26th and Broadway, where David McAtee was killed. Mattingly got shot because he and his fellow officers made a horrible decision based on lies and arrogance.

I advised the Mayor to fire all 4 officers, not because I thought he would win the personnel hearings, but because it would have cost the city less to fight that battle than the one I knew we'd spend the next year fighting in the streets.

We don't want what the system says is fair; we want what is just. We wanted them all fired and charged. Of course, we're not saying a Mattingly firing would have been upheld in a hearing. In fact, it probably wouldn't have, and that's the point. Any system that won't build in fail-safes to rid itself of those who intentionally, unintentionally, or with reckless disregard, harm those they are sworn to serve and protect, is so flawed, it doesn't warrant preservation. Any system that would allow the government to enter the home of a sleeping woman and kill her because of the response of a frightened occupant—in a stand your ground state—is flawed beyond repair. Any system that allows an officer to write a book and profit from the notoriety gained by his hand in killing an innocent woman, is beyond despicable and conducive to a culture that lacks humanity.

Before you say it, I know there are good officers, but at the end of the day, they are rowing an oar off the side of the Titanic. The damage is in the structure of the ship itself, so even the good ones aren't enough to fix the system of policing in America.

Morale is down, and departments should not and will not be able to recruit. So ultimately, policing is going to kill itself. And what will we do then? We will create something that can serve and protect in every zip code for every person.

We need alternative responders right now. We need another number to call for something that requires immediate attention but not a gun.

Who do I call when a man is harassing my child as she walks our dog? We don't need the harasser to be shot, but we need intervention. Use the money for beds for drug treatment and supportive services, which is at the root of his problem. Use the money to pay for mental health workers and to build $400 a month rental housing in every zip code in our city.

Take the money we spend on law enforcement and use it to recruit culturally competent teachers, to lower student-teacher ratios, and to focus on closing the achievement gap. Use the money to ensure that every K-12 student has baseline knowledge and technological capability. Invest in universal Pre-K for every child in Louisville.

But first, use the money to prosecute the police. Arrest the cops that killed Breonna Taylor.

BLACK QUEER DISSENT IN DANGEROUS TIMES:
HOW THE INCLUSION OF BLACK LGBTQ+ COMMUNITIES IS INTEGRAL TO BLACK LIBERATION

Kaila Aida Story, Ph.D., Audre Lorde Endowed Chair in Race, Gender, Class & Sexuality Studies
University of Louisville

"…we sometimes find it difficult to deal constructively with the genuine differences between us and to recognize that unity does not require that we must be identical to each other"
--Audre Lorde[1]

I didn't know my dream job was in Louisville, Kentucky. I arrived in July of 2007 and in the fifteen years that I have lived here, I have met so many extraordinary people. The Black community I encountered upon my arrival was a committed, vibrant, and politically visible one. However, I did notice that in many of the most progressive Black spaces throughout the city, and within many Black activists' initiatives, plans of action, and the like, there wasn't any attention called to Black identity and how it intersects with gender identities and/or sexualities. I noticed that these supposed radical Black spaces weren't inclusive of Black queer and Black trans voices or issues. Many Black churches, organizations, and Black elected officials didn't even make mention of the intersections of race and sexuality in their calls to action, sermons, community upliftment programs, or empowerment endeavors.

At the same time, I also noticed upon my arrival in Louisville that we also had a dedicated, vivacious, and civically engaged LGBTQ+ community, but there was also an absence of Black queer and Black trans seats at the table. Many White LGBTQ+ leaders didn't speak to how sexuality was complicated by race when it came to everyday things such as housing and public accommodations, and they certainly didn't have Black queer and Black trans lives in mind when it came to their festivals, community proposals, or entertainment venues.

The intersection that I have lived within and throughout my life was an intersection that community-engaged folks erased, silenced, or, worse, didn't even think about. Throughout the years I've spent here, I have been extremely pleased to

---

1   Lorde, Audre. (1985). "I Am Your Sister: Black Women Organizing Across Sexualities in Burst of Light" in Freedom Organizing Series No. 3, Issue 3. New York: Kitchen Table Women of Color Press.

see not only the Black LGBTQ+ community grow, but I have also been able to bear witness to the ways that Black LGBTQ+ community leaders and changemakers have influenced both progressive Black collectives and spaces as well as White LGBTQ+ communities, expanding their conceptions of unity and illuminating the fact that how far we can go as a unified community rests upon our commitments to diversity and inclusion.

As the Audre Lorde Endowed Chair at the University of Louisville, I have been able to create original curriculum that explores the intersections of race and gender. This has allowed my students who live at these intersections feel seen in ways that they haven't been in exclusively Black cis-het and/or White queer and trans spaces, organizations, and groups.[2] My podcast Strange Fruit, now in its eighth year of production, delineates on what it means to be both Black and queer, discusses the realities of Black trans identities, and explores how these lived experiences intersect with anti-blackness, anti-queerness, and transphobia, making its listeners know and understand that their lives matter and are valued.

Over my fifteen years in Louisville, I have been pleased to see longtime Louisville activist and one of the founders of the Fairness Campaign, Dawn Wilson, become a Human Relations commissioner, showing our city how much better it can become if the voices of Black trans women are taken into account and amplified. I have witnessed Victoria Syimone Taylor, a Black trans woman, become the city's premiere disc jockey, spinning at almost every venue within our great city.

I have seen both Alé Betts, founder, owner, and director of Waterworks Dance Theater and John Keen, founder, owner, and director of Keen Dance Theater — two Black gay men — create public spaces that allow Black queer, Black non-binary, and Black trans folks feel as if they can bring their whole selves into a space when they want to express themselves through dance.[3] I have seen my former student, Talesha Wilson — a Black lesbian woman — become the founder and director of her own organization Diversity at the Table. She has taken the knowledge learned within the classroom to create a collective that teaches our Black, queer, and trans communities about Black feminism and Black queer studies in accessible and decipherable ways. I have also witnessed Black lesbian art curator Tamika Dozier engender art shows for Black queer and Black trans people where they are showcased and exalted as works of art.

We also have within our great city Black gay Pastor LaRon Hobbs of Fresh Fire Church and Black lesbian Pastor LaShondra Lias-Lockhart of Heart of an Evangelist, creating Black religious spaces that are inclusive to those of who are of faith and also are Black queer- and trans-identified — reminding us that our Black queer lives are inherently divine.

We have Black lesbian personal stylist and women empowerment advocate RaeShanda Lias-Lockhart, who created All is Fair in Love and Fashion, showing our city that there are benefits to body inclusivity. We have Black and queer visual artist Prince Crittenden, founder of the Blacks Organizing Strategic Success (BO$$) collective, who creates networking and socializing events for everyone in our community. We have the Black queer founder of Sis Got Tea, Arielle Clark, who created her teahouse with the aim of creating a space for Black queer and Black trans folks

---

2   According to Queer Dictionary, the term Cis-Het is used as both an adjective and a noun. The term describes a person who is both cisgender and heterosexual. A person is cishet if they identify with his or her assigned-at-birth gender, as well as identify as heterosexual. See: http://queerdictionary.blogspot.com/2014/09/definition-of-cishet.html.

3   According to Queer Dictionary, the term Non-Binary describes a person who does nor identity within a gendered binary of male and female; woman and man. See: http://queerdictionary.blogspot.com/2014/09/definition-of-nonbinary.html.

to gather, network, and build relationships without the backdrop of nightclub setting.

We also have Black gay wedding planner and event coordinator Darien Dickerson-Green of Special Moments Wedding and Event Planning, ensuring that Black queer and Black trans people within our community can have access to affordable and diverse packaging when it comes to planning for their special day. We have the hilarious and talented radio personality at WCHQ (100.9 FM), Shane Dickerson-Green, who amplifies our experiences and realities as Black queer and Black trans people, and Black lesbian activist Desi Carr, who created our city's first ever Black queer and trans awards and the Black Gay Games. We have Hannah Drake, a Black lesbian and world class poet who reminds us that racism and homophobia lives right here in our city. While all of these endeavors, businesses, houses of worship, etc., are wonderful, they are all individual and/or small collective efforts. One of the most exhilarating moves in the right direction was the 2022 election of Keturah Herron, former policy strategist for Kentucky's ACLU, Herron, an out Black lesbian became the state's first Black LGBTQ+ person to hold the office of State representative. As a former policy strategist for the ACLU, Herron also created Breonna's law, in honor of Breonna Taylor, Louisville EMT who was murdered by LMPD using a no-knock warrant. Herron ensured through Breonna's law that no-knock warrants became an impossibility for law enforcement in the city of Louisville, preventing any future violent and terroristic harm to come to Black Louisvillians in this way.

So, you ask what is the state of Black queer & trans Louisville? What do we need from this city? We need the support of Black organizations and Black elected officials to fund Black queer and Black trans futures. That means hiring Black queer and Black trans people and supporting Black queer and Black trans initiatives with dollars and resources. We need the Black community in Louisville to make sure that the missions of their churches are expressly inclusive of Black queer and Black trans people. We also need monies donated to expressly Black queer and Black trans causes. The same way White gays and Black cis and straight men and women have structural and institutional support and power, we as Black queer and Black trans folks need the same thing. If you call yourself a Black religious leader, Black civic leader, or a Black politician, your politic must include Black queer and Black trans people. If it does not, then I hope you realize that your politic is inherently anti-Black.

Our current times are too terrifying to forget how integral Black queer and Black trans people have been and are to the history and contemporary manifestations of Black liberation. From James Baldwin to Bayard Rustin. From Lorraine Hansberry to Langston Hughes. From Angela Davis to Audre Lorde. From Marsha P. Johnson to Laverne Cox and Janet Mock. We must always remember that where we are now as a global Black community has everything to do with them and has everything to do with us. I urge all of us who say we are committed to Black lives and Black communities to heed the word of Audre Lorde: "…we sometimes find it difficult to deal constructively with the genuine differences between us and to recognize that unity does not require that we must be identical to each other". Our differences, nuances, and intersections should always remain a source of celebration and unity, and not one of silence or erasure.

In solidarity!

COVID WAS THE CATALYST:

THE REAL DRAMA OF THE HAVES AND HAVE NOTS

Chanelle Helm

I'm writing to correct the story of 2020. You know the storytellers are not going to tell it right. They're going to tell a story about this political moment in Louisville's history and tie it to the mainstream news. By the time they finish, Breonna Taylor's death will look like the catalyst for a multiracial movement. But the catalyst was COVID.

COVID changed the way that non-white people were seen, non-working people were seen, non-housed people were seen… all the have nots. COVID changed the narrative around what and why the have nots don't have.

See, your have nots were tired. Fed up. The majority of people in the streets weren't Black. The majority of people in the streets were white folks. I don't want to talk about the 50% of white people that were there in guilt. I want to recognize the other 50% of white people who have always been there- the ones who were ready for this shit. They knew they were living a legacy of a lie and they knew that it was a legacy that gave them more privilege and power just because of the color of their skin. These allies were tired of the system and motivated to work with the people who were most impacted. They were with the brown folks as they migrated from Central America to America and got their children taken away. They've been with Black folks since John Brown.

These are the folks who have modeled for their peers what it means to collectively move in an action. Together, we began to do what was necessary for folks in mutual aid. And so as time passed from the total shutdowns of February, we began building out these mutual aid spaces for our most vulnerable–Black elders.

We were also in an election year. We were serving elders who were proud of the fact that they fought to vote in any type of way they fought to vote, even by existing. Yet, they were vulnerable to being left out of national conversations because of their lack of access to the story generators. Our elders kept saying, "People have forgotten about us." We weren't hearing about their daily lives on the news. We weren't getting ready to see them on anybody's Facebook video because they didn't have access to that. They could not access the narrative generator.

So access became the war. That's what set off the uprising of 2020. At stake was access to the narrative, access (or lack thereof) to hope, access to safety, access to health care, and access to food. Access in general was like an inverted pyramid; those on the bottom had the least access to everything from the narrative to food.

Black elders were the people at the bottom of this pyramid, and while we are coordinating mutual aid efforts to take care of them, Breonna Taylor is shot and killed. Our partners in mutual aid remain our partners in this fight for justice, and we keep meeting with our folks in adjacent spaces to make sure we're on the right track. In short, the fight for justice for Breonna was built in the company of elders whose lived experiences and wisdom informed our actions, our strategies, and even our responses to sabotage.

For example, when rumors were circulating about my involvement in actions that had nothing to do with Black Lives Matter, I'd get advice from Ms. Tammy[1], one of the elders I look up to, would pose the same set of questions: "Who are these people? At the end of the day, do they even know who the fuck they are?"

I'm boosting her question for all of us who are interested in doing movement work. Do we even know who we are? Do we know the shape of social hierarchy in Louisville, and do we know why we are positioned where we are? Do we even know the danger of telling a "2020 Turning Point" narrative that ends in celebration?

2020 was a very active year, but the first step in political movement isn't even action. The first step is making sure that we understand where we are. The second step is being able to move from a place of inaction to producing strategies and steps that take care of everyone. We just can't have community without making sure that our most vulnerable are okay.

For the most vulnerable groups, there has absolutely been no change since 2020. Corporatization got stronger, and people moved into legal and nominal organizations. They built themselves off of work from the have nots, and the have nots still continue to have not at a greater disposition. The gap got wider; it has not closed just because people who already have access to communications, to news, and to resources are able to utilize those resources. The skills are still not there, and people are still dead and dying.

So there is nothing phenomenal about where we are after 2020. Reparations are still very much needed. Until we get those, the small amount of reparations in the form of investments are still useful. But they're not closing this gap in any type of way whatsoever, so it's just been really interesting to watch investors call for celebrations of success. They are calling for numbers that defy stereotypes about communities that have always been under scrutiny. They want to see the impact of their investments on the stereotyped people they watch from afar. Meanwhile, the have nots still do not know that their investments exist. They have no access to those spaces of celebration for a ship that, to them, hasn't yet come in. I'm sure the elders we continue to serve are wondering what our celebrations even mean. I'm sure they are wondering, like Ms. Tammy, if we even know who the we are.

---

1   Name changed to protect anonymity.

AMERICA AS A 14-YEAR-OLD WHITE BOY

Marc S. Murphy, Political Cartoonist
Courier-Journal

There have always been walls in America. I grew up on the White side of the tallest wall. The wall drawn sometimes with red lines and other times with prison-barbed wire.

It was also a wall of lies. It still is.

I was raised in Eastern Kentucky in a White public high school in the 70s. Not segregated, just isolated. The history of America we were taught had two colors only when it was comfortable.

In 1976, in the midst of the nation's self-congratulatory celebration of its 200th birthday, Alex Haley published *Roots*. The movie series of the book became the country's first Must-Watch TV event.

Haley's family's American saga, which began with the kidnapping and enslavement of a young African man, could have been an opportunity to reflect upon the country's original sin. After all, we were in the midst of the country's Bicentennial orgy.

Instead, we were asked to write our own stories. To stand on Kunta Kinte's bloody shoulders, already scarred by the slave master's whip, and revel in our own — no matter who we were or how much money we had — privileged roots.

The moment passed. The history books remained the same: White Americans telling other White Americans which Black people they should know. Whom they should cheer for. And why.

ARE WE NOT ENTERTAINED?

My 10-year-old, basketball-crazed self was invited to cheer the Harlem Globetrotters because they were the Clown Princes of Basketball.

We celebrated Henry Aaron — I took his name in my Catholic Confirmation! But we weren't told he had to start his career in the Negro Leagues in Indianapolis. Also as a Clown.

We only learned later that as he chased Babe Ruth, White Americans threatened his life daily, and that when he ran those record-setting bases, he feared the exuberant White fans running with him were there to kill him.

It was not reported that when the great Bill Russell travelled with the Celtics to Lexington, he couldn't share a meal or a bed with his own teammates. Whites were never told the hate didn't begin at the Mason-Dixon Line, either, and that 11 NBA titles were not enough for the white people of Boston to accept him.

And it's impossible to for me to describe to you now how much Louisville's Ali was hated by the white people even in his home state, on our side of the wall. Even in death, among the millions of words floating like butterflies above his funeral service, little was said in white America about the segregation he, his brother, his family, and their neighbors all knew. That there was a wall around his part of the city, too. So when he said white Americans were his Opposers, not the Viet Cong, the words landed like his lightening fists, caught white America by surprise, and hurt.

We should not have been surprised. We built the wall. Every generation from which the truth is withheld makes that wall higher until an American football player kneels and white America asks why, ignores the answer, then demands that he stands. Like a clown.

RECOGNIZING THE LEGACY OF SLAVERY

Michael Aldridge, Former Executive Director
ACLU of Kentucky

For nearly 100 years, the American Civil Liberties Union (ACLU) has been our nation's guardian of liberty, working in courts, legislatures, and communities to defend and preserve the individual rights and liberties that the Constitution and the laws of the United States guarantee everyone in this country.

Whether it's achieving full equality for LGBT+ people, establishing new privacy protections for our digital age of widespread government surveillance, ending mass incarceration, or preserving the right to vote or the right to have an abortion, the ACLU takes up the toughest civil liberties cases and issues to defend all people from government abuse and overreach.

Yet, until June of 2019, the ACLU was on the sidelines as advocates championed the fight for reparations. Through the leadership and advocacy of those in the reparations movement, the ACLU has finally come to accept what so many have known for so long: if this country ever wants to achieve true racial justice, then we must examine the impact and legacy of slavery — and start to make amends through reparatory justice.

Slavery didn't end in 1865. Its legacy continued for decades through Jim Crow laws and Black Codes, and it lives on through mass incarceration, police brutality, and de facto segregation in Louisville and every part of the country.

America used 246 years of enslaving millions of African Americans to enrich, develop, and create our nation. The United States was a slaveholding country for nearly 100 years longer than it has been a truly "free" one. We cannot ignore the continued afterlife of slavery today.

The ACLU has committed to fostering a dialogue to reach consensus on what reparations should mean. On a national level, the ACLU supports H.R.40, the "Commission to Study and Develop Reparation Proposals for African-Americans Act." The bill was first introduced by former Congressman John Conyers in 1989 and has been re-introduced by Congresswoman Sheila Jackson Lee as the lead sponsor. An important (and historic) Congressional hearing was held on the bill in June 2019, but the legislation has yet to be called for a vote.

On the local level, the ACLU of Kentucky is eager to follow the lead and help raise the voices of advocates who have championed the fight for reparations for decades. These actions are part of a larger commitment to racial justice affirmed by a Values Statement developed for our 60th Anniversary in 2015. The statement reads as follows:

> **Sixty years ago when Jim Crow segregation was the law, the ACLU of Kentucky was founded, and the new organization's legal docket was designed to address racial discrimination. We have defended communities of people who have been historically, and are currently, denied certain rights that are extended to others. These communities continue to endure discrimination and inequality denying them access to resources and opportunities.**
>
> **Racial justice has been, is now, and will continue to be central to our mission. We dedicate ourselves to pursue cases designed to have a significant and wide-reaching effect on communities of color, to work in coalition with other civil rights groups and local advocates to lobby in local and state legislatures, and to support grassroots movements. Through these efforts, we strive to educate and empower the public on how racism impacts the issues that we work on — including but not limited to criminal justice reform, reproductive freedom, LGBT and immigrants' rights — and we commit to consider racial impacts when making hiring, policy and administrative decisions for the organization.**

FROM SLAVERY TO LYNCHINGS TO STRUCTURAL VIOLENCE

Rashaad Abdur-Rahman, MSSW
CEO/Founder Racial Healing Project

Black Louisville, and Black America for that matter, have never been the beneficiaries of humanizing narratives that center our strengths, assets, and contributions. It has always been up to us to tell our own stories. To protect our own truths. This is no different when we talk about complex community challenges like violence.

More often than not, the causes and blame of community violence are laid to rest in total at the feet of youth and families. It is argued that, surely, if people would simply change, then we would no longer have these issues. Worse yet, based on this kind of oversimplified analysis, we have pursued a path for decades that has accelerated mass incarceration — an economically incentivized, exponentially ballooning prison population in our country. This has made the United States the country with the largest amount of incarcerated people in the world, and Kentucky the state with the second highest number of incarcerated parents.[1]

The return on investment in the interest of public safety is non-existent.

More insidious is that these actions occur in an intellectual and historical vacuum. Without question, there is far greater understanding in our city of how policies like redlining have created the economic and social inequities that sustain problems like housing instability, poverty, violence, and mass incarceration. Any cursory examination of the data reveals the racialized nature of these outcomes (e.g., it is impossible to have a fact-based conversation about poverty without discussing racism). Yet, we fail to characterize these broad sweeping actions as violence in and of themselves.

These forms of violence, called "structural violence," have devastated generations of families in Louisville.

---

1   Kentucky Youth Advocates. (2018). Minimizing the Impact of Parental Incarceration on Kentucky Kids. Retrieved from https://kyyouth.org/minimizing-impact-parental-incarceration-kentucky-kids/

It is a form of violence with population-level reach and ramifications impacting not only quality of life, but the ability to live at all.

What our city has yet to do is two-fold: understand the legacies of slavery and lynching represented in the current legal system (structural violence), and make a broad commitment to anti-racism (structural peace). There are approximately 4,084 documented lynchings stretching across our country,[2] and countless more we may never know. This form of White supremacist, extrajudicial terrorism took place across Kentucky counties as well with the expressed goal to guarantee the dehumanization and sub-class status of Black people.

This kind of anti-Black brutality does not simply go away. Rather, it evolved in ways that remain codified in law. It's why being poor and innocent leads to worse outcomes in our legal system than being wealthy and guilty. It's why institutions like the death penalty, cash bail, and lifetime felony disenfranchisement must be dismantled. Their very existence invalidates what the U.S. Constitution claims to guarantee, and the preservation of any hierarchy sustains all hierarchies.

In addition, we all have the opportunity to commit to anti-racist principles and practices. Scared of the phrase "anti-racist"? You shouldn't be. It would be more productive to be afraid of elements in our groups, organizations, and lives that perpetuate outcomes stratified by race. In fact, an anti-racist framework provides for the universal guarantee of equity across dimensions inclusive of gender, age, religion, sexual orientation, etc.

Embracing anti-racism is committing to a journey where we no longer accept that the color of one's skin or their zip code should determine one's quality of life. This commitment is demonstrated in how we deploy resources, what policies we enact, which policies we dismantle, our mission statements, our holiday dinner table conversations, our places of worship, the choices we make in the voting booth, our art, committing to reparations, and whatever portion of Earth you happen to be occupying.

It's the way we have to start living. Inequity and injustice have been done, and it can be undone. By us. In this city. Now.

---

2   Equal Justice Initiative. (2017). Lynching in America: Confronting the Legacy of Racial Terror. Retrieved from https://eji.org/reports/lynching-in-america/

ORGANIZATIONAL COMMITMENTS TO ANTIRACISM RING HOLLOW
(BUT THERE IS ANOTHER WAY)

Rashaad Abdur-Rahman, MSSW
CEO/Founder Racial Healing Project

Breonna Taylor, David McAtee, George Floyd, Ahmaud Arbrey, and countless other Black folks have been murdered by police, the National Guard, and other white supremacists who endorse the notion that Black life is conditional; Black life may be permitted to exist insofar as it does not transgress white comfort and dominance. I doubt the Louisville police officers who murdered Breonna could meaningfully articulate the ways their actions demonstrate their allegiance to white dominance (or would care to), but their powers of articulation are hardly required where their actions have sufficed.

This is the crux of the matter: **words will never outweigh actions**.

Throughout the summer of 2020, we saw a "mad dash" by Louisville organizations to articulate a commitment to justice. We saw these statements carefully (or not so carefully) crafted by the mayor's office, the business community, nonprofits, universities, and even philanthropy. The commitments made covered the imaginable spectrum, from racism as a public health issue to the standard "DEI" (Diversity, Equity, and Inclusion) fare. Paradoxically, many organizations embraced antiracism as a new ideal with little evidence of understanding that paradigm. Nonetheless, the commitments being made seemed endless. Websites were updated, Black faces were on the front of brochures and materials, and a few Black faces were welcomed onto the boards of some organizations. Was this substantive or, as they say in Texas, "*all hat and no cattle?*"

What the research tells us is that, overwhelmingly, these efforts are uniformly ineffective and fail to produce real change. First, any organization that ostensibly seeks to end racial inequity, yet fails to deal with white supremacy, by definition cannot succeed. Srivastava and Francis[1] completed research indicating that any attempts to do racial equity work while avoiding the impacts of white culture create barriers to success. The authors point out that the invisibility of whiteness allows white people to remain passive participants and unimplicated, while placing excessive burden and emotional labor onto Black and Brown folks who suddenly become objects of knowledge to be displayed, interrogated, or dismissed. Additional research conducted by Robinson[2] illustrates how white supremacy thrives in organizational settings by establishing and sustaining one set of rules and expectations (often unofficially) for white employees and another set of rules for employees who are Black, Brown, Indigenous, etc. Another lesson we can learn from the research literature is that an essential ingredient to successfully reduce racial inequity is to redistribute power in the organizational setting[34] (Alfred, 2001; Bell et al., 2018). It makes sense that if there are separate rules which reward proximity to whiteness, that there must be a disruption of that reward loop. This kind of disruption requires the creation of new power structures.

If all of this sounds like something you haven't heard before, it is likely because the vast majority of DEI endeavors rely on interventions that are several decades obsolete and have been sterilized in corporate settings. Unfortunately, many DEI approaches continue to rely on what is called the "contact" hypothesis[56]. The contact hypothesis promotes the idea that if White people simply had greater contact with Black, Brown, Indigenous, and other people of color, this contact would be enough to humanize us in the eyes of White folks and therefore result in more humane treatment by said White folks. Sound familiar? It should. We have been told that if police just spend more time in the Black community, then they won't harass or shoot us as much.

We have had over 400 years of "contact" on this continent and several hundred more prior to the colonization of these lands. We can see plainly with our own eyes that the contact hypothesis is not correct, yet corporate DEI approaches continue to rely on it almost exclusively. This should tell us something, fundamentally, about the lack of desire to really solve these problems. It should also evidence that actions in Louisville have yet to demonstrate the commitments and words that were spoken over two years ago. I don't think organizations in Louisville could articulate how central the contact hypothesis is to their thinking, but as we observed earlier, actions will suffice. We must be clear eyed to the reality that the resilience of white supremacy is in part due to the ways many continue to benefit from it. Oppressive white supremacist institutions like police departments and jails enjoy large city budgets because they **benefit** elected officials who seek to remain in office by touting "public safety." Foundations continue to pay out less than 5% of their total assets (despite earning 6% to 8% on

1   Srivastava, S., & Francis, M. (2006). The problem of 'authentic experience': Storytelling in anti-racist and anti-homophobic education. Critical Sociology, 32(2 – 3), 275 – 307.

2   Robinson, O.V. (2014). Characteristics of racism and the health consequences experiences by Black nursing faculty. The ABNF Journal, 110 – 115.

3   Alfred, M. (2001). Expanding theories of career development: Adding voices of African American women in the white academy. Adult Education Quarterly, 51(2), 108 – 127.

4   Bell, M. P., Leopold, J., Berry, D., & Hall, A.V. (2018). Diversity, discrimination, and persistent inequality: Hope for the future through the solidarity economy movement. Journal of Social Issues, 74(2), 224 – 243. https://doi.org/gdtb24

5   Goldberg, D. (1993). Racist culture: Philosophy and the politics of meaning. Cambridge, MA: Blackwell.

6   Hiranandani, V. (2012). Diversity management in the Canadian workplace: Towards an antiracism approach. Urban Studies Research, 2012, 1 – 13. https://doi.org/gb8fsk

their investments) and call that "charity" because it provides tax **benefits** to the elite while growing their wealth indefinitely. Large corporations champion "DEI" on the surface because it **benefits** their image, while continuing to prioritize shareholders and record profits at the expense of Black and Brown communities. *I don't believe what you say because I see what you do.*

There is good news, I promise! It isn't too late. There are effective organizational strategies that can turn words into meaningful actions. Studies at the intersection of organizational change management and antiracism indicate that if you can analyze whiteness, disrupt harmful practices, and redistribute power in an organization that these approaches can be transformative. That is certainly easier said than done, and it does require a great deal of courage to weather the push back that accompanies any threat to white dominance. However, there are powerful examples of organizations that have made real commitments and are engaged in the necessary work to make justice in their space a reality. These case studies are becoming more abundant and serving as proof points that courage and clarity can shift the ground you are standing on.

We must believe that it is, in fact, possible to break the back of white supremacy. It can be done. It requires us to stop doing what feels safe, or what caters to the comfort of white folks in white dominated spaces. If Louisville organizations felt morally compelled to produce statements, I would simply ask what more these organizations are compelled to do. The feel-good statements, the "safe" DEI committees, the new websites…these things are all deeply insufficient. Our work requires a new paradigm that does not preference the comfort of a white audience. Moving at the pace of "when they are ready" is a failed strategy, surely, we can see that. This new paradigm must preference justice, human rights, and shared liberation urgently. I will end with a quote from the artist and activist Lilla Watson, "If you have come here to help me you are wasting your time, but if you have come because your liberation is bound up with mine, then let us work together."

BLACK LOUISVILLE AND PRETRIAL INCARCERATION

Shameka Parrish-Wright
The Bail Project

The Bail Project is a national, nonprofit, revolving bail fund with local networks that focus on disrupting pretrial incarceration by paying unaffordable cash bails. We collect needs-based data to know who our clients are and to monitor their progress and case outcomes as they navigate the judicial process. We started this work in Louisville in May 2018. Over 1,600 clients later, we have seen that the need for our services are great.

We work with community partners to help connect clients and pay bails, including the Louisville Community Bail Fund and the Louisville Metro Public Defenders (who provide 95% of the referrals we receive). It's important to note: less than 20% of our clients ask for more services and, more importantly, almost all clients have better outcomes. Most just need to get out of jail as soon as possible to keep their jobs, housing, family, health and sanity.

Undoubtedly, Black, brown, and poor people are disproportionately represented in our local jails and prisons. We know that 80% of the people in our local

jail are held pretrial. Even more staggering, most Black people in Louisville become justice-involved as the direct result of alleged traffic violations.

The state of Black Louisville when it comes to reducing pretrial incarceration is this: do not be pulled over for any reason by any means necessary.

Our very first client, a 67-year-old Black man, had the deck stacked against him because he lives and frequents west of 9th Street. It is no secret our city's West End community is plagued with over-policing. He has been pulled over more than ten times in the last two years for vehicle registration and car insurance issues. He assumed his insurance was tied in with his mortgage payments.

When we interviewed him at the jail for our project, he was so broken and visibly confused. When we got involved and paid his $800 bail, he was also sick and lacking the medications he needed, so much so that he had to be hospitalized immediately after we got him out. His case was resolved when he was able to produce paperwork verifying his new insurance. Yet, he continues to be pulled over because once you get pulled over in a vehicle like his in the West End, it happens over and over again.

I know this to be true on a personal level. My husband James was pulled over when we lived near 37th & Broadway. After that first encounter, he was soon pulled over a second time. Finally, after the third time, I told him to sell that truck and he hasn't been pulled over since.

There is no way to prevent "driving while Black" in Louisville. There are also many factors that contribute to the incarceration of Black, brown, and poor people like low wages, homelessness, landscape, hunger, and limited public transportation.

At The Bail Project-Louisville we try to offset the biggest issue people have in getting to court: transportation. It's a major barrier for our clients, so we offer free bus and rideshare rides to their court appearance dates. This, paired with court reminder calls and texts, has been most effective in reducing failure to appear rates. We must change the narrative that when someone misses court, it's because it's intentional.

Pretrial incarceration for Black Louisville is also attributed to implicit biases in our judicial system when it comes to bail setting. Two people can be charged with the same exact offense and mirror in age and justice involvement, but if one is Black, more often they are given a higher bail and/or stricter conditions of release. Black boys and men are far more impacted by higher bails and harsher jail sentences.

It seems unbelievable, but someone could literally start with a traffic ticket and end up with a felony — especially Black and brown people.

Everyone in Jefferson County is a stakeholder. We want judges that readily use every option they have in their judicial discretion toolbelt to give everyone their day in court, to grant opportunities for less punitive toutcomes, and to restore faith in the judicial process. We need lawyers — especially prosecutors — to recognize their power of influence in the courtroom and to support restorative justice practices at every level. We need the community to continue to build awareness, diligently researching the systems that impact us. We also need the community to support support the organizations that work hard to hire, counsel, house, treat, and stop recidivism for those impacted by incarceration.

We thank our growing list of community partners including Louisville Showing Up for Racial Justice, Louisville Family Justice Advocates, Louisville Urban League, Presbyterian Church USA, Louisville Metro Public Defenders and, especially, Attorney Ted Shouse, who is working pro bono to keep our revolving community bail fund going strong by fighting forfeitures of monies when people miss court.

None of our work happens without community. From access to the local jails; to meeting clients through Louisville Metro Corrections; to being able to process bails in bulk through the Administrative Offices of the Court; it will take all of us and more to end cash bail and help people get on with their lives … because poverty is not a crime in our compassionate city.

AMERICA'S FORBIDDEN ZONE

Kevin Cosby, D.Min., Pastor/President
St. Stephen Church/ Simmons College of Kentucky

The 1968 science fiction blockbuster *Planet of the Apes* was a movie about a future world turned upside down. Astronauts somehow had transcended *chronos* and landed on a strange planet where the social order that they knew on earth had been inverted. On this new planet, humans held the status and privilege of apes, while apes had the status and privilege of humans. Apes were the predominant species while humans were oppressed and enslaved.

But the movie based on French novelist Pierre Boulle's 1963 novel *La Planète des singes* was more than a movie about a strange future world where apes rule. It also was a movie about what happens when history is covered up.

The movie centered around a section of the planet called, "The Forbidden Zone," a restricted region where both apes and humans were forbidden to enter. All sectors of society from civil to religious cautioned against entering the Forbidden Zone. Nevertheless, at the end of the movie, astronaut George Taylor (portrayed by Charleston Heston) took his intellectually undeveloped female companion and ventured to enter the Forbidden Zone. And when one of the primate leaders was asked by a fellow primate what Taylor would find there, the leader replied, "He will find his destiny."

The most poignant scene in the movie is when astronaut Taylor sees the Statue of Liberty protruding from the ground. It is then that Taylor realizes the true history of the planet. This was once a planet controlled by humans that had come under primate domination after a nuclear explosion. The nuclear fallout inverted the natural order — placing the apes in a hegemonic role above humans.

The Forbidden Zone was deemed a dangerous place because the truths it concealed exploded the myth of ape supremacy and human inferiority.

The movie addressed many of the dominant themes of the turbulent 1960s. There were concerns about the danger of nuclear weapon proliferation and Cold War politics. However, the primary theme of the movie was the issue of racial hierarchy and human ignorance regarding how these racial grades came to exist. The movie was an allegorical commentary on how America's racial history has been covered up.

When it comes to our racial history, most Americans live in the "Forbidden Zone," because discovering America's true racial history will explode the myths of white supremacy in all its forms and establish for Black American Descendants of Slavery (ADOS) a unique justice claim with the United States government and society.

The ADOS movement was founded by Yvette Carnell, a graduate of Howard University who served as a congressional aide to Senator Barbra Boxer, and Antonio Moore, an attorney practicing in Los Angeles. The ADOS cause is driven primarily online through their podcasts, Breaking Brown.com and Tone Talks.

ADOS promotes the following assertions:

1. Native Blacks in America who are the descendants of slaves should be designated as a unique and distinct category of Americans. Grouping ADOS with other groups to form a broad and ambiguous new category – people of color, minorities, multicultural, disadvantaged groups, distressed groups – waters down the unique experiences of native Blacks. Terms such as these lack specificity and are mere decoys designed to divert attention from the unique justice claims of native Blacks.

2. Blending native Blacks with other groups camouflages the progress of ADOS. For example, by using such broad categories, school boards can present distorted reports on minority students' progress and success because minority groups include Asians, East Indians, and White Latinos. But when ADOS is singled out apart from these groups, the data does not look as compelling.

3. ADOS is a distinct group because no group in America has experienced similar levels of government-sanctioned oppression as native Blacks. Here are some of the distinctions:

    -   Native Blacks are the only group that did not come to America voluntarily.

    -   Native Blacks have been denied our humanity by the federal government. We were designated as 3/5ths of a person in the U.S. Constitution. The Dred Scott Decision of the U.S. Supreme Court determined that native Blacks, "had no rights that the white man was bound to respect."

    -   Native Blacks were slaves for 246 years, deprived of the right to enjoy the fruit of our own labor.

    -   Native Blacks were denied the right to participate in government.

    -   Native Blacks are the only ethnic group denied the right to vote.

    -   Native Blacks are the only group by law denied the right to get an education.

    -   Native Blacks are the only group to fight in all of America's wars, but whose mother country never fought against America.

    -   ADOS forebears have been in America since 1619, one year before the arrival of the Mayflower. We have been in America longer than 99 percent of all other ethnic groups.

    -   Free Black labor was the foundation of America's wealth and prosperity.

    -   Native Blacks are the only racial group denied the right to conduct business in communities beyond our own.

ADOS seeks narrowly focused policies that address the unique experience and justice claims of the American Descendants of Slaves. The primary policy ADOS advocates is a program of reparations that has as its intent to close the Black-White racism wealth gap. Whites have 10 times more wealth than Blacks.[1] This is directly attributable to the fact that Blacks were exploited through slavery, sharecropping, and convict leasing. Not only were Blacks exploited by these practices, but they were also excluded from the government programs that created the White middle class and the wealth disparity. The New Deal and the Fair Deal created the White middle class.

But while Whites were getting a new deal and a fair deal, Blacks were getting a raw deal.

Just like the humans on the planet of the apes, in every social and economic measurement, Blacks are at the bottom. Whites are 60 percent of the population, yet they control 90 percent of the wealth. Blacks who can trace their lineage back to American slavery are 13 percent of the population, yet control only 2.7 percent of the wealth.

According to research conducted by Prosperity Now and the Institute for Policy Studies, by the year 2053, the median level of Black wealth will equal zero.[2] [3] White family median wealth is now $133,000, while Black family median income, minus depreciating assets, is $1,700. Blacks almost have no wealth upon which to draw at times of crisis or emergency. Blacks are worse off financially today than they were in 2000. The median income for Black households at the new millennium was $41,363; today that median is $39,490.

Despite the successes of the Civil Rights Movement and the U.S. having had its first Black president, African Americans are doing worse today than we were 50 years ago. In 1968, unemployment for blacks was at 6.7 percent. In 2017, it was at 7.5 percent. These numbers are, in fact, much higher when factoring in Blacks who are incarcerated.

Black home ownership has leveled since the 1960s, which was 41 percent then; today, that figure sits at 40 percent. Meanwhile, Black incarceration rates tripled between 1968 and 2019.

Imagine two drivers taking the 6,000-mile trip from New York to Los Angeles. One driver is given a 4,000-mile head start. After being told to wait, the second driver is allowed to begin his journey. The first driver is wondering why the second driver is behind. He was never told he was given privileges that the second driver did not receive. He is unaware that the second driver was held back to work so he could pay for the first driver's gasoline and automobile. The first driver deduces that the second driver is behind because he is lazy and takes too many rest stops or he simply isn't smart enough to read a roadmap. The facts are concealed that the second driver not only was held back but also paid the price for the first driver's success.

Most Whites never think about how the conditions of gross inequity came to be for Blacks. Part of the privilege that Whites have in America includes

1   Hanks, A., Solomon, D., & Weller, C.E. (2018, February 21). Systematic inequality: How America's structural racism helped create the black-white wealth gap. Center for American Progress. Retrieved from https://www.americanprogress.org/issues/race/reports/2018/02/21/447051/systematic-inequality/

2   Prosperity Now. (2017, September 11). Black and Latino households are on a short road to zero wealth, hollowing out America's historic middle class. Retrieved from https://prosperitynow.org/blog/black-and-latino-households-are-short-road-zero-wealth-hollowing-out-americas-historic-middle

3   Institute for Policy Studies. (2017, September 11). Report: The road to zero wealth. How the racial wealth divide is hollowing out America's middle class. Retrieved from https://ips-dc.org/report-the-road-to-zero-wealth/

playing the colorblind card, which wipes their mental memory clean of centuries of racism. The new racism in America is colorblind, which seeks to downplay the importance of race as though it doesn't matter. Yet, amazingly, most Whites tend to be very color conscious when it comes to who they marry, the neighborhood in which they live, the church they join, and the friends they choose.

The myth of a colorblind society is further reinforced by the racial virtual reality of television. The racial harmony depicted in advertisement and mass media are not representative of the real-life experiences of the great majority Americans. Three quarters of Whites in America cannot claim one friend from another race.[4] Even if the virtual integration we see in media existed in the real world, that would not solve the problem of fundamental racism in America – the racial wealth gap.

ADOS seeks reparations. The agenda calls for a new deal for Black America which includes, but is not limited to:

- Set asides for American descendants of slavery, not "minorities."

- Once affirmative action is streamlined as a government program only and specifically for ADOS, the program should be fully reinstituted.

- The protections outlined in the Voting Rights Act are essential to protecting the rights of ADOS in America. Reinstituting the protections of The Voting Rights Act is a key part of our agenda.

- Successful entrepreneurship requires capital, therefore, the ADOS agenda demands that 15 percent of SBA loans be distributed to ADOS businesses.

- A multi-billion-dollar infrastructure plan targeted to ADOS communities including, but not limited to, the Black Belt, Flint, Michigan. A Reuters examination published in 2016 found 3,000 cities with poisoning rates higher than Flint.

- The Justice Department must also institute protections which exact heavy fines and federal criminal prosecution for future offenders of environmental protections.

- Mass incarceration has wreaked havoc on Black American families. We demand an immediate assessment of the numbers of the ADOS prison populations at the state and federal levels. We also demand that there be review if punishment is being levied at unfairly high levels on ADOS based on gender and race for similar crimes to other groups. We demand that there be real prison reform in the form of investment into counseling, job training, and rehabilitation for our incarcerated.

- ADOS calls for legislation to triple the current federal allotment to Historically Black Colleges and Universities (HBCUs). The federal government must fully endow HBCUs at a dollar amount that meets the budgetary needs of each institution. In addition, ADOS students who attend HBCUs should receive a discount in the form of a 75 percent tax credit. ADOS who choose schools outside of the HBCU network should receive a 50 percent government funded credit.

---

4   Ingraham, C. (2014, August 25). Three quarters of whites don't have any non-white friends. The Washington Post. Retrieved from https://www.washingtonpost.com/news/wonk/wp/2014/08/25/three-quarters-of-whites-dont-have-any-non-white-friends/?arc404=true

- According to a study by Rutgers University professor Hal Salzman, American colleges graduate more tech workers than tech companies need, hence the H1-B program reduces opportunities for ADOS searching for careers in technology. The government must strictly limit the number of H1-B Visa workers tech companies that flow in each year.

- Audit banks for patterns of racial discrimination in lending, and require these banks to extend loans to ADOS businesses and lending to Black businesses and institutions.

- Mandate that the government's advertising budget include Black media and incentivize through legislative action that all major companies spend 10 percent of their advertising budget with ADOS media in exchange for tax credits.

- ADOS college debt should be forgiven in the same way losses were forgiven for the banks on Wall Street.

- A health care credit to pay for medical coverage for all ADOS.

- H.R.40 must be rewritten to include reference to ADOS as the recipient group, cash payments, and additional supportive measures implemented.

Through Simmons College of Kentucky, Louisville has become the *de facto* national headquarters of the ADOS movement. In October 2019, Louisville hosted the ADOS national conference, and [served as host again in 2021]. In November 2019, the *New York Times* featured a cover story about the Louisville conference and the movement.

Kentucky is an excellent location to give stronger

footing to the ADOS movement, given the state's aggressive role in suppressing the ability of native Blacks to have all of the rights and privileges of their White counterparts. After Emancipation, the Commonwealth of Kentucky passed a number of laws that were expressly designed to deny equal opportunities to Black people.

Between 1866 and 1960, at least nine miscegenation laws were passed in Kentucky, reinforcing the prohibition against marriage or cohabitation of mixed-race couples. Multiple laws were passed during this same timeframe to prevent Blacks from having access to the same education, goods, and services as Whites.

In 1912, Kentucky passed a law that "Residential Building permits for building Negro houses in white communities, or any portion of a community inhabited principally by white people, and vice versa prohibited. Penalty: violators fined from $50 to $2,000, "and the municipality shall have the right to cause said building to be removed and destroyed."[5] Further, all schools were required to be racially segregated (1934) and there were to be no state funds distributed to non-segregated schools (1957).

The law prohibited Whites from marrying any African American who is more than 12 percent African American (meaning having a blood relation up to the third generation to an African American). Penalty of not following this law was a felony that was punishable by imprisonment in the state penitentiary up to five years.

African Americans were allowed to attend white colleges and universities (1950) only if comparable courses were not available at Kentucky's African

---

5   Wikipedia. (n.d.). List of Jim Crow law examples by state: Kentucky. Retrieved from https://en.wikipedia.org/wiki/List_of_Jim_Crow_law_examples_by_state#Kentucky

American college in Frankfort, Ky., and the school's governing body had to approve of this act.

All businesses were prohibited from permitting any dancing, social functions, entertainments, athletic training, games, sports or contests on their premises in which the participants are members of the White and African-American races. All public parks, recreation centers, playgrounds, etc. were required to be segregated (1956). The race of each candidate was to be written on the ballots (1956).

In the minds of most Americans, eliminating racism means Whites liking Blacks. If ending racism is defined as a matter of liking one another, then in the words of author Nancy DiTomaso in *The American Non-Dilemma* are true: "Most Whites conceive of racism as a people who harbor ill will toward nonwhites doing bad things to them" (pg7).[6] By relying on this definition, Whites can absolve themselves of being considered racists because they can say, "I harbor no ill will toward Blacks, neither have I done any bad things toward Blacks." In fact, they might say, "I detest any White person who does."

Ending racism is not a matter of Whites beginning to like or accept Blacks, but rather Whites lifting Blacks from the dungeon to which White America consigned Blacks beginning with slavery. We will never fix racism until we have the courage to cross over into the forbidden zone of American history and see the brutalities and blocked opportunities that have prevented Blacks from enjoying citizenship as full Americans with all rights and privileges.

Racism is a power dynamic that Whites have with

Blacks. Racism is White control of a disproportionate amount of wealth, power, and resources gained through historic injustices against Blacks. The dilemma for Blacks is that it is a history that White America has taken to the forbidden zone. Not only is it a history about which Whites are woefully ignorant, it is a history about which Whites are *willfully* ignorant. William Faulkner once said, "What we don't have the courage to fix we simply ignore."

America's ignorance of race is willful. Immediately after the end of Reconstruction, a group emerged called the Daughters of the Confederacy. Essentially, their goal was to rewrite racial history in America. The tragedy of Daughters of the Confederacy is how they were able to spread this disinformation into the curriculum of school systems across America. When one factors in 246 years of slavery, along with another 100+ years of slavery, Black descendants of slavery have a unique justice claim.

For the past 30 years, there has been a bill in Congress called H.R.40, introduced by Michigan Congressman John Conyers in 1989. The bill did not call for reparations; it called for the study of slavery in America. For thirty years, the bill has not been able to get out of committee. To do so would mean going to America's forbidden zone. Going to the forbidden zone would mean rejecting the myth of White exceptionalism as well as the myth that Black suffering is the result of inherent laziness and inferiority.

South African theologian Allen Boesak observed, "It is absolutely imperative for the oppressor to preserve their innocence, just as it is imperative for

---

6   DiTomaso, N. (2015). The American non-dilemma: Racial inequality without racism (p. 7). New York: Russell Sage Foundation.

the oppressed to destroy it."[7] Most Whites will do everything to avoid the forbidden zone of American history. Those who venture there are accused of living in the past or stirring up racial hostility. We are accused of being an angry Black man or woman. We are ostracized and excluded from opportunities and jobs.

If you are trying to get our nation to the Forbidden Zone, expect, in the words of Robin Deangilo, "silence, defensiveness, argumentation, certitude, and other forms of pushback." No White person gets to Forbidden Zone without intentionally deciding to go. Nothing in White space will ever create an awareness of a Forbidden Zone. But for those who dare to venture into this unchartered space of American history, I suggest a few books, movies, and documentaries:

Books

- "The Half Has Never Been Told: Slavery and the Making of American Capitalism" by Edward Baptist. Basic Books, 2014

- "White Rage: The Unspoken Truth of Our Racial Divide" by Carol Anderson. Bloomsbury USA, 2016

- "When Affirmative Action Was White: An Untold History of Racial Inequality in Twentieth-Century America" by Ira Katznelson. WW Norton & Co Inc., 2005

- "The American Non-Dilemma: Racial Inequality Without Racism" by Nancy DiTomaso. Russell Sage Foundation, 2013

- "The New Jim Crow: Mass Incarceration in the Age of Colorblindness" by Michelle Alexander. The New Press 16, 2012

- "Frederick Douglass: Prophet of Freedom" by David Blight. Simon & Schuster, 2018.

- "Southern Baptists and Southern Slavery: The Forgotten Crime Against Humanity" by Alvin Carpenter. Amazon Digital Services LLC, 2013

Periodicals, Articles, and Research Reports

- "The Case for Reparations". Ta-Nehisi Coates. The Atlantic, June 2014. https://www.theatlantic.com/magazine/archive/2014/06/the-case-for-reparations/361631/

- "The Case for Funding Black Led Social Change". Susan Taylor Batten. Association of Black Foundation Executives (ABFE), 2017. http://www.blacksocialchange.org/wp-content/uploads/2017/02/BSCFN-Case-Statement.pdf

- "Foreclosed". Ryan Cooper and Mat Bruenig. The People's Policy Project, 2017. https://www.peoplespolicyproject.org/wp-content/uploads/2017/12/Foreclosed.pdf

- "Dreams Deferred". Chuck Collins, et al. Institute for Policy Studies, 2019.

- https://inequality.org/wp-content/uploads/2019/01/IPS_RWD-Report_FINAL-1.15.19.pdf

- "Billionaire Bonanza". Chuck Collins, et al. Institute for Policy Studies, 2017. https://inequality.org/wp-content/uploads/2018/11/Billionaire-Bonanza-2018-Report-October-2018.pdf

- "The Road to Zero Wealth". Emanuel Nieves, et al. Prosperity Now, 2017. https://prosperitynow.org/resources/road-zero-wealth

---

7   Boesak, A., & Hansen, L., editors. (2009). Globalisation: The politics of empire, justice, and the life of faith (p. 69). Stellenbosch: Sun Press.

- "What We Get Wrong About Closing the Racial Wealth Gap". William Darity, et al. Duke University, 2018 https://socialequity.duke.edu/sites/socialequity.duke.edu/files/site-images/FINALpercent20COMPLETE%20REPORT_.pdf

Movies and Documentaries

- "Twelve Years a Slave"

- "Reconstruction" (PBS/Henry Louis Gates)

- "Slavery by Another Name" (based on the book by Douglas A. Blackmon), PBS

- "Eyes on the Prize" (PBS)

- "13TH", Ava DuVernay (Netflix)

Immersing yourself in this material will help you discover what is in the forbidden zone of America's racial divide. It will expand your perspective, create much-needed empathy for America's racial victims, and move you toward asking yourself the critical questions essential to change:

- Why?

- Why are things the way they are?

- Why do I live in White space while Blacks live in poor space?

- Why do Blacks only have a fraction of the wealth that Whites have?

- Why are so many Black men in jail and so many few Blacks in STEM careers?

Without going to the forbidden zone of American history, we are left to conclude that the defect is intrinsic to Blacks themselves and not how society has been structured to pick the winners and losers solely on the basis of race.

- Why not?

- Why not commit ourselves to fixing America's 400-year-old race problem?

- Why not move beyond the superficialities of kumbaya relationship to true justice, repair, and equity in the distribution of the opportunity and resources?

- Why not empower all people to exercise self-determination in order that they might realize their full potential?

- Why not me?

The primate leader in *Planet of the Apes* knew that George Taylor would find his destiny in the planet's Forbidden Zone. We too shall find our destiny as we embark on the chartered path of our country's forbidden zone of history!

MY OLD KENTUCKY HOME

Hannah L. Drake
Author, Poet, Spoken Word Artist, Activist

Last year, I had the privilege to teach a workshop on Music/Lyrics & The Movement at the Children's Defense Fund Freedom Schools in Knoxville, Tennessee. It was such a beautiful sight to see hundreds of young Black leaders coming together to study, learn, grow, converse, share, listen and ultimately, pause, take a breath, and then exhale. These young people accepted the call to help facilitate and impact the next generation of young leaders and game changers. Many of the instructors work in communities that have been ravaged by drugs, violence, and poverty, yet they are committed to making a change. This was wonderful for me to see because lately the narrative of change, revolution, and reform has been whitewashed.

The Freedom Schools was birthed out of the Civil Rights Movement under the leadership of Marian Wright Edelman. Despite any narrative that is being told, it is young Black people that drew the blueprint for revolution.

Every morning, the Children's Defense Fund Freedom Schools' retreat started with a Harambee session — a time for celebration and encouragement. Harambee is Swahili for "all pull together" and that is what we focused on during the workshops, how we can all learn and grow together. We spoke of our pain and sorrow, but also of our joy and happiness. I left the Freedom Schools training feeling energized and believing that I could run on and see what the end will be.

On the way home to Kentucky, my daughter and I decided that we would stop and get something to eat. No sooner had we pulled off the exit, a truck decked out with a Confederate flag made its way in front of us.

And it hit me that the safety, insulation, and liberation

I felt at Freedom Schools was gone. I was back in my old Kentucky home.

My old Kentucky home, a state that remained neutral during the start of the Civil War.

My old Kentucky home, a state that was a slaveholding state that benefited economically from the suffering of countless Black people.

My old Kentucky home, where two cities, Louisville and Lexington, were major slave markets that profited from selling Black bodies down the Ohio River.
My old Kentucky home, land of tobacco crops cultivated by slaves.

My old Kentucky home, where over 100 Black men and women were lynched.

My old Kentucky home, where in the 1850s, 23% of White males owned slaves.

My old Kentucky home, where Kentucky protected the right to own slaves.

My old Kentucky home, where a Black man was lynched in Louisville because a White woman felt threatened because he asked was her husband home?

My old Kentucky home, one of three states that rejected the 13th Amendment and didn't ratify it until 1976.
My old Kentucky home, where by 1860, Kentucky had the third-largest number of slaveholders of any southern state, and nearly one-fourth of Kentucky's families owned at least one slave.

My old Kentucky home, the title of the official song of the Bluegrass State since 1928 that was not modified to change the word "darkies" to "people" until 1986.

And in 2018, as my daughter and I pulled into the Taco Bell parking lot, my daughter did not want to go inside and asked that I use the drive-thru. I asked her why and she said, "I do not want anyone to spit in my food if they see that I am Black."

Here, in my old Kentucky home.

My old Kentucky home, where Reverend William Barber, along with hundreds of other protestors of the Poor People's Campaign (a campaign fueled by economic justice started by Dr. Martin Luther King Jr. and the Southern Christian Leadership Conference), was denied access to the Kentucky State Capitol unless they went in two at a time.[1] When I saw the photos, I was angry, embarrassed, and ashamed. The images looked as if Kentucky has rewound time, perhaps to a time that it thought it achieved greatness.

What are we doing, Kentucky?
What are we becoming collectively as a state?

Is this what we want to be known for — a state that stands on the wrong side of history?

When our grandchildren and great-grandchildren read about Kentucky in the history books, will they be proud of us? What will be written about us? What images will be shown? Who are we as a community of Kentuckians?
I challenge you, Kentucky, to finally make a decision.

---

1   Schreiner, B. and Lovan, D. (2018, June 4). Anti-poverty group denied access to Kentucky Capitol. Lexington Herald Leader. Retrieved from https://www.kentucky.com/news/local/article212527724.html

Draw a line in the sand because this time, you do not have the luxury of claiming neutrality.

Either we are going to be what we say we are or we are not.
Either we are going to respect Black lives, or we are not.

Either we are going to provide sanctuary for immigrants, or we are not.

Either we are going to care about the health of Kentucky residents, or we are not.

Either we are going to tear down/remove and place Confederate statues in a museum with historical reference and not just relocate them to other parts of the state, or we are not.

Either we are going to treat teachers with respect and dignity, paying them what they are worth, or we are not.

Either we are going to stand on the principles Kentuckian Muhammad Ali spoke of — Confidence, Conviction, Dedication, Giving, Respect, and Spirituality — or we are not.

As fellow Kentuckian, Florence Reece asked, "Which side are you on?" As the Good Book says, "I know your deeds, that you are neither cold nor hot. I wish you were either one or the other!"

How long do you want to remain lukewarm, Kentucky?

Take a look around you! Choose you this day, Kentucky. But know, that remaining neutral is no longer an option.

RACE, JUVENILE JUSTICE, AND OUR COMMUNITY

Judge Brian Edwards, Circuit Court Judge
30th Judicial Circuit

(Author's note – This article was originally written and published in 2019 prior to the closing of the Jefferson County Youth Detention Center. The issues and concerns raised in this piece are not only still relevant but have, in fact, worsened with detained youth now being housed hundreds of miles away from their family and attorneys while awaiting disposition of their cases.)

Imagine if your children, and the other children in your neighborhood, were exponentially more likely to find themselves incarcerated than children who live in other neighborhoods?

On any given Monday, the Hall of Justice and the Judicial Center are amongst the busiest buildings in our city and in the Commonwealth of Kentucky. Lawyers arrive in droves prepared to fight on behalf of their clients. Law enforcement officers arrive to provide testimony in support of arrests they have made. And countless other individuals, some accused of wrong doing, others victims of wrong doing, will come and go. As they leave these busy buildings to get to their cars or to walk back to their offices, many will pass up a building on the left-hand side of Jefferson Street with a non-descript sign out front which reads Jefferson County Youth Detention Center (JCYC).

JCYC is where we detain children who have been charged with criminal offenses and whom have been adjudicated to be unfit to be released to the community pending disposition of their charges. According to research prepared by Louisville Metro Youth Detention Services — provided to Maria Gurren and the Louisville Criminal Justice Commission — on an average day in 2017, there were 67 children being detained in JCYC.[1] Approximately 77% of those children were African American. And, of those children who were admitted to JCYC with documented addresses, over 50% came from just five of the 70+ zip codes that make up Jefferson County. The zip code that produced the most children who

---

1   Louisville Metro Youth Detention Services. (2017). Data file provided to Louisville Criminal Justice Commission.

were admitted was 40211 which, alone, produced over 16% of those housed at JCYC.

These children have been charged with a variety of offenses ranging from burglary and drug possession to robbery and murder. For those of us who have spent years working inside of the criminal justice system, JCYC is sometimes referred to as baby jail for kids. In theory however, JCYC is not supposed to be "jail". According to the mission statement listed on the front page of Kentucky's Department of Juvenile Justice website:

> *The Kentucky Department of Juvenile Justice provides a range of services to sentenced, committed, probated, and detained youth and their families, creating opportunities for those youth to develop into productive, responsible citizens while enhancing public safety.*

Unlike our adult detention facilities, it is the professed mission of our Juvenile Detention facilities to give children the tools they will need to take positive advantage of second chances.

This unassuming building located just west of the intersection of 8th and Jefferson currently serves as home for those children. It is where they ate their Thanksgiving dinners and where they will spend Christmas and usher in the New Year. And it is where they are learning to navigate the difficult world of burgeoning adolescence.

As an African American male whose first home was on South 45th Street in the same 40211 zip code where so many of these children come from, these numbers and this reality hit home. To be honest, it breaks my heart. I see these kids and I see myself. I see the bright and talented boys and girls that I once played with. And I ask myself, is this where they need to be? I ask why are these children so overrepresented inside of JCYC? I ask what we as a community can do to address this problem. And finally, I ask if these overrepresented neighborhoods were on the east and north east sides of town as opposed to the west and southwest, would there not be outrage?

As we transition into a new year and get past the hustle and bustle of the holiday season, I hope that those of you reading this will begin to think a bit more about the children inside that building on 8th and Jefferson. As you drive by it, perhaps consumed with concerns of how best to navigate rush hour traffic in order to get out of downtown to pick up a child on time, perhaps we should think about the children inside that building. And we should ask ourselves whether we would pay more attention to this building if the majority of those children inside of it were from the neighborhoods we lived in when we were children or the neighborhoods where our own children currently live.

SOCIALLY DISTANCING FROM PARTISAN POLITICS

Timothy E. Findley, Jr.

Partisan politics have failed Black people. That's no secret. Not just today, but consistently and systemically for generations. Yet the only viable options on the table, or so they would have you believe, are Democrats or Republicans. But is that really true? Hear me out.

I believe this is the time and moment for Black People to "socially distance" themselves from both Democrats and Republicans. Year after year, Black voters must choose between a Republican Party which has actively worked against our interest for decades and a Democratic party that has long struggled to meaningfully address race and racism, such as economic, education, and police reform.

For so long Black people have voted Democrat and given Republicans ambiguous, at best, stance on racial issues. In the words of Justin Giboney, "The truth is, the Republican Party has never fully divested itself of the vestiges of the Southern Strategy, which

in the late 1960s and early '70s invited segregationists into the party to secure a majority."

Too many conservative elected officials and civic organizations still readily accept and are dependent on the votes and money of their less than racially tolerant constituents. This isn't to suggest that all Republicans are racist or uninterested in improving race relations, but the party's leadership still humors racist voters, especially during primary season."

Yet therein lies the formula, the decades long formula, for being taken for granted. Democratic leaders know that Republicans aren't a truly viable option for most Black people. To that end, the Democratic party doesn't have much incentive to court members of its most loyal Constituency (except for the time-honored tradition of begging for pulpit time during election season in Black churches).

As former FiveThirtyEight senior reporter Farai Chideya wrote back in 2016, Black voters are so loyal that they're considered "captured"[1] — a theory put forth by Paul Frymer, a professor of politics at Princeton University, in a 1999 book titled *Uneasy Alliances: Race and Party Competition in America*. In other words, they're ignored by one major party and taken for granted by the other.

Today's lopsided Black vote for the Democratic Party is often tied to 1964 Republican presidential nominee Barry Goldwater's vote against the Civil Rights Act. This was certainly a significant event, but the story starts earlier.

Democrat and Republican positions on civil rights were essentially indistinguishable between 1920 and the mid-1940s, blacks' party loyalties were also split. In fact, the NAACP declared in 1926 that, "Our political salvation and our social survival lie in our absolute independence of party allegiance in politics …" (Yes, in 1926 they were also suggesting we distance ourselves from both parties).

In 2022, we're still being sold the falsehood that the Black community's interests align with conserving the power of the Democratic Party. It's a narrative that protects the party at our expense. Competition for the Black vote is the ONLY way our community is going to gain the real power necessary to impact policy in this country.

The truth is as clear as the racism at a Trump Rally or the absence of Democrats once we cast our vote. Neither political party cares enough about the issues that we care about. Neither seems particularly concerned with recruiting new faces, minds, and leadership within either party structure.

Black voters in America are well familiar with what happens to our community every election year. Our issues are paraded and talked about every election season, only to be placed on the back-burner , or taken off the stove completely, after election day. It's a tired, pathetic cycle.

The moment Black America became a guaranteed block of voters for Democrats, was the moment the relationship became one defined by broken promises and offensive compromises that leave us bruised and waiting for reforms that never ever come.

We are actively suffering from a widening racial wealth gap, mortgage denial rates, pandemic vaccination and illness rates, police violence, and a myriad of other bad legislation from local and state politicians in our country.

Black voters decide elections, but the only real attention we receive is questions around voter turnout. Who we vote for is always assumed and that assumption dilutes our power as voters every time we vote. In a country that loves to celebrate independence, it's time that Black voters distance ourselves from the disrespect of both parties, form new coalitions, and embrace our political independence.

---

1   Chideya, F. (2016, September 9). Black voters are so loyal that their issues get ignored. FiveThirtyEight. https://fivethirtyeight.com/features/black-voters-are-so-loyal-that-their-issues-get-ignored/

ORGANIZING OUR COMMUNITIES

Celine Mutuyemariya, Electoral Justice Organizing Director
Black Leadership Action Coalition of Kentucky (BLACK)

Throughout American history, Black people have had few options but to oscillate from one of the major political parties in the United States to the other–with increasingly fewer distinctions between the two–in the hopes of improving the conditions of our communities.

In 1961, Black voters in Louisville aligned with the Republican party because the Democratic administration at the time had failed to realize calls to desegregate public accommodations.[1] That year, under the leadership of the Louisville Non-Partisan Registration Committee (NPRC), tens of thousands of Black people in Louisville registered to vote, left their party affiliation, and collectively chose to elect a slate of candidates from the opposing party.

This organized effort resulted in a public accommodations ordinance being passed, an effort that Democrats had failed to achieve in the three years prior. The fall election of 1961 was not the first time Black Kentuckians worked together to influence local and state races, and it would not be the last.

In August 2022, Black Leadership Action Coalition of Kentucky (BLACK)–a statewide organization working to build a voting bloc that has the power to impact political races up and down the ballot across Kentucky–will join the Black activists, organizers, and organizations who came before us in launching a statewide Electoral Justice campaign focused on increasing the political participation of Black Kentuckians in four regions of Kentucky.

For BLACK, increasing political participation means building power at and beyond the polls. From getting people registered and increasing voter turnout to investing time and resources into building trust and community with a base that is unified by a shared vision and shared values.

Increasing political participation also means building a strategy around our votes so, like those who came before us, we can leverage electoral wins

---

1   Farrington, J. D. (2011). "Even I voted Republican: African American voters and public accommodations in Louisville, Kentucky, 1960- 1961. The Register of the Kentucky Historical Society, 109(3/4), 395–431. http://www.jstor.org/stable/23388026

and translate them into socio-economic gains and liberated communities.

Over time, our work will require that we think about **how we shift from the limited political pathways our current governing systems offer in order to build new, inclusive, community-driven governing systems that center the well-being of people, above all else.**

For Black people, engaging in elections is not simply about getting an individual into power. When we vote, we are actively working to protect ourselves, our families, and our communities from the state-sanctioned violence, disinvestment, and disenfranchisement that have ravaged our communities for years.

Voting, alone, has not and will not save us.

BLACK understands that the sense of apathy and disillusionment people experience about the electoral process is not because we don't care; it is because when we vote, we don't see transformational changes in the conditions of our communities.

And yet, the individuals who win on election day will have considerable influence on the lives of Black people across the state of Kentucky.

This is why it is critical that we link electoral organizing to grassroots community organizing because, **throughout our collective history, whenever we have poured time, energy, and resources into organizing ourselves and our communities, we have won.**

In 2018, one of BLACK's founders, Alicia Hurle,

published an essay in the State of Black Louisville report titled Black Political Power and Civic Engagement[2] offering a number of policy recommendations for building Black political power statewide. Two years after this essay was published, Black Leadership Action Coalition of Kentucky (BLACK) was born in the midst of the 2020 racial uprisings.

As recommended in 2018, BLACK will offer ongoing political education and engagement to develop shared political analysis; opportunities for intergenerational sharing and learning about Kentucky's Black political history; and inclusive spaces for Black leaders of various backgrounds to work together to create and mobilize around a political agenda that seeks to improve the quality of life for all Black Kentuckians.

Organizing our communities has always been the method by which Black communities have made the most significant gains in social and economic policy change and BLACK intends to build on this legacy. BLACK will be a political home that supports the development, care, and coordination of new, emerging, and experienced organizers across the commonwealth. Together, we will work towards a future where all Black Kentuckians have access to just, equitable, and inclusive socio-economic systems.

To learn more or join our efforts, please complete this form or visit bit.ly/joinBLACK.

2   Hurle, A. & Cowherd, K. (2018). Black political power and civic engagement. LEO Weekly. https://www.leoweekly. com/2018/03/black-political-power-civic-engagement/

THE CHURCH MUST INTERRUPT

Timothy E. Findley, Jr., Pastor
Kingdom Fellowship Christian Life Center

The question that continues to beg, plead, for an answer, in my estimation, is a Yes or No question. It is a question that I and countless others have been asked from street corners to beauty and barbershops to community forums. It's a question that brings into visibility the compassion and engagement (or lack thereof) of that local assembly.

It's a simple question surrounding the idea of violence reduction and the reality of social injustices in communities of color. Does the church play a role in changing the ongoing story of violence and injustice in the marginalized neighborhoods beneath the glimmering gentrified skyline across our city?

The answer is Yes. Yet, I would take it a step further. The church doesn't simply play a role. It is the critical, indispensable key to addressing violence and ALL of the root causes that plague so many of our communities.

The story is told of an incident in the life and ministry of Jesus Christ found in the Gospel according to Luke 7:11-15:

Soon afterward He was on His way to a town called Nain. His disciples and a large crowd were traveling with Him. Just as He neared the gate of the town, a dead man was being carried out. He was his mother's only son, and she was a widow. A large crowd from the city was also with her. When the Lord saw her, He had compassion on her and said, "Don't cry." Then He came up and touched the open coffin, and the pallbearers stopped. And He said, "Young man, I tell you, get up!" The dead man sat up and began to speak, and Jesus gave him to his mother.

While this particular miracle speaks of the power and authority of Jesus Christ, it has always struck a chord with me. I have always felt compelled and inspired by this text to interrupt funerals. That procession is going one way, and Jesus and His disciples, the other. They come in contact, and His power arrests the march, sending the dead back living and the mourner glad.

I believe the passion and power of the church must be to interrupt the funerals. Interrupt them before they begin. Interrupt the violence. Interrupt the silence surrounding missing Black girls and women. Interrupt systemic racism. Interrupt the policies that continue to hold people of color underneath the dark waters of discrimination gasping for air. We must pray. Prayer is necessary. And there must be action with our prayers. We must be engaged and learning congregations. We must build our capacity in this work and learn to see youth not as projects, but partners in God's economy. It's not a 'they' and 'them,' but a 'we' and 'us.'

We must be engaged. Engagement may look different in 2020, and that's okay. The church might not be at the center of social change today like it was in the 1960s, but perhaps by not occupying the center, churches can fill a role of actively supporting, collaborating, hosting, and resourcing justice-based initiatives. We must NAME IT and SPEAK TO IT! Naming structural oppression resulting from "poverty, policy, police, prisons and privilege" in our preaching, education, and public theology is hard work, but not doing so creates further oppression.

Finally, we must be OPEN to collaboration within the faith community! Learning what others are doing allows the body of Christ to see itself whole, for the left hand to know what the right hand is doing, and for reflection to turn into action.

"If the church does not recapture its prophetic zeal, it will become an irrelevant social club without moral or spiritual authority."[1] — Martin Luther King, Jr.

---

1   King, Martin Luther, Jr. (1963, June 5). A knock at midnight. Retrieved from https://kinginstitute.stanford.edu/king-papers/documents/knock-midnight

THIS IS WHAT DEMOCRACY LOOKS LIKE

Representative Keturah Herron
Policy Strategist, Organizer, Youth Advocate, Activist
KY State Representative, House District 42

These are a few of the titles given to me before 2020. Things changed quickly as we faced the global pandemic and the height of racial injustice in Louisville, KY and throughout the nation. Upon learning about the pandemic, I started to organize with other directly impacted people to ensure our incarcerated brothers and sisters were released from our local jails and prisons. A statewide reentry group was formed to request that the Kentucky Executive Branch release people and give them access to a reentry guide upon release. We launched a campaign, Liberation Identification, to ensure people had a state issued ID when they came back to the community. We worked with the Chan Zuckerberg Foundation to secure funds for local grassroots organizations to support people with housing and other essential needs upon release.

While we were doing this work, our city learned about Breonna Taylor, a 26-year-old Black woman who was murdered by Louisville Metro Police Department as they served a no-knock warrant. The date of Breonna's murder coincided with Governor

Beshear shutting down the state due to COVID-19 and the global pandemic. The local media had minimal coverage of Breonna Taylor's death. As different stories were being released, we had to depend on the family of Breonna Taylor to share the truth. Late April is when I learn what really occurred the early morning of March 13, 2020.

I was angry, sad, confused and unsure about the community I lived in. As a Black, Queer, masculine-centered woman, I was unsure if I was safe to be in my home like Breonna Taylor. There was a call between a group of local and national people to strategize the actions to take in the pursuit of justice. At that moment I decided to work towards a ban on no knock warrants. I had no idea how I would do it. However, I recognized my privilege as a policy strategist at the American Civil Liberties Union of Kentucky and had access to the tools to make it happen.

I contacted Terrance Sullivan, Executive Director of the Kentucky Human Rights Commission, to talk through researching and drafting a local ordinance to ban no knock warrants. During this time, I had many conversations with Hannah Drake, Cassia Herron, and Phillip Bailey about launching a campaign called #nomorenoknocks to get people involved. We designed tee shirts that said #nomorenoknocks, then asked people to wear them and post a video or picture on social media demanding no knock warrants be banned. During the campaign, I learned Metro Council was in the process of presenting a similar ordinance. Working with both drafts, they combined language and presented Breonna's Law to the Metro Council.

On June 11, 2020, Breonna's Law became an ordinance effectively banning no knock warrants in the city. From the time the #nomorenoknocks campaign was launched until the day Breonna's Law passed, it was just 17 days. That day showed protesters, activists, and allies that the people truly can make a difference. Breonna's Law was a grassroots effort fueled by the people. That is how the paradigm has shifted. A new ground swelling of people realized they can change this community and state. They were from all walks of life. People from all social and economic backgrounds witnessed the power they have. That day on the steps of City Hall is when people realized they can make a difference. We must be prepared for politics to be done this way. There is no going back.

The pandemic, Breonna Taylor, and George Floyd are the catalysts which shifted how we do policy in Louisville, in Kentucky, and throughout the nation. It was regular everyday people who are Black, LGBTQ, directly impacted and who are struggling mentally, emotionally, financially, and spiritually to get by. Typically, policy is created by elected officials, mainly white male elected officials. Not this time. It was the people who saw that something needed to be done. We knew the solution. We demanded change. This

was the first time people in my generation were a part of something so huge. This will be the new way to do policy.

We have witnessed Councilman Jecory Arthur become the youngest person to serve on Metro Council. He has filed and co-signed over 70 pieces of legislation, most of which have passed. From housing ordinances to line items in the budget, he has brought the people into the process at Metro Council. People like Councilman Arthur and myself (now a Kentucky State Representative serving House District 42) and many others across the nation have run for and been elected to office. Not only have we changed the face of policy and politics, but we are also changing the process. We must practice what we want to see. Nothing About Us, Without Us.

Moving forward, I offer the people of my city, my state, and my nation the opportunity to understand our collective power. We must understand we can craft policy, we can get elected, and we can find the solutions to the problems impacting us daily. We must know and understand we are part of a larger ecosystem, and we all have our roles. Some are to protest, some are to cook, some are to disrupt every damn meeting that happens, and some of us must be the ones who sit at the table to ensure the voices of the people are included when decisions are being made.

Voting is an integral component of our collective power. We must free the vote!! Voter registration, engagement, and education must become part of everything we do. If we are bringing water to an event, we must bring voter registration cards to the event. As we have learned in 2022, independents are the largest number of new registrants in Kentucky.

The two-party system is not working, and people care about issues not party affiliation.

We must train people how to organize, teach them how to do policy, and bring them into the election process. How do we do that? We must fund and pay for this work. Historically, Black people have been left out of this process– not because they don't want to participate; it's because they have been shut out or don't have the financial resources to participate. Other cities and states know the importance of paying organizers. Louisville and Kentucky must get on board!!

We must amplify the voices we lost in body, but not in spirit. We must remember the question our late brother Chris Wells frequently asked, "What y'all doing?" We must remember the many times our late brother Travis Nagdy said "Keep going." The people we are looking for to change the city, state, and nation are looking at us in the mirror.

THE STATE OF BLACK LOUISVILLE IS VIBRANT

Amber G. Duke, Interim Executive Director
ACLU of Kentucky

Working in the civil rights and civil liberties space in Kentucky my days are filled with grim data that show the impacts of racism on Black people, limited quality healthcare, lack of access to justice in the criminal legal system, gaps in educational opportunities, barriers to the ballot box, violations of religious freedom, denial of basic civil and human rights… the list goes on.

However, when I reflect on Black Louisville, I can't help but smile. The State of Black Louisville is VIBRANT!

Black Louisville entrepreneurs are creating jobs. Black Louisville artists are capturing our grief, pain, sorrow, AND our joy.

Black Louisville activists are holding government officials' feet to the fire and building power in communities.

Black Louisville educators are pouring into their students as some try to ban and censor their classroom materials.

Black Louisville churches are investing in scholarships, organizations, and important community programming.

Black Louisville organizers are registering people to vote.

Black Louisville historians are uncovering stories we once thought were lost to time.

Black Louisville children are smiling, laughing, dancing, and playing their way through each day.

Black Louisville engineers, welders, electricians, and plumbers are building the city's new landscape.

Black Louisville executives are calling out white supremacy culture in our organizations and companies and demanding investment in BIPOC people.

Black Louisville women are doing anything and everything.

Black Louisville is thriving in the face of a health pandemic, political tumult, and systems designed to keep us down.

As we consider the challenges we face, we can never forget our people's uncanny ability to persist and resist.

YOUTH ARE OUR FUTURE, YOUTH LEADERSHIP MUST BE OUR NOW

Darryl Young Jr., Executive Director
Coalition Supporting Young Adults

Much has been made about normalcy and what that means as we still struggle to navigate a post COVID society. Many of us are still trying to piece together remnants of our past lives, looking for the comfort of the familiar as we face the daunting uncertainty of the present and what is to come. We are desperate to reconvene our old routines and go back to the world we thought we at least had a pretty good grasp on.

However, while some clamor for their pre-mask-mandate lives, there are others who realize that the old way wasn't as great as we thought, and it certainly wasn't working for everyone. While some felt like their rights and freedoms were being intruded upon, others felt like theirs were never fully realized or guaranteed. And while many saw so much of what made up their daily lives come to a sudden stop, others watched on in horror as the murder of Black men and women still continued with macabre precision. It is hard to contextualize the pandemic without thinking about the social unrest caused by the continued slaughter of Black bodies by police and white vigilantes. It was almost unfathomable

to think that even with a country-halting virus, the destruction of Black and Brown people still seemed to follow its morbid routine. Yet when we look at history we realize this destruction is not some modern-day phenomenon. Names like Breonna Taylor, Ahmaud Arbery and George Floyd weren't anomalies; they were just new additions to a blood-stained ledger with enough pages to fill multiple libraries.

During this current iteration of the fight against white supremacy and police brutality there was an occurrence that might have seemed new or different to some. Youth were in the front. Young people, some still with fresh faces and pre-pubescent voices were chanting, marching, locking arms and blocking intersections. They were live streaming (going live on social media) to update folks of what was happening in the streets. They were writing op-eds and organizing other youth to flood the phone lines of politicians and the police department, demanding justice. Calling for change.

To be clear, young people have always been part

of movement building. It is ahistorical to suggest otherwise. Before there was the SNICK some of us watched on Saturday nights on Nickelodeon, there was SNCC (pronounced Snick), the Student Non-Violent Coordinating Committee. Although elders made up much of the Southern Christian Leadership Conference (SCLC), there was a growing number of young radicals who would go on to jump start the Black Power movement.

However, although there is a wealth of evidence of youth movement leading and building, we have consistently struggled to nurture and grow youth leadership and voice. Too often adults are antagonistic to young people, falling back into the adage that youth should be seen instead of heard. We hold them in contempt more often than see their value to the work. Meaningful opportunities to co-lead are instead set aside for hollow and patronizing symbolic gestures. Youth are brought to the photo-op but rarely if ever brought to the table. And even when invited, youth are still maligned and often silenced.

We can no longer allow this cycle to continue. To invoke another saying, if youth are to be our future they must be afforded the ability to serve now in the present. Youth are not as compromised as adults. They are not as tethered to careers, titles and the other trappings of respectable living that have dimmed the fire of many adults into glowing embers. They are on the cutting edge of trends and technologies that allow their thoughts and words to reach farther than more traditional means. Their adept use of social media allows them platforms that reach innumerable audiences.

The Coalition Supporting Young Adults is an advocacy organization that works to provide resources and support to organizations that serve "opportunity youth"- youth 16-24 who are currently or at risk of being disconnected from school and work due to systemic barriers and issues. Youth voice and autonomy is at the center of our work and guides us as an organization. Some of the ways we exemplify this are by inviting youth to serve on our board of directors and paying them for their service. We involve youth in our research projects and allow them to help in the framing and implementation. We develop youth focus groups for every project we undertake, and we pay participants for their time. We also create and support programming to help mold young leaders.

We don't have time to follow another cycle of youth engaging, leading and ultimately being pushed away by the old guard. Now is the time for us as leaders, not gatekeepers, to nurture this current crop of new leaders and entrench them into our current movement for liberation. What does that mean, and what does it look like? They need to serve on boards. They need platforms that give them meaningful opportunities to speak. Opportunities that offer them chances to shape and mold, not just receive empty and condescending platitudes from adults who don't intend to actually implement what they hear. Young people deserve the space to analyze and critique the spaces they are in, to help inform what does and doesn't work for them. And if money is involved, they need a say in how it is spent. Finally, if everyone else in the room is getting some money, youth should get a check too.

If we are to do this work authentically, equitably and genuinely, we must require youth to be our partners and invite them from the back of the room to the front.

FROM PROTEST TO PRODUCTIVITY

Dr. F. Bruce Williams
Bates Memorial Baptist Church

Recently it was announced that four officers of the Louisville Metro Police Department (LMPD) were indicted in relation to the Breonna Taylor Case. For years justice loving people have been working, fighting, and praying for some meaningful progress toward justice for Breonna Taylor. While indictments are not convictions, they are a hopeful step in the right direction. This new and hopeful development is, among other things, the fruit of our relentless protests.

Scores of people worked hard on multiple fronts to get to this moment. Community leaders, activists, pastors, attorneys, political leaders, artists, judges, and just plain everyday people came together, of every age, race and socio-economic status, to make their contribution. Petitions were signed, political leaders were pressured, law enforcement was challenged, votes were cast, educators were invited, the apathetic were stirred, and masses were beckoned to join the struggle to uncover the truth and bring justice to Breonna Taylor and her grieving family.

Among the many actions taken to help bring Breonna Taylor justice, the most overt, dramatic, and perhaps most controversial actions taken were the scores of protests that took place throughout the city, state, country and indeed throughout the world. Repeatedly concerned citizens took to the streets demanding justice for Breonna Taylor. Louisville started the spark that led to the flame of protests that spread around the world. In the face of an attempted coverup, masses of people took to the streets disrupting traffic, shutting down businesses, and clogging thoroughfares in a dramatic attempt to bring attention to Breonna Taylors case, expose the corruption, and uncover the facts that resulted in her murder.

Dr. Martin Luther King said, "...the great glory of American democracy is the right to protest for right."[1]

---

1   King Jr., M.L. (1955, December 5). The Montgomery Bus Boycott. Holt Street Baptist Church, Montgomery, AL, United States.

America is no stranger to protest. Her very inception was conceived in the fires of protest. And when it comes to the issue of police brutality and the pain it has historically visited on the Black community, both America and her Black citizens are no strangers to protest.

Frederick Douglas declared that "without struggle there is no progress." And when it comes to the struggle for justice in America, including in the city of Louisville, justice has never come rolling in on wheels of inevitability for Black people. We have had to fight every step of the way. And one of the tools used for the struggle for justice is massive protest.

Protests in Louisville were met with harsh criticism, erroneous claims, and sometimes brutal and even deadly police force. Even some who claimed to be sympathetic to the cause reviled the protests claiming that they were useless and served no productive purpose. In my judgement, those types of comments are typical of status quo keepers, and are often made by those who are more concerned with order than justice. Some people would rather change come in a nice, orderly, nonthreatening way than by the disruptive nature of physical protest. But usually those who prefer the former have a superficial understanding of the nature of systemic oppression. In other words, they really want things to change as long as they stay the same. Many of us have come to know that Dr. King was right when he said, "Freedom is never voluntarily given by the oppressor, it must be demanded by the oppressed."

The recent light-at-the-end-of-the-tunnel that shines from the indictment of four LMPD officers would never have happened had it not been for the relentless quest of courageous protestors who put their very well-being on the line to make sure that Louisville responded to the demands for justice. Our protests led to productivity. The irony is that many who condemned the protests will be the very ones who benefit from its fruit.

EDUCATION

WE NEED A PLAN TO FIX JCPS NOW

OUR CHILDREN'S LIVES & OUR ECONOMY DEPEND ON IT

Sadiqa N. Reynolds, Esq, President and CEO
Kish Cumi Price, Ph.D., Director of Education Policy & Programming
Louisville Urban League

We have defended educators as they were threatened and verbally assaulted for fighting for their own rights amid a backdrop of low scores and low performance in Jefferson County Public Schools (JCPS).

We have stood with parents and other community organizations to defend the district and its opportunity to create solutions, and we have met with district leaders to hear their proposals. Now, we need to see the deployment of the additional resources we expected educators to be provided to help them adequately meet and address the needs of JCPS students.

According to recent K-PREP scores, less than half of students tested were "proficient" (i.e. knew what they should know at their respective grade levels) in reading, math, writing, and social studies.[1] Only 24.9% (1 in 4 students tested) scored as proficient in science. Only 30% of Black youth scored at grade level in reading across grade levels.

The proficiency rates are even more alarming for Black students' scores in math (e.g., 21%, 19% and 13% in elementary, middle, and high, respectively). In other words, an estimated 70% to 80% of Black youth tested in Louisville were not at grade level in core subject areas — enough to fill every seat at the Louisville Slugger Field.

JCPS' two-star ranking is proof that the system is failing its Black students and students living in poverty. This is made even more complicated by the fact that these are generally children from families that every other system is failing too.

When the problem has deep roots, our tendency is to talk about the issue and present surface-level solutions instead of having deep and vulnerable

---

1   Kentucky Department of Education. (2019). School report card: Jefferson County. Retrieved from https://www.kyschoolreportcard.com/organization/5590?year=2019

discussions that lead to considerate strategies with measurable outcomes.

We know there are those who believed these students to be incapable of learning, so we advocated for the creation of W.E.B Dubois Academy to prove that with the right leadership, care, and expectations, our children could thrive. It turns out we were right. Our children can learn, and they can thrive, and we have created a system within the system to prove it.

To be clear, it is not about resegregating our schools, but about recognizing that we are trying to educate children in a system not designed to teach them and one that heretofore has been unwilling to adapt to their needs. So, DuBois Academy was an exercise in testing our own theories. Over and over we hear the resegregation criticism, but generally it comes from people who have little to no evidence of ever really caring for our children.

Systemic Racism and Poverty

Let's be honest. It is impossible to talk about the achievement gap without dialogue on systemic racism and poverty. It was racism that caused Black communities across the country, including Louisville, to be redlined out of wealth-building opportunities. Now, years later, we can overlay a map of redlined areas and match them almost perfectly with the housing occupied by children who are on the lowest end of the achievement gap. In other words, children forced by biased and broken systems to be raised in poverty also have the poorest educational outcomes. And here's how you know it's systemic: they also have the poorest health outcomes, poorest quality of life,

and the least amount of access to quality grocery stores and healthcare.

Let's pull back the layers of our "racial equity speak" and address our educational woes as if all of our children are the ones showing up in the bottom 5% of schools across Kentucky. This is not a Black problem. It is a societal problem and one that school leaders, parents, community organizations, and policy makers must swiftly address.

Supporting our teachers means supporting *all* our students. That means funding for additional human resources in the schools. We know teachers are buying Kleenex, but what are we willing to pay for success when we realize the old models aren't working? Addressing equity gaps as a priority will be evident when the district's budget reflects it.

How much are we willing to invest to offer attractive stipends for more seasoned teachers to go into low-performing schools? Turnover is an issue. Are we willing to invest in retention? If we don't want police in schools,[2] are we willing to bring in culturally competent and caring adults who are willing to serve as another set of eyes and hands? Many students act out because they are distracting teachers from larger, harder issues. If we had time for heart engagement, we would need fewer handcuffs. For clarification, culturally competent doesn't always mean Black; we know cultural competence is in reach of good educators in every racial group.

Black and Brown Suspension Rates

Last year, 77% of suspensions in JCPS were attributed to the suspension of Black and Brown youth.[3] These gaps in suspension rates exist even when Black

2   McLaren, M. (2019, August 7). There won't be any more resource officers at JCPS: What parents should know. Retrieved from https://www.courier-journal.com/story/news/education/2019/08/07/jcps-wont-have-any-more-resource-officers-at-schools-what-to-know/1941550001/

3   Jefferson County Public Schools. Suspension incidents 2018-2019. Retrieved from https://www.jefferson.kyschools.us/sites/default/files/jcpsdbk255.pdf

students and White students commit the same infractions. Are we ready to admit that some of those within the educational system view the actions of students of color through the lens of intentionality and criminality, while excusing similar behaviors of their White counterparts? Can we love our children enough to admit that we have biases we don't leave at the front door when we walk into our jobs?

Despite being in a city deemed as compassionate, many students of color are not being educated with the same compassion and consideration that their White peers receive even within the same classrooms. Just think; the crack-epidemic among Black people spurred the "war on drugs," which led to higher incarceration rates. On the other hand, the opioid addiction, currently primarily being experienced by Whites, is resulting in take-back programs and officers armed with life-saving drugs. These responses are compassion-in-action examples that Black people have never been afforded.

We also recognize that the insidious criminalization of students of color has occurred even in the face of heavy circulation of buzzwords such as "adverse childhood experiences," "trauma-informed approaches," and "racial equity plans."

This is not check-the-box work. This cannot be the responsibility of one department, but the work of a district or, dare we say, a community. While we see widespread data-sharing and professional development trainings, the current educational approaches and racial equity plans implemented in many of our schools are failing most of our children because there is no standardization and, therefore, no true ability to scale or replicate. Can we open the doors of the University of Louisville, Simmons College, and Bellarmine University and bring all of

our teachers in for live simultaneous, continuing education? Inconsistent training leads to inconsistent application, which affects the authenticity of the model.

Ill-Equipped Educators, Parents

Certainly, the district's decision to increase mental health professionals across schools is a step in the right direction, but taking slow steps in the right direction when we should be running is false progress. There remains a pressing need to have enough compassionate educators and leaders in every learning environment.

We also understand the district is offering a faster path to certification, and we are excited about it, but how much will be invested in supporting new educators when they walk into these overwhelming situations? They are often placed at schools that are considered low-performing and under-resourced with little to no mentorship. These conditions can dramatically impact the ability to retain teachers of color. Do we plan to appeal to retired educators to return, even on a part-time basis, to assist these new educators? We want to see the plan with identified community support.

Parents need to realize that most teachers care about our children and want to successfully manage their classrooms but may feel ill-equipped. What if parents and administrators took the time to understand that most teachers feel stressed? According to a recent survey, approximately 70% of JCPS teachers surveyed reported that they did not have adequate training in restorative practices.[4] That is stressful. How do you implement something you don't understand? How quickly does JCPS intend to address this?

Educators and administrators must be willing to

---

4   Voices of Teaching Equity. (2019, December 2). Understanding and improving difficult student behavior. Retrieved from https://edvotejcta.com/2019/12/02/understanding-and-improving-difficult-student-behavior-in-jcps/

acknowledge that parents love their children and want what is best for them, but many parents are stressed and may feel ill-equipped as well. We see them showing up in community settings emotional and exhausted. They don't deserve to be demonized any more than teachers do.

And what if our legislators focused on how actions like stripping education budgets and shaming teachers negatively impact school performance, teacher creativity, and innovation? Consider funding solutions that include educators – not only, but especially, Black educators and educators of color working alongside caring adults who prioritize education for students.

Research supports that children are most successful when they have at least one caring adult in their lives. Sometimes that is the parent, and sometimes that caring adult is in the school. Let's just deal with that reality.

We want JCPS to provide a written plan for the 36 schools identified as needing Comprehensive Support and Improvement (CSI).[56] Let's include viable strategies coupled with intentional execution to produce measurable outcomes of success. Truancy reduction plans and volunteer recruitment efforts are a great start. After all, the problems within our education system demand the attention and resolve of a compassionate community, a supportive state legislature and a deliberate district. Our children's lives and Louisville's economy depend on it.

---

5   Kentucky Department of Education. (n.d.). 2019-20 Comprehensive support and improvement school roster. Retrieved from https://education.ky.gov/school/prischedrecov/Documents/CSI%20School%20Roster.pdf

6   JCPS has releases updated plans for CSI schools since this aricle was wriiten. Plans can be found here: https://www.jefferson.kyschools.us/department/accountability-research-systems-improvement-division/research-and-systems-improvement-4

INVESTING IN OUR FUTURE MEANS UNDERSTANDING OUR PAST

Marland Cole, Executive Director
Dr. Matt Berry, Chief Scholarship and Policy Officer
EVOLVE502

Evolve502 has a grand vision: all children in Louisville are prepared for college, career, and a successful productive life.

To achieve that goal, we are betting big on the power of education. In fact, a key to our strategy will be building a scholarship fund that would give all Jefferson County Public Schools (JCPS) graduates the opportunity to earn a two-year degree or certificate tuition free[1]. This is a significant investment of resources and, to be effective, it will require the entire community to rally around supporting our students and families. If done right, efforts like ours can unlock the power of higher education as the great equalizer in American society.

The truth is, however, that access to scholarship opportunities alone isn't enough to achieve the equality we strive for. We know that the size of the investment won't matter as much as its equitable distribution. That distinction is critical because, while higher education has been the source of opportunity for many, for many more it has been a perpetuator of inequality.

For generations of African Americans, access to the promise of higher education has been limited or wholly denied. Post-Civil War segregationist policies laid the foundation for the legal exclusion of Blacks from colleges. It also allowed similar statutes — such as the Day Law in Kentucky, which prohibited White and Black students from attending the same school — to survive until the mid-1950s.

More subtle means of exclusion also existed. The GI Bill of 1944 was perhaps the single greatest expansion of access to postsecondary education and home ownership in American history, but because racist policies and practices were in place, African American veterans found it difficult or nearly impossible to take advantage of the benefits they had earned.

These examples of intentional racist practices and

---

1   Evolve502 has begun offering scholarships. Details are available here: https://evolve502.org/scholarship-for-students/

others are why Evolve502 is dedicated to equity in our actions. For example, we'll be offering grants beyond tuition and fees for our lowest-income students to help with books, supplies, or unexpected expenses that challenge persistence in college. We're also working with our partners to coordinate and target comprehensive support services for students and families that will remove barriers to learning. We are building systems to better identify students in need so that they can be matched with interventions which will help them remain on track for success.

These are strategic steps which we believe will bring us closer to our vision of success for ALL children, and they are a recognition that achieving equality in outcomes will require equity in our investments. Dr. Martin Luther King Jr. once said, "if one gets behind in a race, he must eternally remain behind or run faster than the man in front. You've got to give him the equipment to catch up."[2] Education, coupled with the right supports, will provide the right equipment for those who have been left behind and left out to catch up — a necessary investment for our community to grow and thrive.

---

2   Dr. Martin Luther King Jr. (1963, December). Speech presented at Western Michigan University, Kalamazoo, Michigan.

PERMISSION TO BE BRILLIANT

Shashray McCormack, District Resource Teacher
Diversity, Equity & Poverty Programs

What is often taught in our educational system is rooted in a struggle over whose knowledge and experiences should be included. Most often, curriculum priveleges Eurocentric/ White ways of knowing.

When I taught African American history as an elective at Mill Creek Elementary, accomplishments and achievements of African Americans were not limited to Dr. Martin Luther King Jr. and Rosa Parks. I taught a deep understanding of complex social problems and real-world issues to encourage change agents.

Our narrative did not begin with African American life in slavery. In the classroom, we started with the essential questions such as "What do maps have to do with social equality?" We discussed African governmental structures from which other governments were designed and we learned the history of race and ethnicity and how they influenced the world politically and socially.

Giving students permission to be brilliant gives them the right to question and be critical of what they are being taught. Permission to pose questions such as "Why would Europeans want to engage in Native American genocide and create boarding schools where language, culture, and beliefs were literally stripped away?" Permission to question the westward "expansion" as "conquering and civilizing the savages"

and then conclude that it really was an entitled takeover of other people's lands. Permission to make the case for reparations.

Giving students permission to be brilliant teaches them to be critical of what they have learned. Our students must be taught what injustice looks like so they will fight for justice. It is important they learn the history of 40 acres and a mule, the govrnment's first systematic attempt to provide a form of reparations to newly freed slaves, and Jim Crow's ongoing impact on institutions, systems, and individuals that will address the wrong that has been done to Black people by paying money to or otherwise helping those who have been wronged.

My students use their brilliance to become critical thinkers and to question, "Why are achievements and accomplishments of Black, Brown and First Peoples left out so often?"

But for me, the most important question to ask is why students are not taught to develop a critical consciousness so that they will never stop asking why people are missing from histories and why reparations are important. They never stop questioning distortion and the role teachers can take in changing that status quo and speaking to White-centered history.

REDLINING BLACK RELEVANCE AND GENTRIFYING BLACK REALITY:
HOW CURRICULUM BUILDS SEGREGATION

John Marshall, Ed.D., Chief Equity Officer
Jefferson County Public Schools

The state of Black Louisville is one that is not difficult to understand. It is not an unexplainable phenomenon that requires deep discourse and discovery. In truth, Louisville, Kentucky is what many urban districts are and have been for a while: redlined and gentrified.

Many Louisvillians can speak to the impact of redlining and gentrifying neighborhoods and communities. I, although having seen gentrification of certain parts of Louisville and knowing that redlining cost my family, see clearly that the redlining of our relevance in history is just as damning. The curricular gentrifying of our being has silenced and sliced our understanding of who we are.

Why are we so omitted from history? Why are we taught so little about the greatness of Black men and women? Because an integrated curriculum upends a segregated psychosis that creates White benefactors and exalts Whiteness as opulent, open, and honest.

Being redlined and relegated to snippets of history in our curricula cost Black Louisville, and Black America, millions of minds and millions of dollars. The gated communities of White America far exceed the brick and mortar and blockaded border of 9th and Broadway. The gated communities of honesty and Black exceptionalism are abandoned in our schools.

Whitewashed lessons lead to battered, befuddled, and bounded Black minds. The 9th Street divide, although only taking five minutes to cross physically, is gaping and vast when you think about the polarizing pedagogy and colorblind teaching that excavates the pages of history, science, literature, and math books. The state of Black Louisville is housed under the shadow of a lesson that White America has built. Black Louisville is lied to by design and, in truth, the lies traverse neighborhoods.

It is a different kind of redlining. It is a redlining that feeds the phony and relieves philanthropies from funding and reversing the damage done to communities. The psychosis of curriculum subtly inoculates us all to believe that blight and Blackness are synonymous, that the founding fathers (who founded nothing) were not philanderers and gangsters, but were patriots and protectors and protagonists. The omission of founding mothers is an intersection of the redlined thoroughfare that our Black sisters, particularly, are boarded out of.

I submit that the physical status of our predominantly Black neighborhoods are bulldozed and blockaded by banks and (school) books. The sinister schema of overcharging to buy a house is met and multiplied by the schema to under-develop and deconstruct the extraordinary history of a people that bankrolled the genesis of White Louisville and White America.

In urban (school) districts and cities throughout America, bulldozers, cranes, and jackhammers are readying cities for newness and modernity. Be reminded that the real or, at minimum, just as important blueprint to building and repairing a city starts with teaching Black Louisville and Black America that the high-rise business towers and gated communities is a mentality as much as it is a reality.

The education system must teach — not 'bleach'. The redlining of Black relevance and gentrifying of Black excellence is 'built' into the blueprint and fiber of America. Building a new building in any part of the city means nothing if Black reparations in education are abandoned or never built.

PHILANTHROPY, GENTRIFICATION, AND SCHOOL SAFETY

Corrie Shull, Ph.D.
Board Member, 6th District , Jefferson County Board of Education
Pastor, Burnett Avenue Baptist Church

The prolific twentieth-century novelist James Baldwin helpfully illuminated that "people who cling to their illusions find it difficult, if not impossible, to learn anything worth learning: a people under the necessity of creating themselves must examine everything…" The past year serving as the Sixth District Representative for the Jefferson County Public Schools (JCPS) system has repeatedly reinforced this lesson for me.

Illusions are powerful and sometimes lead people to accept things that are not in our personal or collective best interest. One such thing, in my data-informed opinion, is police in public schools. The illusion is that police in schools make schools safer when, in fact, national data does not corroborate this. Schools with School Resource Officers (SRO) see more student arrests than their counterpart schools without SROs for behaviors that would ordinarily lead to school-based behavior interventions. Yet, for students in schools with SROs, it leads to increased occurrences of justice-involvement.

This is a critical and important distinction in the conversation concerning police in schools and the ways in which SROs increase the likelihood of youth being justice-involved — particularly Black, Latinx, and children with disabilities. I am convinced that there are ways to provide a safe environment for students and teachers without criminalizing minority students, and national data should be what informs our approach, not politics or personal opinions.

School personnel need to be equipped with resources and skills to deescalate negative behavior and to mitigate against safety concerns. All too often, it seems that the only strategy in schools is to call the SRO. Aaron Kupchik, in his book *Homeroom Security: School Discipline in an Age of Fear*, argues that "part of the problem is that most Americans are so wedded to a particular solution to the problem of school crime, despite a lack of evidence that the solution works. Strategies such as police in schools, security cameras and zero-tolerance measures resonate with widely shared ideas about crime prevention: that more police and punishments will keep us and our children safe."[1]

The criminalization of students has become an acceptable practice in American schools that feeds the prison industrial complex system and further disenfranchises Black youth. Philanthropy can positively impact schools by investing in the creation of healthy school culture within school buildings, which will make schools safe places where children want to be. This must be a community effort!

1   Kupchik, A. (2012). Homeroom security: School discipline in an age of fear. New York, NY: NYU Press.

STATEMENT REGARDING JCPS STUDENT ASSIGNMENT PLAN

Louisville Urban League

June 1, 2022. The Louisville Urban League is prepared to support the proposed plan if the Jefferson County Teachers Association (JCTA) supports the plan in a meaningful way because the plan will not be successful without some changes to the collective bargaining agreement that is currently being negotiated.

Our teachers and administrators deserve raises, and we hope the new contract reflects substantial pay increases for these heroes. Heroes who have pushed through a pandemic to help ensure that our students not only survived, but learned, despite obstacles and challenges. We know the criticism and critique of broken systems and even have our own, but we understand that our educators are the best example of what is working for our students, even in spaces where the system itself might be failing.

It is not our teachers, but these historical system failures that cause concern. We believe the Superintendent and his team have worked to propose a student assignment plan that centers students' needs. We also understand that the only way the plan can be successful is complete implementation, thus it is imperative that we highlight the pieces of this puzzle that are incomplete without buy-in from all, including but not limited to JCTA.

In order for the student assignment plan to work, JCTA must hold true to its mission - not a part of its mission but all of it. We highlight this tonight because we are being asked to endorse a plan that can only work if the union contract, currently being negotiated, is adjusted for its success.

We see and have joined some of the battles that JCTA has fought in our state and know that in such a contentious world, it is easy to get so caught up in fighting for retirement benefits and putting in place guard rails to protect educators, that they forget that our teachers signed up for this work in order to ensure the success of every learner. While JCTA must advocate for the rights and interests of its members as it relates to salaries and benefits, JCTA must also fight to advance the reason its teachers became teachers in the first place. There is always a simultaneous need to prioritize promoting success for every learner. There is always a simultaneous need to advance human, civil, and economic rights for all.

There is always a simultaneous need to serve as the active voice for excellence in public education.

To that end, the current contract rightfully allows teachers to choose which schools they apply to work in. This often leads to the best-performing schools with the lowest rates of poverty having the most tenured teachers. In other words, the average tenure of a teacher at the former Roosevelt Perry might be 4 years, whereas the average tenure at St. Matthews might be 15 years. As a result, personnel costs at lower-performing schools are less each year. The result is as inequitable as the investment.

The union contract can fix this. We understand that the superintendent has proposed an increased stipend for those working in our Choice schools. We expect that stipend to be no less than $10,000 in additional income per year per employee. We suggest this change in order to see an increased investment in schools that have higher poverty and lower resources and can be seen as less desirable assignments. CHOICE schools need support to build up a base of mentors with tenure who can help stabilize the infrastructure of those schools. We must end the revolving door in these schools, and we understand that the union must help us to do that because their mission requires that they not only promote the success of every learner, but also advance human, civil, and economic rights for all while serving as the active voice for excellence in public education. We support the student assignment plan only to the extent that things like a $10,000 pay increase will be negotiated and reflected in writing between the district and JCTA because these are the moving parts that will help to make the plan successful.

We also believe that the student assignment plan will be strengthened by prioritizing hiring in Choice schools. There really is no other way to ensure the staffing necessary to manage the concentration of such high-need students. So, for example, we believe the union leadership will agree that should a Choice school and another school have openings for a Certified science teacher, the hiring in the Choice school will be prioritized.

We do not want to see the creation of more high-poverty schools; this is and has been a recipe for disaster for educators and students. Our expectation is that if we find that students in Choice zones are not exercising their choices, the board and administrators will work to review the challenges rather than allowing schools with numbers like 85% poverty to exist in our community. The success of the plan will also require that the choices put before our families and students be *quality* choices.

We also believe that the student assignment plan cannot be successful if the funding set aside for AIS schools is not enough or is not committed long term.

In a nutshell, we support the plan if JCTA supports its full implementation and if this board and the current and future administration of JCPS are willing to be committed to our students in a way that is responsive to the data that we will gather after a year or two of implementation of this plan.

We support the plan if this board agrees that the funding for CHOICE schools will be put in place and will stay in place from day one of implementation.

We support the plan if we will see a reduction in the concentration of poverty in any particular school and an increase in financial and human resources in schools where poverty is highest.

We support the plan if this board, the administration,

and JCTA can agree to prioritize staffing in the CHOICE schools.

We support the plan if proposed curriculum changes are implemented across the board aligning academics in schools across the district.

We expect JCTA to help us hold the board and district accountable on whether or not the proper supports are put and kept in place in our AIS schools. As the plan is enacted, we need an analysis of turnover in our choice schools compared to others in the district. We need the board and administration to be in constant review and response to the data around the achievement and success of our students. That information should be shared publicly, and we need effective responses and adjustments to the information being shared. As steps like these

are taken, it will ensure fidelity to the plan that our Superintendent and his team have worked so hard to put forward.

In summary, the Louisville Urban League is prepared to support the proposed plan if JCTA supports the plan in a meaningful way because it will not be successful without some changes to the collective bargaining agreement, which we again highlight, is currently being negotiated. This is a historic moment and a historic plan with consequences that will affect generations to come. The board, the administration, the community - we will all be judged by how we collectively rose to meet tonight's moment and every consequential moment that will result from the full implementation of this student assignment plan.

BE BRAVE

Louisville Urban League

June 25, 2021. The time to act is now. Pre-pandemic, 63% of JCPS students weren't proficient in reading and 70% weren't proficient in math. One out of every two white students is behind. Four out of every five Black and Brown students are behind. This is not a new issue and the current Board and Superintendent, along with teachers and administrators are working tirelessly; and still, those numbers represent thousands more underperforming students than seats in Louisville Slugger Field. And that was all before. Before an acute global health crisis was layered on top of the chronic crisis of racism.

Right now is the time to focus squarely on closing the widening achievement gap. For the next three years, we have one-time money through the American Rescue Plan to do just what the name implies and rescue our students. We must use these unprecedented dollars to drive unprecedented results. "Gone is the time of doing things the way we've always done them," declared Dr. Marty Pollio,

JCPS Superintendent, in his 2021 State of the District address, and we couldn't agree more.

Here are 11 recommendations for ways JCPS can invest its federal dollars and immediately reshape the futures of our students and our city. Louisvillians, democrat, republican, Black, White, citizen, resident, and immigrant; we are in this together.

1. **Provide access to intensive tutoring services for high school students not meeting proficiency standards.** This request will cost JCPS $111,000,000 ($111M) over three years to make intensive tutoring programs like Kumon, Sylvan, Scholar Factory, Mathnasium, Equitas Prep, Decode Project, Langsford Learning, etc. accessible for every student striving for proficiency. These intensive tutoring programs are proven to produce significant gains in student achievement. The funding will be used to pay

for intensive tutoring in math and reading for 12,000 students, and math or reading for approximately 3,000 students.

2. **Invest in our teacher workforce.** With over 80% of our teachers having obtained a Master's degree or higher, the issue is not with teacher qualifications, but rather the number of teachers we have in the classroom. The hybrid model used to return students to the classrooms during the pandemic helped to reduce teacher-student ratios and allow for more uninterrupted instruction time. As we return for fall classes, students already suffering through traumas prior to the pandemic cannot come back to crowded classrooms and disruptions. Not only is this not conducive for students learning, but it also is not good for our teachers. There is a need for a smaller student-to-teacher ratio. We must have more teachers in the classroom immediately.

To achieve this, retired teachers and administrators need to be allowed to return to our schools while we spend the next few years recovering from the pandemic. More teachers are going to be needed in every school across the district as we work to combat the proficiency gap. Their long-term return will take two things. First, we are asking Governor Beshear to issue an executive order allowing retired teachers to return to the classroom without foregoing their retirement benefits for the next three years. In addition, we are asking JCPS to invest funds into paying the salaries of these teachers. For 300 retired teachers to return to the classroom at a salary of $70,000, this equates to an investment of $63M over three years.

3. **Intentionally recruit Black and minority teachers.** JCPS must be intentional about recruiting teachers who reflect the students

in the classrooms across the district. According to the National Education Association, tens of thousands of black and minority teachers were pushed out of the classroom when integration of schools occurred. JCPS still has not recovered from these losses. Across the district, a little more than 16% of teachers are teachers of color, while students of color make up over 52% of the students in JCPS. As we make up for the teachers that we lost, we will also raise JCPS test scores and graduation rates. We know from research conducted by Johns Hopkins University that having even just one Black teacher in elementary school reduces the probability of a Black, low-income student dropping out of school by 29%. Staff who look like students instill confidence and create higher expectations. They raise the bar, and students meet it.

Further, approximately 3% of teachers nationally are retiring each year. JCPS can't afford these losses. To entice the best and brightest teachers to our district, we suggest a direct recruitment strategy that would pay the student loans for up to 600 teachers coming into our district over the next three years. Based on estimated public university costs of $125,000, the total investment by JCPS will be approximately $75M over the course of three years. These teachers would also receive a $10,000 sign-on bonus to commit to working in an identified underperforming school for five years. This is important because we need to reduce turnover in these schools. In total, JCPS will invest $81M in the recruitment of teachers.

4. **Retain teachers by offering a $20,000 annual incentive for teachers in CSI schools.** CSI - comprehensive support and improvement- schools are among the lowest 5% in academic performance or have graduation rates below 80%. We need to

do all that we can to reduce the amount of turnover in these schools, including providing resources needed to ensure the success of teachers and thereby students. Just like in a company with high turnover, when teachers are not retained, it leads to an influx of new teachers in a school. This, in turn, leads to new teachers being forced to learn the school, policies and procedures, along with the needs of each student. These new teachers are forced to learn all of these things without the guidance of veteran teachers. Students and parents are often already dealing with inconsistency in many avenues of their life -- classroom inconsistency should not be an additional one. In the current environment, there are 36 CSI schools with a collective 1,377 teachers. Implementing this recommendation equates to an investment of $27.5M a year or $82.5M over three years.

5. **Invest in technology for students.** The need for digital connectedness and the reality of the digital divide has been made more clear than ever through the COVID-19 pandemic. A 1:1 technology ratio is essential for students to survive in our world today, and every company in our community benefits when young people graduate with digital skills. We urge JCPS to purchase 32,000 more Chromebooks as they did during the 2019-2020 school year for $11.4M.

6. **Commit to providing educational experiences that will enhance the learning of students in the lowest-performing schools in the district.** A full 36 of the 50 lowest performing schools in Kentucky are JCPS schools. The principals, administrators, and teachers that lead these JCPS schools know what their students need to succeed. They need the resources to address the challenges their students face inside and outside of the classroom. We recommend $1.5M to each of these schools to offer students the programmatic offerings their leaders determine are necessary to achieve student success.

7. **Increase cultural competency.** We have a majority-minority school district. The level of cultural competency among JCPS employees, including but not limited to teachers, must be greatly improved. Our students will succeed in classrooms with teachers that understand them and can address issues that arise through a lens of knowledge. To do this, we are encouraging JCPS to require cultural competency education for all employees. This should also be incentivized and provided consistently over the three years, helping to improve the culture in many of our schools. We suggest a $3M budget over three years. This training delivered in a group setting could be as low as $55 per person; with 18,000 employees in JCPS, this would equate to $1M per year over three years for the training.

8. **Invest in technology for out-of-school time providers.** Out-of-school time providers are integral to the success of our students. They provide academic enrichment, social and emotional support, exposure to higher education, a sense of belonging, and more. Just like the schools, these programs require the technology needed to meet the needs of students in a digital world. An estimated $10M should be allocated to these providers to support their technology capacity and infrastructure.

9. **Address Trauma.** Simply put, our children are experiencing unprecedented levels of trauma, and our schools need the resources to address it. Social workers and mental health workers should be contracted through our colleges and universities to support the emotional needs of our students during the school day. This requires agreements

for information and record sharing that will warrant the use of project managers to fully effectuate these changes in record-setting timeframes. In 2019, JCPS had 136 mental health practitioners across the district. We need to quadruple the amount of these practitioners on staff, bringing the total number of mental health practitioners to 544 across the district. This would require an additional investment by JCPS of approximately $50M over three years.

10. **Support JCPS Human Resource Department.** We are fully aware that the JCPS administration must invest in additional Human Resources staff who can execute these recommendations. From making contact with colleges and universities, to ensuring coordination of intensive tutoring services with out-of-school-time providers and families, JCPS will need contractual staff to help handle the load as we work to improve and quickly utilize these resources.

11. **Establish Universal Pre-K.** JCPS should use the funding to establish more early childhood classrooms so that our city can be at the forefront of offering universal pre-K. The data is clear - with high-quality early childhood programs, people are more likely to have a higher income in their adult life, graduate high school on time, and have less of a need for interventions later in their educational career. Head Start and Early Head Start serves the nation's most at-risk children from birth through a "whole child' model which includes education, health, nutrition, health and social services. Head Start goes further by helping parents with their educational literacy and life goals. This stabilizes families and lifts them from poverty. Despite Head Start's documented successes, it is underfunded reaching only 50% of the eligible kids. Early Head Start reaches only 5%.

JCPS must convene early childhood leaders like Head Start providers Ohio Valley Education Cooperative and The Family and Children's Agency as well as private and other nonprofit providers. With the expertise of these leaders, we encourage JCPS to address the lack of early childhood classrooms by investing in our youngest students -- specifically in those areas where students are further behind and where early interventions can therefore help the most. JCPS can do this by first establishing 4 early childhood classrooms in the 26 one-star schools across the district. This investment will cost approximately $48M, with $22M for staffing and $26M for costs related to the startup and continuation of the programs.

These recommendations are grounded in data and lived experiences, and most importantly, they can be done. They meet our children where they are. For the first time in a generation, we have the money to invest in change. It is education that pulls families out of poverty. It is education that helps to build safe communities. We have the funding to transform this entire community, and the lives of hundreds of thousands of residents. We have the funding but only we can decide if we have the will.

Do we have the courage to empower our children to be a better generation? Do we want better for them? Do we believe they are capable of greatness? We say, yes! The question is, are we? As JCPS Chief Equity

Officer Dr. John Marshall said, "Equity doesn't have to be hard. It's just got to be brave." Let's be brave.

Louisville Urban League
Louisville Urban League Former CEO, Benjamin Richmond
Louisville Urban League Guild
Louisville Urban League Young Professionals
15,000 Degrees
Alpha Kappa Alpha Sorority, Inc., Eta Omega Chapter
AMPED
Antioch Missionary Baptist Church
Art Thrust
Bates Community Development Corporation
Bates Memorial Baptist Church
Beargrass Missionary Baptist Church
Broadway Baptist Church
Canaan Christian Church
Canaan Community Development Corporation
Canon to the Ordinary, Episcopal Diocese of Kentucky
Center for Neighborhoods
Central Presbyterian Church
Christ Church Cathedral
Cities United
Closing the Gap Consulting
Coalition Supporting Young Adults
Congregation Adath Jeshurun
Emmanuel Baptist Church
Evolve 502
Exploited Children's Help Organization (ECHO)
Gifted By Design Leadership and Consulting
Highland Baptist Church
Jewish Federation of Louisville
Kentucky Alliance Against Racist and Political Oppression
Kingdom Fellowship Christian Life Center
Kingdom Fellowship Life Development Corporation
Louisville Alumnae Chapter of Delta Sigma Theta Sorority, Inc.
Louisville Alumni Chapter of Kappa Alpha Psi Fraternity, Inc.

Louisville Alumni Chapter of NPHC
Louisville Central Community Center
Louisville Kappa League
Minority Mental Health Project
Molo Village Community Development Corporation
NAACP Kentucky State Conference
New Horizon Baptist Church
No More Red Dots, Inc.
Play Cousins Collective
REBOUND, Inc.
River City Drum Corporation
Simmons College of Kentucky
Sowing Seeds with Faith
St. Matthew's Episcopal Church
St. Peter's United Church of Christ
St. Stephen Church
The 40 & 1 Company
The Bail Project (Louisville)
Until Justice Data Partners

A NEW DAY?

JCPS, BLACK STUDENTS AND STUDENT ASSIGNMENT

Corrie Shull, Ph.D.

Board Member, 6th District , Jefferson County Board of Education
Pastor, Burnett Avenue Baptist Church

Just before her death at ninety-six years old, Cicely Tyson released *Just As I Am,* a fascinating memoir in which she makes the tremendous observation that "social transformation is not measured in weeks or months but in generations."[1] In June of 2022, the Jefferson County Board of Education unanimously voted to take a step toward social transformation as mediated through public education by revising the district's Student Assignment plan. Since 1984, Jefferson County Public School's Student Assignment plan, which determines where students attend school, prioritized the preferences of White, wealthy, East End families. The former plan allowed this group to stay close to home while assigning Black and/or poor students living in Louisville's West End to schools outside of their communities. This plan often required Black students to endure long bus rides each morning and evening. This negatively impacted at least one generation of students matriculating through the Jefferson County Public School System underscored by ever declining rates of academic achievement, student belonging and attendance. After nearly four decades, there is a new Student Assignment plan that district leaders believe will usher in a new day for Black students in JCPS. The new Student Assignment plan gives West End families the option of choosing to attend a school closer to home, aligning the district's magnet programs with the standards of Magnet Schools of America and funding "Choice Zone" schools more equitably. However, the question remains: will the changes be enough to usher in a new, more equitable, day for Black students wherein both academic success and proximity to one's address are accomplished simultaneously?

In my estimation, the answer to this question revolves around JCPS' commitment to equitably resourcing schools within the "Choice Zone" as well as other schools that have been designated as "Accelerated Improvement Schools." It is not enough for the JCPS Board of Education to vote in favor of sweeping changes to the Student Assignment plan and then precipitously allow for funding to be

---

1   Tyson, C. & Burford, M. (2021). Just as I am: A memoir. HarperCollins Publishers.

reduced for the necessary wrap-around-services that these schools will demand when no one is paying attention. What the current JCPS Board of Education knows is that schools within the "Choice Zone" will have high concentrations of poverty. Schools having high concentrations of poverty does not mean that students within those schools cannot learn but it does mean that those students must overcome more barriers to achieve academic success. The barriers that those students must overcome necessitate more mental health resources, behavioral supports, and learning supports than schools that do not have as high concentrations of poverty.

The need for additional resources must be reiterated for every succeeding board member elected and every succeeding superintendent hired to lead JCPS, as neither the current superintendent nor the current board members will hold their positions for the duration of time that it will take to implement, or assess the effectiveness of, the changes called for in the new Student Assignment plan. Without question or equivocation, current and future district administrators and school board members must give unwavering commitment to resource allocations that will ensure the success of "Choice Zone" and Accelerated Improvement Schools. Otherwise, the most recently adopted Student Assignment plan will be merely another well-intentioned document that has no transformative consequences for Black students.

To put it simply, the game has changed. The foundation for a more equitable, inclusive, district is in place. Now, the community must be as vigilant about budgetary matters as we are cultural responsiveness and cultural reflectiveness. It is a wonderful thing that students living in Louisville's historic Black communities- such as the West End and Newburg- will now be able to choose to attend schools that are closer to their homes. This choice

could provide greater opportunities for family involvement in the school community, shorter commutes, and a reduction of chronic absenteeism. However, proximity to one's address should never come at the expense of equitably-resourced schools that will provide a myriad of well-resourced academic and extracurricular offerings.

Over the long-term, ensuring that this balance of quality and proximity with fidelity is up to the community. After all, elected officials and superintendents change and with those changes come different agendas and sophisticated schemes to manipulate the ways in which resources are allocated. Our community cannot afford to take our eyes off the implementation of the new plan. Regardless of who is at the table, we must hold the district accountable for its promises to our children and our community.

To be sure, the new Student Assignment plan can be an opportunity for a new day for Black students in JCPS, but the quality of that new day will be dependent upon resource allocation that empowers school-based personnel to successfully create school environments that produce extraordinary outcomes for Black students. Unfortunately, if Ms. Tyson's words are true, we may not be able to fully assess the success of this new plan for another generation. Still, when that assessment is finally made, it will tell a story about all of us— elected officials, JCPS administrators and community. May the future story be that our work in this generation ensured better outcomes for the next generation.

UK IS BEATING UofL AGAIN

THIS TIME IN FIGHTING ANTI-BLACKNESSS

Ricky L. Jones, Ph.D.., Professor and Chair, Department of Pan-African Studies
University of Louisville

It was jarring when I arrived at the University of Kentucky as a new political science graduate student fresh out of the Naval Academy and Morehouse College three decades ago. The department had very few Black graduate students and no Black professors. "Man, this is a really white space," I thought. As I learned more about the Bluegrass State, I realized many people thought things were better 70 some-odd miles away at the University of Louisville. Many considered U of L the "Black school" when compared to UK.

That's changed!

In recent years, Kentucky, not Louisville, has been the university to seriously invest in fighting anti-Blackness and changing the course of its campus. UK has pushed a robust Black faculty hiring plan that has yielded impressive results. Currently, according to Derrick White, Professor of History and African American and Africana Studies at the University of Kentucky, UK has 76 full-time Black faculty members in its College of Arts and Sciences alone. That rivals or exceeds U of L's total number of full-time Blacks across its entire university.

University of Louisville shamefully began last school year with only 24 Black professors in Arts and Sciences, its largest college. Ten were in one department: Pan-African Studies (PAS). Multiple Black scholars left during the year, dropping that already paltry number into the teens. It's unclear how many have been replaced.

For many years, Louisville bragged that it housed the state's only Black Studies department at a public university. Indeed, Pan-African Studies is one of the oldest in the country and celebrates its 50th anniversary in 2023. What is not currently discussed is that several moves have been made over the last few years at Louisville that endanger PAS, its only academic unit solely dedicated to studying and teaching about the Black experience.

University core curriculum changes have funneled student traffic away from PAS. Budget model changes have stripped it of funds, an area where it was previously among the strongest in the country. Its full-time faculty has almost been slashed in half with no current plan to address the losses. University of Louisville has reduced PAS's general funds budget literally to $0. Meanwhile, UK's administration has developed the "Commonwealth Institute for Black Studies," hired multiple faculty members to work with it, and dedicated $200,000 a year of guaranteed money to it in perpetuity.

Full-time Black faculty numbers have dropped like a

stone across U of L. The environment is so bad that most refuse to even entertain counteroffers to stay. The school's interim provost recently claimed there is now a long-requested plan to address and correct this problem. That remains to be seen.

Readers may say, "Wait! Didn't the University of Louisville claim that it aspired to be the nation's premier antiracist university back in 2020?" Yeah, that's over. The president who made that proclamation is long gone. Word is that U of L's current leadership is loath to even use the phrase "antiracist university" for fear of retribution by conservative Kentucky legislators and community pushback.

Apparently, the behind-the-scenes party line is they'll "do the work" without the "antiracist university" language. Even though both white people and strategically placed Black people at the school will take umbrage, the so-called "work" they are currently doing where Black folk are concerned is questionable. Like many white-dominated spaces, it can be argued that U of L has joined in on the "DEI (diversity, equity, and inclusion) lie." They talk about diversity when challenged (rarely about Black folk specifically, mind you) but do very little of consequence when the curtain is pulled back.

The commitment to silence where anti-Blackness is concerned is becoming a pattern for U of L. When the state's Republican-dominated legislature pushed anti-Black laws attacking the substantive teaching of race (in the guise of anti-critical race theory), Louisville's leadership said little to nothing. Black faculty who cared felt hung out to dry. That silence was (and is) deafening. No wonder so many Black staff members are leaving.

Dr. Brandon McCormack, the director of the University of Louisville's Anne Braden Institute and associate professor of Pan-African Studies, opined in 2020, "Listen. The University of Kentucky apparently gets it. You can't say Black Lives Matter without demonstrating, with resources, that Black studies matter. Period." That's quite an admission from McCormack, who is a Louisville graduate and no fan of that Big Blue school up the road.

Of course, U of L's terminal decision-makers will explain it all away. There will even be a few low-expectation-having, institutionalized, anaesthetized Black people who will join them and say, "It's not all that bad, we're doing more than you know" and call criticisms such as this one "extreme" or "unfair." They will say to those who care about fighting anti-Blackness that it's very difficult or impossible for the school to dedicate resources to this issue because it has no money. According to them, Louisville is all but broke.

Maybe that's true. Maybe U of L simply isn't a financially viable institution anymore (outside of paying athletic coaches, of course). Or maybe the school is just fine financially. Maybe the university's current decision makers just don't care deeply about Black issues. Or maybe they do. Who knows at this point? What we do know is UK has come a long way since I became only the second African American to receive a Ph.D. in political science there 26 years ago. Meanwhile, U of L has regressed. Nobody can say with a straight face that U of L is the "Black school" when compared to UK anymore.

It would be a stretch to argue the University of Kentucky has evolved into an institution that's great for Black folk. In the grand scheme of things, it may not even be good just yet. But it's trying and is damn sure better than the University of Louisville right now. And that's pretty doggone sad.

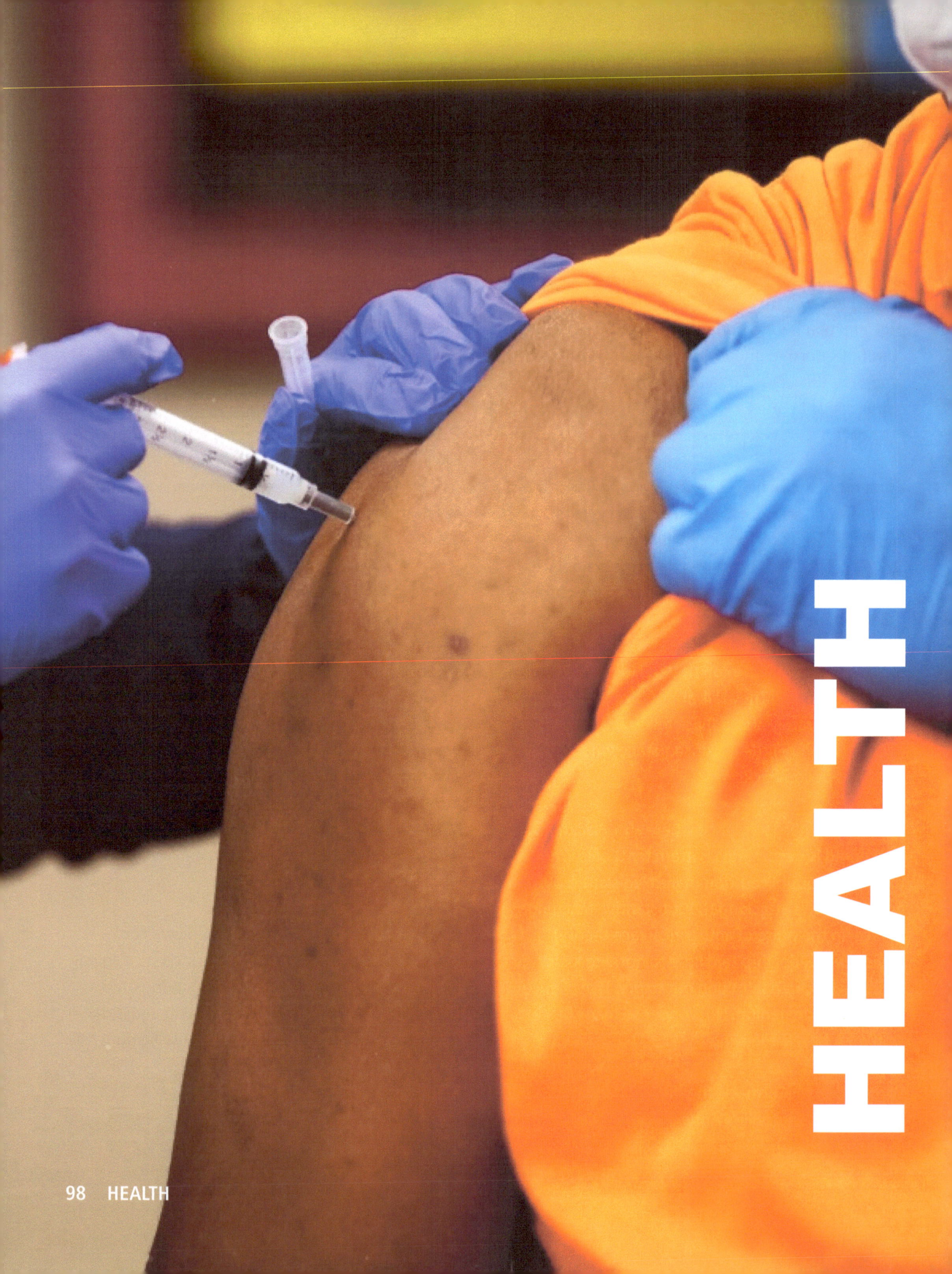

HEALTH

ADDRESSING CANCER SURVEILLANCE AND SURVIVORSHIP IN THE BLACK COMMUNITY

Janikaa C. Sherrod, MPH, Cancer Control Specialist
Kentucky Cancer Program
University of Louisville
James Graham Brown Cancer Center

Out of every 100,000 Americans living in Kentucky, approximately 207.4 African Americans in contrast to 197.8 Caucasian Americans will die of breast, colon, lung, and cervical cancer.[1]

Although this racial disparity has decreased, cancer continues to burden the Black community at a disproportionate rate. Therefore, for the African American community, the color of cancer is not pink, blue, or purple, but different shades of black and brown. Social causes such as socioeconomic status, housing, education, accessibility to health care, and environmental surroundings does increase individuals' risk of getting cancer. Unfortunately, for the Black community, these factors are a consistent struggle towards attaining equity.

Limited access to healthcare is a major contributor to racial disparities. Lack of healthcare increases the chance of Blacks not receiving recommended cancer screenings or delayed screenings from a healthcare profession when early treatment would have been effective. Blacks are less likely to receive preventive services and more likely to receive low quality healthcare. The same social factors that contribute to higher death rates in the Black community are the same factors that cause a gap in the five-year cancer survival rate among African Americans.[2]

Lower-income African American survivors are in the group of individuals that is not receiving surveillance

1   Kentucky Cancer Registry. (2018). Cancer incidence/mortality rates in Kentucky. Retrieved from https://www.cancer-rates.info/ky/

2   American Cancer Society. (2019). Cancer facts & figures for African Americans. Retrieved from https://www.cancer.org/content/dam/cancer-org/research/cancer-facts-and-statistics/cancer-facts-and-figures-for-african-americans/cancer-facts-and-figures-for-african-americans-2019-2021.pdf

and follow-up treatment, leading to a widening gap in survivorship. Moreover, socioeconomic status is associated with housing, environmental surroundings, and education causes, which influences cancer risk and outcomes along the cancer continuum.

According to the American Cancer Society, African American women have an 81 percent breast cancer survival rate compared to a 91 percent survival rate in white women.[3] This racial disparity is consistent across cancer types. Black women have a cervical cancer five-year survival rate of 56 percent compared to white women's 68 percent; acolorectal cancer survival rate of 58 percent compared to white women's 65 percent; and lung cancer survival rate of 16 percent compared to a 19 percent survival rate in white women. This is a significant problem that will change the way we approach healthcare in the African American community.

We need to move beyond past and present policies that have fueled such social factors. Not only do we need continued multi-sector collaboration to address this racial disparity, but in order to see significant decreases in cancer mortality rates among African Americans, systems of dominance that have long oppressed the African American community must be redressed to change the circumstances that obstruct Black people's ability to move forward. In addition, healthcare professionals must explicitly acknowledge that race and racism factor into healthcare.

---

3   American Cancer Society. (2019). Cancer facts & figures for African Americans. Retrieved from https://www.cancer.org/content/dam/cancer-org/research/cancer-facts-and-statistics/cancer-facts-and-figures-for-african-americans/cancer-facts-and-figures-for-african-americans-2019-2021.pdf

USING DATA FOR ACTION
MOBILIZING FOR A HEALTHY BLACK LOUISVILLE

Dr. Billie Castle, Executive Director
Oasis Living in Freedom and Excellence (LIFE) Center

"In Louisville, health equity means that everyone has a fair and just opportunity to be healthy and reach their full human potential."[1]

The Center for Health Equity (CHE) provided comprehensive data and an overview of the current health status of the city in their 2017 Health Equity Report.[2] The report details historical injustices, and we can see where white supremacy and capitalism have shaped concentrated wealth and concentrated scarcity. Daily, white supremacy and capitalism impact local and statewide decisions that continue to harm Black Louisville. We have overwhelming amounts of data that show us exactly what needs to be done and where. Now is the time to balance the emphasis from what is wrong to what we need.

Black Louisville needs to be at the baseline of the median indicators of Louisville Metro in order for us to be the top-tier city amongst our peers such as Charlotte, North Carolina, St. Louis, Missouri, Cincinnati, Ohio, Omaha, Nebraska, and Kansas City, Kansas.[3] While reparations are past due, they are not the sole answer to moving Black Louisville forward. Reparations are an ADDITION to creating a city where the life expectancy map is dark green for ALL of Louisville Metro (See map). To move forward, Black Louisville needs to first be moved UPWARD. Upward within the median income. Upward towards closing the educational achievement gap. Upward of eliminating poverty. Upward in access to food. Upward in safe and affordable housing, WITHOUT displacement and gentrification. Upward towards safe and healthy communities.

In the 2017 report, the Center for Health Equity offered this policy recommendation: "Implementing a state-level Earned Income Tax Credit (EITC) to aid

1   Center for Health Equity. (2017). Louisville Metro health equity report. Retrieved from https://louisvilleky.gov/sites/default/files/health_and_wellness/che/health_equity_report/health_equity_report.pdf

2   Center for Health Equity. (2017). Louisville Metro health equity report. Retrieved from https://louisvilleky.gov/sites/default/files/health_and_wellness/che/health_equity_report/health_equity_report.pdf

3   Costello, D. (2019, March 26). Report: Louisville hasn't jumped ahead of peer cities. Here's how it compares. Courier-Journal. Retrieved from https://www.courier-journal.com/story/news/politics/metro-government/2019/03/26/greater-louisville-project-report-how-louisville-compares-peer-cities/3269992002/

wealth building and alleviate poverty." This is one example of a policy Black Louisville can mobilize around in the creation of healthy communities. Mobilization depends on Black Louisville's understanding of and functioning by mutual aid — "giving each other needed material support, trying to resist the control of dynamics, hierarchies, and system-affirming, oppressive arrangements of charity and social services."[4] We must reject white supremacy culture and the culture of economic exploitation, respectability, and love for Black capitalism in community building. We must also ensure that the actions we create and advocate for do not replicate the harm we have internalized at the hands of the current systems and structures.

Free African Society, New African Society for Mutual Relief, Phoenix Society, and various Negro mutual benefit societies in Philadelphia are examples of what W.E.B. DuBois called, "the first wavering step of a people toward organized social life."[5] During times when austerity measures are being taken at all levels of government, Black Louisville needs to create a community that models these examples of mutually beneficial societies.

The Louisville Urban League is positioned to lead Black Louisville into such a model through the organization's key five areas of jobs, justice, education, health, and housing. Its new Norton Healthcare Sports & Learning Center will provide Black Louisville with the opportunity to access much of the needed resources for extending our life expectancy rates. Many of the early mutual assistance societies functioned within these areas providing job training, educating the Black community, and providing healthcare and other basic needs to protect and sustain the community. The time is now to invest in our community and receive the investments owed to Black Louisville to ensure the community is healthy.

We need to create a shared vision for how we will model our institutions and sustain our communities free of white supremacy. We need to heal together, protect each other, and build for each other. We need to imagine what our community would look like without the extraction of capitalism and violence of sexism, queerphobia, ableism, and classism.

---

4   Big Door Brigade. (n.d.). What is mutual aid? Retrieved from https://bigdoorbrigade.com/what-is-mutual-aid/
5   National Humanities Center Toolbox Library. (n.d.). Mutual benefit. Retrieved from http://nationalhumanitiescenter.org/pds/maai/community/text5/text5read.htm

WATER EQUITY

Tony Parrott, Executive Director
Sharise Horne, Director of Community Benefits
Louisville and Jefferson County Metropolitan Sewer District

The US Water Alliance defines water equity as "just and fair inclusion–a condition in which everyone has an opportunity to participate and prosper. Water equity occurs when all communities have access to safe, clean, affordable drinking water and wastewater services; are resilient in the face of floods, drought, and other climate risks; have a role in decision-making processes related to water management in their communities; and share in the economic, social, and environmental benefits of water systems."[1] [2]

The economic, social, and environmental benefits is a triple bottom line approach that not only advances equity, opportunity, and fairness as an economic driver, but one that ensures a prosperous future for the upcoming generations, our community, and our country. Economic inclusion tools and strategies that connect underrepresented groups to new jobs and economic activity are essential in social mobility and economic empowerment.

Three strategies in Metropolitan Sewer District's (MSD) toolbox are used to accomplish the integration of water equity, economic inclusion, and alignment with Metro Louisville's Resilience Plan:

Resilience = Equity + Compassion + Trust

-   Equity = Maximizing the overall investment in infrastructure as part of a job creation strategy

-   Compassion = Create opportunities for local businesses owned by women and members of minority groups

-   Trust = Economic inclusion — conduct Disparity Study to verify

A key component in fostering economic growth

---

1   US Water Alliance (2105). The pillars of water equity. Retrieved from http://uswateralliance.org/wec/framework

2   US Water Alliance (2017). An equitable water future: A national briefing paper. Retrieved from http://uswateralliance.org/sites/uswateralliance.org/files/publications/uswa_waterequity_FINAL.pdf

and competitiveness is the public investment in our infrastructure. Public infrastructure like water and sewer systems, bridges, roads, transit lines, and communication lines are fundamental to economic vitality. Public investment is one of the most effective job creation strategies. Infrastructure connects workers to jobs and educational opportunities, increases business efficiency, revitalizes distressed neighborhoods, and fosters growth. That is the formula for water equity!

In 2018, MSD completed a comprehensive Disparity Study which examined our contracting practices over a five-year period. Disparity Studies review government or utilities rules, regulations, and ordinances for public contracting. The study also performed a comprehensive analysis of potential bidders to determine which firms are ready, willing, and able to bid on contracts. The study found a disparity existed regarding underutilization in the award of MSD prime and subcontracts among African Americans and other people of color. As a result of the findings, we have committed to implementing new programs and enhancing others to ensure our policies advance equity and opportunity for all. You cannot discuss equity until you first acknowledge that there is inequity.

MSD is committed to ensuring we are maximizing the economic, environmental, and social benefits from our large-scale infrastructure projects. We formalized a Community Benefits Program to leverage capital investments in water infrastructure to benefit ratepayers through workforce development, education, and economic development. The program not only provides a workforce pipeline for careers in wastewater infrastructure, but it also includes procurement policies that incentivize vendors to provide community benefits through volunteer hours, in-kind services, or financial contributions to local non-profits, community-based organizations, and schools. In addition, MSD has vested resources to ensure our revamped Supplier Diversity Program is not only sustainable and measurable, but enforceable. The companies MSD directly and indirectly contracts with must adequately reflect the diversity of our community and the residents we serve.

To enable an equitable future for all, a community that is resilient, equitable, compassionate, and trusted, leaders in Louisville must recognize that policies and practices must be intentional and focused on the needs of the most vulnerable communities so the entire city and metro area can realize its full potential.

The planned investments in water and wastewater will provide a platform where existing policies can be modified and new programs developed to ensure Louisville is creating job opportunities for the local workforce — now and for generations to come.

LOUISVILLE'S DADS MAKING A DIFFERENCE

Armon R. Perry, MSW, Ph.D., Professor
Kent School of Social Work
University of Louisville

Contemporary society requires much more of men to earn the title of a good father today than in days gone by. Historically, securing gainful employment and providing for one's children were sufficient parenting goals for men. However, in the last 30 years, research indicates that fathers have become more receptive to expanding their parenting repertories[1]. Consistent with this expansion, researchers, practitioners, and policymakers have begun to recognize the multidimensional nature of fatherhood which now includes equal emphasis on financial responsibility, increased accessibility, and engagement in caregiving[2].

Unfortunately, fathers face many barriers that limit their ability to act on their intentions to take more active roles in the lives of their children. Among these are individual and interpersonal barriers are: conflictual co-parenting relationships[3], maternal gatekeeping behavior[4][5], as well as macro-level barriers such as structural racism manifested in disparate criminal justice involvement[6], and economic shifts that have led to the outsourcing of manufacturing work that many low and semi-skilled men relied on to earn a wage that could

1   Mazza, C., & Perry, A. (2017). *Fatherhood in America: Social work perspectives on a changing society.* Springfield, IL: Charles C. Thomas Publishers.

2   Lamb, M. (1986). *The role of the father in child development: Applied perspectives.* New York: John Wiley & Sons.

3   Perry, A., Rollins, A., & Perez, A. (in-press). A mile in my shoes: An exploration of custodial mothers' perspectives on empathy and its role in co-parenting and paternal involvement. Journal of Child and Family Studies.

4   Goldberg, J. S. (2015). Co-parenting and nonresident fathers' monetary contributions to their children. Journal of Marriage & Family, 77(3), 612-627.

5   Goldberg, J. S. (2015). Co-parenting and nonresident fathers' monetary contributions to their children. Journal of Marriage & Family, 77(3), 612-627.

6   Williams, D., & Perry, A. (2019). More than just incarceration: Law enforcement contact and black fathers' familial relationships. Issues in Race & Society, 47, 85-118.

support their families[7]. For Black fathers, these barriers are exacerbated because of the way that they disproportionately impact men of color[8].

Locally, there have also been efforts to deficit-frame fathers as absent and unconcerned. A few examples include a former television show called *Deadbeat Kentuckiana*, and the Courier Journal publishing the names of child support delinquent parents around Father's Day. There has also been statewide legislation passed which makes non-resident parents ineligible for Supplemental Nutrition Assistance Program (SNAP) benefits if they fall behind on their child support payments. At best, these policies and uses of media are ill-advised efforts to raise awareness. At worst, they are willful and intentional attempts to smear, stigmatize, and punish non-resident fathers who are disproportionately Black.

In either case, beyond satisfying society's interest in getting its proverbial pound of flesh from non-resident fathers, this public parent-shaming does nothing to help fathers act on their intentions to take more active roles in their children's lives. In fact, it only serves to further reinforce the archaic notion that financial provision is and should be fathers' most significant contribution to their children's growth and development. For these reasons, it has been encouraging to see a few recent examples of policies in Kentucky that have the potential to positively impact fathers. The first is the increasingly popular family court law that includes 50-50 parenting time presumptions when parents divorce. In these cases, the law goes beyond traditional joint legal custody which gives both parents decision-making authority. Rather, these laws guarantee that children have access to both of their mother and father based on a schedule agreed upon by both parents, with the possibility of exceptions being made where there is evidence of abuse or when the parents live so far apart that such an arrangement is not feasible.

Another recent policy innovation is the advent of the "self-support reserve." With it, Kentucky lawmakers have developed guidelines that consider the basic needs of low-income parents with limited means when calculating the amount of their child-support obligation. This provision is an attempt to recognize that a low-income parent needs to be able to meet their own subsistence needs while still paying child support.

These recent policy shifts represent the increasing awareness that fathers' roles are unique and irreplaceable. And while they are a great start, there still exists a gap in services that aim to assist fathers in developing their skills as nurturers and caregivers.

In response, the 4 Your Child Fatherhood Program represents an attempt to support fathers in their efforts to increase their capacity for involved parenting. The 4 Your Child program was developed from a federally funded grant to provide parent education workshops and solutions-focused case management services to non-resident fathers. The parent education workshops consisted of 28 hours of content on a variety of topics including parenting, co-parenting, conflict resolution, communication, emotional intelligence, health, mental health, balancing work and family responsibilities, child development, and discipline. The case management component of the program is individualized and most often focused on helping fathers secure more access to their children or improving their socioeconomic status. In addition to participating in the parent education workshops and case

---

7   Edin, K., & Nelson, T. (2013). Doing the best I can. Berkeley, CA: University of California Press.

8   Kerr, J., Schafer, P., Perry, A., Orkin, J., Vance, M., & O' Campo, P. (2018). The impact of racial discrimination on African American fathers' intimate relationships. Race and Social Problems, 10 (2), 134-144.

management services, data were also collected on programmatic outcomes and fathers' satisfaction with the services they received. We found a significant difference between fathers' pre- and post-intervention parenting knowledge, one of 4 Your Child's most important outcomes.

Family is the primary institution in society and as such, many of the challenges facing our society have their roots in challenges facing families. Despite the widespread agreement that contemporary fathers should be financial providers and engaged caregivers, we have not done enough to facilitate fathers' ability to meet these expectations. The 4 Your Child Fatherhood Program represents one of only a few resources in Louisville aimed at supporting fathers. Given the positive gains being made by the fathers that enrolled in the program, local policymakers would be wise to invest in initiatives such as 4 Your Child, 502 Fathers, and the Commonwealth Center for Fathers and Families because doing so has the potential to transform the lives of Louisville's children, families, and communities.

DIABETES IN WEST LOUISVILLE, KENTUCKY:
PREVENTABLE CAUSE OF SUFFERING AND DEATH

Bert Little, Ph.D.
Craig Blakely, Ph.D., M.P.H.
Brad Shuck, Ph.D.
Matt Ruther, Ph.D.
University of Louisville

Type 2 diabetes mellitus (T2DM) is a chronic disease nationally, but in west Louisville, there are alarming trends of increasing prevalence. The prevalence of T2DM in the United States is approximately 12% among whites, 14% among African Americans, and 22% among Hispanics.[1] The prevalence of T2DM in the state of Kentucky is 12.5%. In west Louisville, the prevalence of T2DM is 12.6% to 23.2% depending on age — well above the national average of 12%.[2]

Type 2 Diabetes Associations

Current trends indicate that cases of T2DM are increasing nationally but at even higher rates among African Americans and Hispanics. In predominately African American communities like west Louisville, there are between 12.5% and 20% of adults have T2DM. By contrast, 4% to 8% of adults in predominately white communities like east Jefferson County have diabetes. Because T2DM prevalence is a reflection of overall community health, this upward trend is alarming and requires urgency to identify the contributing factors. Further compounding the problem, an estimated 40% of T2DM cases remain undiagnosed.[3] T2DM is a medically urgent diagnosis because it is associated with six major life-threatening complications: kidney failure, peripheral artery disease (PAD)/peripheral vascular disease (PVD) leading to limb amputation, diabetic heart disease, diabetic retinopathy, neuropathy, and ketoacidosis.

The Link to Poverty

Compare household income[4] with T2DM, and one can clearly see that T2DM prevalence is highest where income is lowest in Jefferson County: west

1   Menke, A., Casagrande, S., Geiss, L., & Cowie, C. (2015). Prevalence and trends of diabetes among adults in the United States, 1988-2012. Journal of the American Medical Association, 314(10), 1021-1029.

2   Behavioral Risk Factor Surveillance System. (2017). Kentucky Department for Public Health and Centers for Disease Control. Kentucky Behavioral Risk Factor Survey Data: 2000, 2011, 2012, 2013, 2015 and 2017. Retrieved from https://chfs.ky.gov/agencies/dph/dpqi/cdpb/Pages/brfssreports.aspx

3   Cabinet for Health and Family Services. (2019). Kentucky Diabetes Report. Retrieved from https://chfs.ky.gov/agencies/dph/dpqi/cdpb/dpcp/2019%20Diabetes%20Report%20latest%5b11610%5d.pdf

4   U.S. Census Bureau. (2019). American Community Survey. Retrieved from https://www.census.gov/programs-surveys/acs/data.html

Louisville. It can be more convenient for a working parent to get dinner at fast food drive-thru than to shop and cook a meal at home. Foods high in carbohydrates are a staple in the fast food industry because they are cheaper to serve than more nutrient-rich, high-protein foods. Fast-food restaurants thrive in poverty-stricken areas such as west Louisville, whereas full grocery stores leave such areas.[5] West Louisville has many more restaurants (green circles on map) than traditional grocery stores (red squares) compared to east Jefferson County.

Poverty and Food Deserts

The link to T2DM in west Louisville is *food availability*, a major social determinant directly linked to poverty[6]. Overlay maps of T2DM, poverty, grocery and restaurants with food deserts, and the association is clear. T2DM is highest in places with high rates of poverty and limited food availability: food deserts.

Major challenges associated with poverty include gaps in educational opportunities, which determine nutritional information and knowledge about healthy eating habits. Poor physical activity is directly associated with high crime rates and lack of safe, accessible places for leisure physical movement (e.g., walking, running, ball games, etc.).

The issue is systematic and multifaceted, placing certain groups of a population at increased risk for obesity and hypertension. Changes in lifestyle to manage tense conditions become huge challenges, especially for those with T2DM. Interventions effective for prevention of T2DM include dietary change, increased physical activity, weight loss (a target body mass index of 23-24), management of blood pressure, and lowering bad cholesterol (i.e. low-density lipoprotein).

The Economic Argument to Prevent and Treat Diabetes

The National Institutes of Health reported that people with diabetes have average medical expenditures of more than $13,700 per year, of which about $7,900 is attributed to diabetes.[7] In Kentucky, the excess expenditures attributable to diabetes are higher, approximately $10,000 greater per year per person with T2DM.[8] Kentucky ranks 6th in the U.S. for prevalence of adult diabetes and 3rd in childhood obesity.[9]

In the immediate future, it is possible to decrease the likelihood of developing T2DM among those with metabolic syndrome (a precursor to T2DM) or pre-diabetes through careful changes in diet (i.e. limiting sugar and carbohydrate intake) and activity (i.e. walking as much as possible). Residents in areas with high prevalence of T2DM need primary care clinics located in the community to help those at risk of developing T2DM, and to treat those who have T2DM. Finally, medications to treat T2DM must be made available, along with appropriate pharmacist counseling, to those who have the disease but are unable to afford the medication or those who must

5. Louisville Jefferson County Information Consortium, (2019).. Retrieved from https://www.lojic.org/maps/map-hub

6. U.S. Department of Agriculture. (2019). Retrieved from https://www.ers.usda.gov/data-products/food-access-research-atlas/

7. Human Resources and Services Administration. (2017) Health Center Data. Retrieved from https://bphc.hrsa.gov/uds/datacenter.aspx?q=d&year=2017&state=KY#glist

8. Cabinet for Health and Family Services. (2019). Kentucky Diabetes Report. Retrieved from https://chfs.ky.gov/agencies/dph/dpqi/cdpb/dpcp/2019%20Diabetes%20Report%20latest%5b11610%5d.pdf

9. Cabinet for Health and Family Services. (2019). Diabetes education services scorecard for Kentucky. Retrieved from https://chfs.ky.gov/agencies/dph/dpqi/cdpb/dpcp/2019%20KY%20Diabetes%20Ed% 20Scorecard%20Final3.pdf

choose between their medications and feeding their family.

The things we can change are the social determinants of disease: increase food availability, create safe zones for physical activity, and improve educational and employment opportunities.

STATEMENT ON ROE

Louisville Urban League

June 24, 2022. Tomorrow our daughters will wake up in a world where they have less freedom than their mothers had the day before. This morning, the Supreme Court overturned the rights to abortion established in Roe v. Wade, which means that as early as today, Louisville citizens were denied quality healthcare because of the decisions of predominantly white male politicians. The trigger ban goes into effect immediately, and Kentucky is one of three states that have immediate bans.

The Louisville Urban League stands with the National Urban League in disavowing any policy that disproportionately, or negatively impacts our community. When the Supreme Court refused to block Texas's abortion ban last week, the National Urban League argued that these laws disproportionately affect members of the communities we serve. It is important that we protect our communities as an organization, regardless of personal beliefs or political affiliation.

The people are our priority, and the people are in trouble. Limited access to safe medical procedures will increase the death rates of women forced to take their health into their own hands. This is a direct slap in the face to women who just yesterday enjoyed reproductive freedom over their own bodies. Furthermore, studies have shown a causative relationship between limited access to abortion and higher rates of child abuse. Kentucky already has the fifth-highest rate of child maltreatment in the country. In 2019, we were in 1st place. "The people" includes our children, who are much more vulnerable to abuse when their very births are sources of resentment.

The Louisville Urban league stands with ThriveKY, a coalition of organizations dedicated to equitable health outcomes for all Kentuckians. We also stand with the Kentucky chapter of the American Civil Liberties Union, an organization prepared to sue the state of Kentucky to protect the rights of its citizens.

Please stand with us. Now is not the time to despair. Now is the time to get involved. You can contact your state and federal legislators directly to voice your opinion, but your voice rings loudest when it is attached to the vote. Now is the time to make sure that you and all eligible loved ones are registered to vote and increase turnout in the 2022 elections. This is also a time to have difficult conversations with friends and family members whose life experiences have not built empathy for desperation. Perhaps they can't even conceive of the decisions women are forced to make when reproductive justice is denied.

Please stay tuned as this tragic moment unfolds.

COMMUNITY DISPLACEMENT, ENVIRONMENTAL CHANGE AND THE IMPACT ON MENTAL WELL-BEING

Vicki Hines-Martin Ph.D., RN, FAAN
University of Louisville School of Nursing

Community displacement is the involuntary movement of a population out of a neighborhood as redevelopment occurs.[1] This displacement frequently occurs as a result of government-funded revitalization projects.

Within the city of Louisville, urban revitalization has had a significant impact on downtown and west Louisville neighborhoods, where most of these neighborhood residents are African Americans.

Revitalization projects focus on innovations that frequently change targeted communities from high-density housing to low-density communities which may or may not cause a net displacement of residents who once called the renovated community home. Revitalization involves investment in economically deprived neighborhoods, and the literature notes negative consequences for vulnerable populations in those neighborhoods, including increasing housing

1   Cohen.R. (2019). Shelter in Place: Reducing displacement & increasing inclusion in gentrifying neighborhoods. Harvard Law & Policy Review, 13(2). Retrieved from https://harvardlpr.com/wp-content/uploads/sites/20/2019/02/20180813-1_Cohen.pdf

costs, involuntary displacement, and loss of social ties.[234]

In addition, this neighborhood transition alters the architectural landscape that contains personal and community history valued by residents of those communities. Populations who are displaced are at risk for: 1) Being relocated temporarily [possibly to a more disadvantaged neighborhood and/or one in which resources and supports must be re-established]; 2) Inability to return to their former neighborhood [permanent displacement due to cost, especially among low-income renters]; and 3) Loss of familiar anchors [cultural/social displacement] that tie individuals and communities to their past and to each other.[567]

The research clearly identifies that most residents of these neighborhoods also experience greater disadvantage in political influence.[8] Although increasing attention is being focused on "Engag(ing) existing community residents and organizations, such as neighborhood associations, churches, and government agencies" to increase residents' voice[9] in the revitalization efforts, dislocation and resulting

changes to individuals', families', and communities' perceived identity and connectedness has had limited discussion.

Imagine calling a city home in which your former neighborhood no longer reflects any ties to your past. You cannot say "I once lived in this house", "This is where I visited my grandparents" or "This field is where all the neighborhood families used to play ball". What if the former neighborhood is one to which you could not return and therefore could not build new memories in a familiar setting? What is the impact on emotional well-being and mental health for individuals that reside in neighborhoods targeted for revitalization?

The lack of focus on the emotional well-being of those who are displaced undervalues the interests of the community residents who are affected. Studies that do focus on mental health identify that low-income residents of communities that experienced gentrification had higher rates of emergency room visits, mental health-related visits, and higher alcohol- and drug-related problems.[10] The significant impact of displacement and neighborhood change

2   Duggan, P. (2016). After a decade of gentrification, district sees a surge in families crushed by rent. The Washington Post. Retrieved from https://www.washingtonpost.com/local/social-issues/after-a-decade-of-gentrification-a-sharp-rise-indc-families-crushed-by-ent/2016/12/23/8c2dba92-c550-11e6-bf4b-2c064d32a4bf_story.html?utm_term=.034f4d76f5bd ill be displaced

3   Grass, T., Cho, S., & Joseph, M. (2016). HOPE VI data compilation and analysis. PD&R Research Partnerships. Retrieved from https://www.huduser.gov/portal/sites/default/files/pdf/HOPE-VI-Data-Compilation-and-Analysis.pdf

4   Office of Policy Development and Research. (2018). Displacement of lower-income families in urban areas report. U.S. Department of Housing and urban development

5   Mehdipanah R., Marra G., Melis G., & Gelormino, E. (2017). Urban renewal, gentrification and health equity: a realist perspective. The European Journal of Public Health, 28(2), 243–248.

6   Joint Center for Housing Studies of Harvard University. (2016). The state of the nation's housing 2016. Retrieved from http://www. jchs.harvard.edu/research/state_nations_housing

7   Meltzer, R., & Schuetz, J. (2012). Bodegas or bagel shops? Neighborhood differences in retail and household services," Economic Development Quarterly, 26 (1), 73–94.

8   Office of Policy Development and Research. (2018). Displacement of lower-income families in urban areas report. U.S. Department of Housing and urban development

9   Office of Policy Development and Research. (2018). Displacement of lower-income families in urban areas report. U.S. Department of Housing and urban development

10   Lim, S., Chan, P.Y., Walters, S., Culp, G,, Huynh, M., & Gould, L.H. (2017). Impact of residential displacement on healthcare access and mental health among original residents of gentrifying neighborhoods in New York City. PLoS ONE, 12(12): e0190139. https://doi.org/10.1371/journal.pone.0190139

on mental health observed by Lim et al (2017) is consistent with another study's findings. Keene, Geronimus and Wethering (2011) identified that temporarily or permanently displaced individuals experienced increases in reports of mental health conditions after demolition of public housing units.[11] Although the causes of displacement may be different, it may be "root shock" that links displacement with mental health.[12][13] Displaced persons no longer have access to the same social networks, may lose community ties, and often suffer disruptions in regular routines, which increase stress and psychological distress.[14][15]

The Matsuoka and Lucky (2017) model illustrates what the literature has identified related to displaced populations (See figure).[16]

What are the policy implications for a city such as Louisville? Policy related to revitalization of any neighborhood must be based on the recognition that dislocation, whether temporary or permanent, has significant potential for additional stress and poor mental health outcomes on a population that already experiences disparities in social determinants of health and health outcomes.

Recommendation for change are as follows:

- Identify poor mental health outcomes as a risk of revitalization and include funding for mental health promotion strategies within the plan

- Include outcomes research related to dislocation in any revitalization plan to build more robust evidence about population needs.

- Add supportive resources based on current evidence to address potential mental health effects of community change.

- Employ community participatory strategies not only for those who are temporarily dislocated, but also those who are permanently dislocated.

- Strategies for community inclusion in the process must extend beyond the planning of the revitalization to post-project development to address population issues.

11   Keene, D.E., Geronimus, A.T., & Weathering, D. (2011). Hope IV: The importance of evaluating the population health impact of public housing demolition and displacement. J Urban Health 2011, 88(3), 417-435. https://doi.org/10.1007/s11524-011-9582-5 PMID: 21607787

12   Fullilove, M.T. (2009). Root shock: How tearing up city neighborhoods hurts America, and what we can do about it. One World/Ballantine.

13   Fullilove, M.T. (2001).Root shock: the consequences of African American dispossession. J Urban Health 78(1), 72-80. https://doi.org/10.1093/jurban/78.1.72 PMID: 11368205

14   Fullilove, M.T. (2009). Root shock: How tearing up city neighborhoods hurts America, and what we can do about it: One World/Ballantine.

15   Center for Disease Control and Prevention. (2017). Health effects of gentrification. Retrieved from https://www.cdc.gov/healthyplaces/healthtopics/gentrification.htm.

16   Matsuoka, M. & Lucky, J. (June 2017). Gentrification and displacement impacts on individual and family health. Power, Place and Public health.

HOUSING

STATEMENT ON AFFORDABLE HOUSING IN LOUISVILLE

Louisville Urban League

October 26, 2021. The Louisville Urban League stands in agreement with residents and our colleagues; housing must be the chief priority of the city's ARP funding allocation. Housing was a major issue before the pandemic, and we can no longer afford band-aid solutions to a critical problem. On October 26, despite an overwhelming consensus from the community and practitioners that real housing solutions be prioritized, the Mayor and other city officials proposed funding for housing development in the amount of $79.5 million. This is not an insignificant amount of money, but it is well short of the $231 million request by advocates- a number rooted in data and Louisville's great need.

There are a variety of areas under the umbrella of housing that need significant support. No one area is going to solve everything and there are not enough available dollars in ARP to fund them all. These issues are rooted in more than a century of bad, racist policies and intentional disinvestment. In response, our approach must be a deep investment sustained over time, but this is a once-in-a-lifetime opportunity to make a significant impact on those problems that have been made worse by the coronavirus pandemic. We cannot afford to squander this opportunity on more half-measures and superficial solutions.

AFFORDABLE HOUSING

The city's 2019 Housing Needs Assessment instructed that when we create new housing units, at least 54% of those should be dedicated as rental units for extremely low-income Louisvillians—those making 30% AMI or less (about $20,000 for a family of three). Taking the 833 households who were living on the streets or in shelters on one night, and multiplying it by $150,000 (the federal dollars needed to create a new affordable housing rental unit after other subsidies), equals $125 million for those on the lowest end of the economic spectrum. Still more supports are necessary for people between 30-80% AMI—those who make more money but still lack affordable housing options.

The League believes any investment must also be done creatively (single-family, multi-family, senior living, tiny homes, etc.), compassionately (reducing barriers to participation), and with pathways to ownership for those who desire it. Failure to include opportunities for mobility across the county concentrates poverty and only exacerbates the problem. Affordable housing should exist everywhere in Louisville and the creation of that housing should not displace people who want to stay in the communities they are in.

HOUSING STABILITY TEAM

As an organization invested in this work daily and serving the most impacted populations, LUL knows we cannot solve the problem of houselessness without 1) building more houses; and 2) building the human infrastructure needed to help people navigate as they seek to transition into new and existing spaces. LUL along with our partners have proposed the creation of a Housing Stability Team to meet this need.

As it stands, many community members—especially those at the lowest income levels—experience barriers related to things like technology, transportation, and understanding certain systems and services. Housing navigators can help bridge these divides and locate resources to address a wide array of needs. Navigators can also act as advocates to help navigate Fair Housing concerns. As of now, no one organization can take on the immense need for housing navigation services. LUL has been doing this work in partnership with the Association of Catholic Ministries, the Coalition for the Homeless, the city, and others, but a more permanent, sustained solution is necessary.

There is a proposal before the city that would establish a team to support community members through every potential phase of the housing process—from those at risk of eviction to those transitioning into more permanent solutions—to prevent houselessness and empower pandemic recovery efforts. This process would include linkage to wrap-around services for ongoing stability.

PERMANENT SUPPORTIVE HOUSING

LUL fully supports significant investments in client-centered housing with wrap-around services. Organizations like Wellspring, St. Vincent de Paul, and others are vital parts of our local housing ecosystem and their work should be fully funded and scaled to meet the actual needs of our communities. This requires an understanding that these organizations do not just provide space, but also individualized medical, mental, and social support services for those in their care.

SAFE OUTDOOR SPACES, TRANSITIONAL HOUSING, AND SHELTERS

LUL recognizes that temporary houselessness may be unavoidable for some, but that does not mean those individuals cannot have safe and dedicated spaces to live. The League supports the creation of safe outdoor spaces to meet the needs of our houseless community members. Additionally, we support the creation and support of safe, dignified, transitional housing for those newly entering our community, returning citizens, and others who need space as they work to stabilize themselves in a new environment. The League emphasizes dignity in the creation and upkeep of these spaces, because no one, regardless of their background or housing situation should be systemically dehumanized through their living conditions.

LUL supports the expansion and renovation of dilapidated shelters, but not at the expense of new permanent housing solutions. While shelters need to be safe, livable, dignified spaces ready to serve a large and diverse population, shelters—as a matter of practice—are not a sustainable solution to houselessness.

DOWN PAYMENT AND RENTAL ASSISTANCE

Continued direct financial support for those navigating housing instability will be a critical need for the foreseeable future. This includes rental assistance to help prevent evictions as well as down payment support for individuals moving into new homes or apartments. COVID has added to the financial instability of many families already struggling economically and there will need to be systems in place to assist those families long term.

HOME REPAIR

Home repair funds are a housing stability mechanism that not only helps to keep families in their homes but also improves property values and the look and feel of communities. Part of the legacy of redlining has been the inability of Black homeowners and property owners in certain areas to be able to receive loans and lines of credit to maintain and improve their property. This can lead to several problems and compounding inequities over time—for individual families and entire communities. Investing here is important to the long-term health and stability of our beloved neighborhoods.

POLICY

In addition to the financial investments in housing listed above, there are many policy solutions the city and state can implement to support housing stability.

Eviction Expungement and Just Cause Evictions

An eviction filing can impact your ability to find new housing which can quickly escalate to homelessness. People should not be completely locked out of housing options because of an eviction filing. Renters should also be protected from arbitrary, retaliatory, or discriminatory evictions by ensuring that landlords offer evidence showing a legal reason for eviction.

Right to Counsel

In Louisville and across the country, most tenants do not have access to legal representation in eviction cases. Estimates show that up to 90 percent of landlords have legal representation, while only 10 percent of tenants do.

Reforming eviction set-out procedures

The trauma and cost of our current set-out procedures can be reduced by working with a local Housing Stability Team who can help tenants move from one home to another without having to throw their children's clothing and family belongings out on the street.

Anti-rent gouging policies or a dedicated funding source for rental assistance

The minimum wage has been stagnant for years. The National Low Income Housing Coalition recently published a study showing that, in several American cities, the minimum wage would have to be at least $24 to afford a 2 bedroom apartment and $20 to afford a 1 bedroom apartment.

Improved enforcement of Fair Housing Policy

Discrimination continues to be a barrier to housing access. As of March 2021, the Louisville Metro Council passed an ordinance adding new protected classes to the law including "Source of Income." Despite this law, some landlords demonstrate little concern for upholding Fair Housing requirements because they know it is unlikely that they will be held accountable in a meaningful way.

Dedicated funding sources for housing subsidies
To help close the gap of over 30k units affordable to those at 30% AMI or lower, we must establish

a dedicated funding source that would cover operational costs.

Land use policy and the development approval process reform

In Jefferson County, 75% of our land is zoned exclusively for single-family residential use. It is critical that we support and engage in this reform because of the way our Land Development Code limits development options. This is a racial justice issue as well because the way land is currently zoned reflects a history of racist housing policy.

Exploring innovations in housing finance and home ownership models

Across the country, communities are engaged in conversations to explore innovations in housing finance and ownership models. One of the policy strategies that has been offered in this conversation is driving housing development through tax policy. An example of this strategy might be to offer a tax credit for commercial owners to convert vacant commercial properties to residential properties. It's critical that Louisville engage in creative and innovative conversations to explore new strategies for financing and home ownership.

COMMUNITY DEVELOPMENT
MAKING THE ORIGINAL RESIDENTS THE PRIORITY

Dr. F. Bruce Williams, *Pastor*
Bates Memorial Baptist Church

In recent years, noticeable neighborhood development is taking place in key areas across the city. One example is the Smoketown neighborhood, the oldest Black neighborhood in Louisville. After decades of social isolation, economic deprivation, political manipulation, and overall neglect, the promise of community development inspired many Smoketown residents to begin to dare to dream of a better community.

Communities like Smoketown desire community development, but too often when cities speak of community development, the focus is on developing land and buildings while ignoring the most valuable asset a community has: the people. The greatest frustration for the original residents is that the development happens not for *their* benefit, but for the benefit of those the new development hopes to attract. This, in a word, is *gentrification*.

Once the development begins, not only are large groups of original residents relocated, but those who remain are at risk of being priced out of the neighborhood by rising housing prices. They are also at risk for being pushed out by new, incoming residents who are looking for, what appears to them, to be an opportunity to live in an area that is on the rise. Usually, this involves the change of culture and color of the community.

Former residents watch their community rise without them, while the remaining residents watch it change, often at the expense of the community's rich culture, history, and valuable legacy. Like others, they dream of living in a neighborhood with good schools, affordable homes, safe, healthy environments, job opportunities, sit-down restaurants, and prospering residents. But it seems that it only happens once they are displaced and replaced.

Black and poor people are tired of being neglected, overlooked, and abused. Black people are tired of city planning models that are outdated and laden with racist policies and practices that disenfranchise them, threatening to make them a permanent underclass.

There is no upside to gentrification for those former residents who lose out on a better community.

There needs to be a new paradigm of community development that prioritizes the original residents! I have no new, silver bullet approach, but I believe that it ought to include:

1. An effort to develop the people as a priority, not just property. It may take longer and it may even cost a little more, but given the city's history of economic neglect, it owes it to the residents to *repair* the damage due to neglect.

2. Guaranteed affordable housing for former residents. Given the history of economic violence due to neglect, *reparations* are in order. Money for homes can perhaps be provided through some type of forgivable loan.

3. City plans should also provide for continued economic investments once the initial development is completed, including expanded opportunities for original residents.

Those who live in struggling communities like Smoketown are valuable citizens worthy of the best that the city has to offer. They should not be neglected, devalued or denied, but offered opportunities to thrive, excel, and prosper. To do this is to treat them with the dignity and respect that they are due, not only because they are fellow citizens, but also because they are fellow human beings made in the image of God.

THE WEST CAN'T WAIT

Kevin Dunlap, Executive Director
REBOUND, Inc.
Jeana Dunlap , Urbanist, Strategic Advisor, Community Investment Specialist
2019 Harvard Loeb Fellow

To many, if not most, homeownership is part of the American dream. For those who have readily available resources, purchasing property and making investments is a straightforward strategy for amassing personal wealth and intergenerational prosperity. For those who don't possess significant amounts of cash, mortgage loans provide a necessary mechanism for purchasing and maintaining homes.

To fully grasp the plight of Black families, you must also understand that west Louisville, which is predominantly African American, has systematically been denied access to fair and reasonable mortgage loans as far back as the 1930s. Federal, state, and local policies were enacted and enforced that influenced and, in most cases, denied access to capital and credit. The result has been a long-lasting effect on residential development patterns, neighborhoods' economic health, and household accumulation of wealth in Louisville's nine western-most neighborhoods.

Despite decades of multi-million-dollar property developments, many African Americans have yet to realize sustainable homeownership or a viable stake in the communities they love. After decades of redlining, disinvestment, and devaluation, many Louisvillians have succumbed to a form of "redline thinking" that unjustly suppresses the Black experience and relegates Black communities to misinformed stereotypes about our human potential and personal ambition. We have a unique opportunity to collectively create pathways for resident investment *now* so that families and neighborhoods can realize the full economic benefit of increased equity in their homes in the future.

Recognizing the most recent surge of economic investment in west Louisville, a coalition of non-profit, affordable housing organizations are gathering to create a bold, unified strategy around **development without displacement**. The West Can't Wait (WCW) will target the former, and arguably still current, 'redlined' areas that are experiencing development pressure and real estate appreciation. WCW member organizations have over

50 years of experience providing housing options for families, seniors, and special needs residents via new construction and rehabilitation.

This ongoing effort demonstrates a commitment to increasing residential options and desirable lifestyle alternatives that people can afford, maintain, and sustain. This will be done while simultaneously advocating for innovative strategies and anti-displacement policies at every level.

It involves our collective hard work navigating complex processes and progressive mindsets to overcome a legacy of redline thinking. As outside investors continue to drive up property values, we know from history that these same investments often prevent those currently living in the neighborhood to remain. NOW is the time to act. We simply can't wait.

GENTRIFICATION AND THE ROLE OF THE URBAN CHURCH

Rev. Dr. Jamesetta Ferguson
Senior Pastor, St. Peters United Church of Christ
President and CEO, MOLO Village Community Development Corp.
Johnetta Roberts
OwnerForty and One
Board Member, MOLO Village Community Development Corp.

The Beecher Terrace (BT) community has lived under a cloud of oppression for over sixty years. This low-income housing partnership was Louisville's answer for African American residents, just like Pruitt-Igoe federal apartments was to St. Louis. The results of both were the same: a high concentration of poverty, public housing with little maintenance, and a concentration of the ills of societies for the city's most vulnerable people.

The demolition of BT and the displacement of the residents all around Jefferson County has set the gentrification of the BT area in motion. Residents have been separated not only from familiar surroundings, but also from their families and friends and even their church. It's a blessing that they no longer have to be limited to one full-service grocery store to serve 9,000 residents, three dollar stores to serve as the primary retail centers of the community, the local liquor store which serves as the neighborhood financial institution, halfway houses

filled beyond capacity, and slumlords renting for subpar housing.

In their new locations, these former BT residents now can enjoy some of these perceived luxuries, causing some not to want to return to BT even though they will have the opportunity under the agreement of the Choice Neighborhoods Initiative.

Whether the old residents return or there are new, young, professional residents, the urban church must find its way in its new gentrified landscape. We at St. Peter's United Church of Christ are one of the many Russell churches affected. Our membership is made up mostly of the former BT residents. Many are no longer able to attend because of lack of transportation from the outskirts of Louisville.

But the church must be relevant no matter who occupies the neighborhood. We've been in Russell for over 125 years. Therefore, St. Peter's United Church of Christ and Molo Village Community Development Corporation teamed up with the Church Building and Loan Fund of the United Church of Christ to shape a vision for the potential use of our existing property for ministry and mission in the future. Because of their support and guidance, we will begin construction on a new 30,000 square-foot, two-story, mixed-use retail and office development in January 2020, to be completed in fall 2020. For our church, we will no longer only provide spiritual guidance for BT residents, but we also see our role as an urban church to be an integral part in the economic revitalization of our community through a $7 million investment providing the amenities and resources that all Louisville residents deserve.

THE STATE OF AGITATION

Rev. Dr. Jamesetta Ferguson

Senior Pastor, St. Peters United Church of Christ
President and CEO, MOLO Village Community Development Corp.

In 2022, Louisville continues to be in a state of agitation. Eighty-five years of little or non-investment in Louisville's west-end communities, redlining, urban renewal, segregation and institutional racism seemingly came to a head one day in 2012 with 6 people shot, resulting in 3 deaths on a west-end street. in Two years later, a 2014 shootout in Beecher terrace killed two men, inspiring the airing of a "Frontline" documentary that took a deep look at the costs and challenges of the criminal justice system on a specific neighborhood in Louisville. In 90 minutes, "Prison State" told the story of four Louisvillians, including two juveniles, who are entangled in Kentucky's criminal justice system. All four were from Beecher Terrace."[1] A State of Agitation.

As we fast forward to 2022, Louisville continues to live in an agitated state due to the COVID pandemic, injustices perpetrated by a small number of racist and unscrupulous police officers recently charged by the Federal Justice Department, increase in residential foreclosures, a growing number of unsheltered people, food insufficiency… the list is too vast to name.

This state of agitation brought on by so much negativity has reminded many Louisvillians of our need for communion with others regardless of racial, social, or economic status. Social isolation due to the COVID pandemic has affected more than those with severe mental or physical illnesses; it has severely affected many of our children. The loss of social life and learning time has caused tremendous increases in mental illness, drug use, and suicide.

Agitation is not always negative; the word also connotes struggle, as when agitation separates oil from water. And yes, this state of agitation has caused the world to open its eyes to the institutions of racism here in America and around the world and to be reminded that racism and bigotry are alive and well in our communities. Our spike in mental illness created an increased awareness of mental health needs in our black communities. This agitated

---

1   Ryan, Jacob. Takeaways From Frontline's Look at Criminal Justice and Louisville's Beech Terrace: wfpl.org, 2014.

state has also shined a brighter light on the lack of medical care, inadequate housing, food insufficiency and subpar education as a way of life for brown and black folk not just here in Louisville, but throughout many urban cities across America. All of the events throughout the many years in Louisville have moved many of us out of our comfort zones. This causes me to reflect on the words of Archbishop Desmond Tutu when he said, "Disturb us, agitate us O Lord, when we are too well-pleased with ourselves."

The lessons for us to learn in 2022 Louisville is for us not to become well-pleased with ourselves. Yes, we have made much economic progress in Louisville with the building of the Village @ West Jefferson, the Norton's Sport Complex, The 18th Street One West Corridor and soon the dismantling of the 9th Street Divide. But have our minds changed to do the hard work of learning the power dynamics in our communities? Are we laying the groundwork to improve the way our institutions work with each other? Does government, businesses, nonprofits, churches and residents all have a place at the table? "Do we have a basic understanding of which leader (s) have following and influence, how they relate to one another, who determines what decisions are made and how money is spent."[2] We cannot continue to work in silos. As Louisville continues in transition, we must move forward together with all stakeholders, but most importantly the residents of the west-end, while discerning a new path for the future. It takes a village to build a community, and we are all part of that village. We must ensure all voices are being heard and that we have an opportunity for action.

Most people know that change is necessary, but it can make us feel uncomfortable, causing anxiety, a hint of trepidation, or worry. But we are to be reminded that each of us were formed in a state of agitation and have navigated our way through change and transformation our entire lives. Second, agitation causes many of us to move outside of the box. In other words, when we are outside the box, we stop putting limits on what can be accomplished. Again, I borrow from Archbishop Tutu, who states, "when our dreams have come true because we dreamed too little, stir us O Lord." Agitate us O Lord, to think beyond what we see. Help us, shake us to dream past the stars in the sky. Finally, let us remember that the world and all that is within it was created through a state of agitation, and it is a world ever moving, changing, transforming, and becoming. Together, Louisville can become a thriving community for all. I have hope that we can get there.

---

2   Gecan, Michael. Effective Organizing for Congregational Renewal. Chicago: ACTA Publications, 2008.

HOW THE USE OF PUBLIC FINANCING EXTENDS LOUISVILLE'S WEALTH GAP

Cassia Herron, Urban Planner, Freelance Writer

In its 2019 annual report, the Metropolitan Housing Coalition states that 22,000 Black homeowners and a yearly investment of $1 billion are needed in order to close the homeownership and wealth gaps between White and Black households in Louisville.

Louisville Metro Government has identified a need for more than 60,000 units to fill Louisville's housing crisis. Yet, between 2014-2019 with over $21 million combined, Metro Louisville's Creating Affordable Residences for Economic Success (CARES) program and the Louisville Affordable Housing Trust Fund created only three units of affordable housing for those at 30% AMI or lower — those with the highest housing need in the city. Elected officials and housing developers continue to bemoan the need for more funding in order to fill the affordable housing need.

Since the city's merger with Jefferson County, Louisville Metro Government has entered numerous public-private partnerships to finance economic development projects. As described below, "pilot agreements" — properties exempted from local property taxes — have been created with Jefferson County Public Schools (JCPS) in order for the district to continue levying its taxes.[1] In these cases, Metro has provided the developer property tax exemption and the use of industrial revenue bonds to finance their projects.

- When the Courier-Journal needed a new building and printer in 2001, Metro authorized the use of an $85 million industrial bond with a 30-year term.

- The University of Louisville and its private student housing development partners in 2008 collectively received over $90 million in public financing through two bonds to fund projects at 7th and Hill Streets at the old American Standard building site. This created 666 units of student housing.

---

1   Copies of all pilot agreements cited were obtained from Jefferson County Public Schools and can be obtained from JCPS or Louisville Metro Government.

- Heaven Hill Distillery received a $10 million, 30-year deal in 2014 for land acquisition renovation and equipment.

The purpose here is to highlight an array of businesses that local government has deemed worthy in which to invest utilizing public bonds and Metro's credit rating. These companies also receive local property tax exemption – removing revenue from Metro's general fund. Recent reporting from WDRB's Chris Otts illustrates how Metro's use of these economic development tools affect public schools.[2]

In 2002, Churchill Downs received a $250 million publicly supported bond with a 30-year term "for the benefit of Churchill Downs" to improve its property. For the next 17 years, Churchill Downs paid JCPS $148,000 in yearly property tax liability based on a $20.4 million property valuation. After its reassessment this year, valuing the property at $112 million, the track's tax liability to JCPS will be $850,000. Otts' reporting does not assess whether JCPS is owed additional tax revenue due to the undervalued assessment used for the last 17 years.

Taking properties off the tax roll and inadvertently undervaluing property are problems with the way Metro has utilized property tax valuation and public bonds for economic development. There is also an equity issue.

From the FY18-19 Metro budget, the Louisville Urban League's Sports and Learning Complex received $10 million in bond financing for its $30 million project. It's a drop in the bucket in comparison to what's needed for the project, West Louisville and the city's poor and Black residents.

To what extent has Louisville Metro Government used bonds to support other developments in West Louisville or that were planned for the explicit benefit of Black and/or poor residents?

What if Metro used bond financing to invest $100 million in affordable housing and home energy efficiency upgrades? Or $25 million for cooperative business development? Or $50 million for environmental clean-up necessary to repurpose much of the vacant land in West Louisville?

Further analysis is needed to assess 1) how bonding and other public financing tools have been used in west Louisville as compared to the rest of the city; 2) the types of projects and what the outcomes have produced; and to determine 3) how economic development tools like bonds and property tax exemption could be used specifically to help close the growing wealth gap in Louisville.

---

2 Otts, C. (2019, April 26). JCPS could get $700,000 boost thanks to Churchill Downs tax change. WDRB. Retrieved from https://www.wdrb.com/in-depth/jcps-could-get-boost-thanks-to-churchill-downs-tax-change/article_d56bc3cc-6858-11e9-9e52-bf15f53f1538.html

THE PAST IS NEVER THE PAST

IS SHIVELY A MODERN EXAMPLE OF SEGREGATION?

Cathy Hinko, *Former Executive Director*
Metropolitan Housing Coalition

One hundred years ago, Louisville's elected officials passed an ordinance that, block by block, mandated racial composition. Imagine the effort and racial animus that went into that effort.

When the U.S. Supreme Court struck down that law in Buchanan v. Warley, those elected officials turned to an alternative method of zoning to create and maintain segregation. The banks and federal housing policy overtly supported this — everyone should look at Louisville's Redlining project.[1] The real estate industry was complicit through techniques like steering, fostering White flight, the use of restrictive covenants (not fully illegal for all uses until 1972), and, most recently, homeowners association rules. This perfect storm of racism has been successful for one hundred years.

You have only to look at Louisville to see how effective it has been and still remains. Between 2000 and 2017, Black homeownership rates declined, Black homeowners experienced disproportionate losses in home values, Black household incomes continued to remain far below the median income of Louisville/Jefferson County, and Black households earned a disproportionately smaller share of Louisville aggregate household income.[2]

All of these facts unveil the scale of the racial wealth gap and the obstacles Black households face in building and maintaining wealth. Addressing these disparities is imperative for a thriving Louisville as we look to the next decade.

While 70 percent of the 225,000 White households in Louisville/Jefferson County are homeowners and creating intergenerational wealth, the ownership rate for Louisville's 63,500 Black households is only 36

1   Poe, J. (2017). Redlining Louisville: The history of race, class, and real estate. LOJIC. Retrieved from https://www.lojic.org/redlining-louisville-news

2   United States Census Bureau. (2018). 2013-2017 American community survey 5-year data profile. Retrieved from https://data.census.gov/cedsci/table?q=&d=ACS%205-Year%20Estimates%20Data%20Profiles&table=DP03&tid=ACSDP5Y2017.DP03&g=0400000US21_0500000US21111&lastDisplayedRow=144

percent, which is the same rate for Latinx households (See Map 2). For all female-headed households, the homeownership rate is 42 percent. This is the legacy of deliberate federal policies that excluded Black people from the same programs for ownership where White households received subsidies to become homeowners. Even homeownership in Louisville is racially charged and the attached map shows that half of all Black homeowners live in just 22 of 198 census tracts.

The case of Shively poses some unpleasant questions as to whether those practices are really in the distant past, or still currently in use. Shively is a suburban municipality that has undergone a racial transition over the last 30 years, shifting from a majority White to a majority Black population and maintaining a relatively high median income when compared with Black households in Louisville.

Between 2000 and 2017, the overall homeownership rate of Shively decreased, from 69.8 percent to 61.8 percent.[3] In fact, Shively's homeownership rate dipped to 60.1% in 2012, when the worst effects of the Great Recession were felt, but increased a percent by 2017. But there was a very large change in who owns the homes. Of all homeowners, the percent that are Black went from 39% to 66.7% and the percent that are White went from 60.9% to 33.3%.

The real median income of all households decreased between 2000 and 2017 (with the biggest dip in 2012, but recovering by 2017). Shively households went from a median income of $45,673 in 2000 to

Map 2: 22 Tracts Containing 50% of Total Black/African American Homeowners in Louisville/Jefferson County (2017)

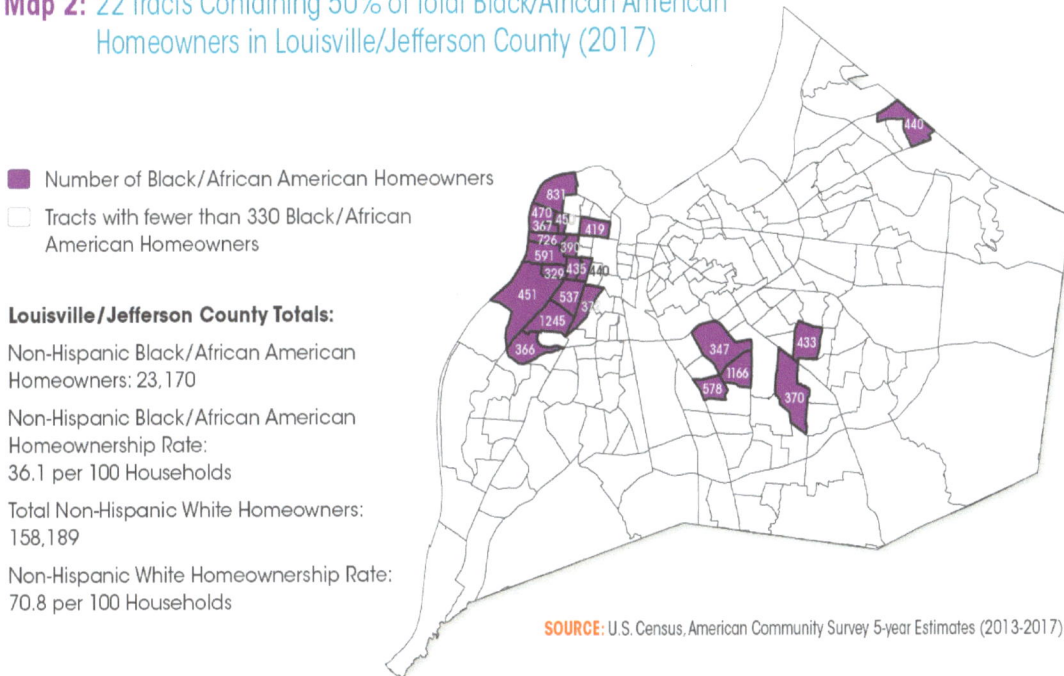

■ Number of Black/African American Homeowners

☐ Tracts with fewer than 330 Black/African American Homeowners

Louisville/Jefferson County Totals:

Non-Hispanic Black/African American Homeowners: 23,170

Non-Hispanic Black/African American Homeownership Rate: 36.1 per 100 Households

Total Non-Hispanic White Homeowners: 158,189

Non-Hispanic White Homeownership Rate: 70.8 per 100 Households

SOURCE: U.S. Census, American Community Survey 5-year Estimates (2013-2017)

---

3   United States Census Bureau. (2018). 2012-2016 American community survey 5-year data profile. Retrieved from https://data.census.gov/cedsci/table?d=ACS%205-Year%20Estimates%20Data%20Profiles&table=DP03&tid=ACSDP5Y2016.DP03&g=0400000US21_0500000US21111

Map 10: Percentage of Population Identifying as Black or African-American

by Census Tract – Louisville/Jefferson County
2016 ACS 5-Year Estimates

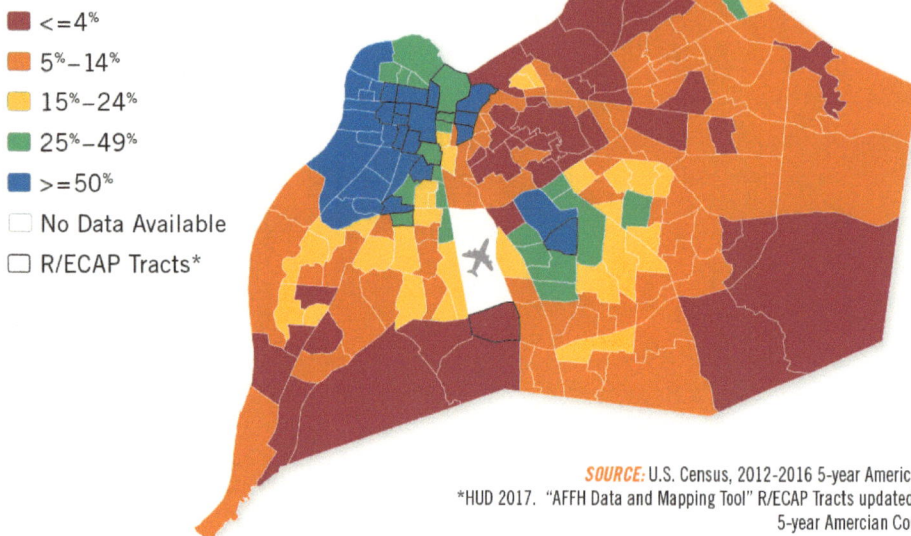

- ■ <=4%
- ■ 5%–14%
- ■ 15%–24%
- ■ 25%–49%
- ■ >=50%
- □ No Data Available
- □ R/ECAP Tracts*

SOURCE: U.S. Census, 2012-2016 5-year American Community Survey
*HUD 2017. "AFFH Data and Mapping Tool" R/ECAP Tracts updated to reflect 2009-2013 5-year Amercian Community Survey data.

2018 State of Metropolatain Housing Report

Figure 12: Housing Tenure

United States, Kentucky, Louisville MSA, and Louisville/Jefferson County 2016

	United States	Kentucky	Louisville MSA	Louisville/ Jefferson County
Total Households	117,716,240	1,718,217	497,174	310,355
Owners	63.6%	66.8%	66.7%	61.2%
Renters	36.4%	33.2%	33.3%	38.8%
Households by Race/Ethnicity				
White Households	81,079,480	1,506,718	396,501	224,570
Owners	71.4%	70.7%	73.7%	70.3%
Renters	28.6%	29.3%	26.3%	29.7%
Black/African-American Households	14,343,764	134,831	70,530	63,585
Owners	41.9%	36.5%	36.6%	35.8%
Renters	58.1%	63.5%	63.4%	64.2%
Hispanic/Latinx Households	14,725,771	37,970	15,596	11,259
Owners	45.8%	35.3%	39.0%	37.1%
Renters	54.2%	64.7%	61.0%	62.9%
Households by Family Type				
Family households	77,608,832	1,136,651	318,689	185,805
Married-couple Household	56,270,862	836,940	228,179	126,001
Owners	79.5%	82.5%	84.7%	81.9%
Renters	20.5%	17.5%	15.3%	18.1%
Male Household, No Wife Present	5,681,312	82,911	24,196	15,241
Owners	53.2%	57.7%	59.2%	55.4%
Renters	46.8%	42.3%	40.8%	44.6%
Female Household, No Husband Present	15,146,112	220,274	66,710	44,990
Owners	45.1%	46.9%	46.4%	42.3%
Renters	54.9%	53.1%	53.6%	57.7%

SOURCE: U.S. Census, 2012-2016 5-year American Community Survey

2018 State of Metropolatain Housing Report

$34,963 in 2012, recovering to $36,525 by 2017.[4][5] With an increasing median income, the property values should be recovering as well. The mystery is why property values continue to decrease in a way that is different from elsewhere. Or maybe it is not a mystery!

In 2000, the median home value in Shively was $112,193.[6][7] By 2012, it was $108,269 and in 2017 it dropped to $97,860. The absolute values have fallen despite the recovery in income. Yet, relative to Jefferson County, the median home value changes are more worrisome. The median home values in Shively fell from 76.5 percent of the Louisville/Jefferson County median home value in 2000 to 61.5 percent in 2017.

Why is there no real estate value recovery? What are the real factors in the change in racial composition of Shively? Considering the percentage of Black homeowners in Louisville/Jefferson County compared to all homeowners, the change does not seem to be accidental. Was there steering? Was White flight encouraged in Shively? What is happening with appraisals? Are they race related?

People have lost their wealth and this needs investigation.

4   United States Census Bureau. (2018). 2013-2017 American community survey 5-year data profile. Retrieved from https://data.census.gov/cedsci/table?q=&d=ACS%205-Year%20Estimates%20Data%20Profiles&table=DP03&tid=ACSDP5Y2017.DP03&g=0400000US21_0500000US21111&lastDisplayedRow=144

5   Consumer Price Index Inflation Calculator. 2017 Dollars. Retrieved from https://data.bls.gov/cgi-bin/cpicalc.pl

6   United States Census Bureau. (2018). 2013-2017 American community survey 5-year data profile. Retrieved from https://data.census.gov/cedsci/table?q=&d=ACS%205-Year%20Estimates%20Data%20Profiles&table=DP03&tid=ACSDP5Y2017.DP03&g=0400000US21_0500000US21111&lastDisplayedRow=144

7   Consumer Price Index Inflation Calculator. 2017 Dollars. Retrieved from https://data.bls.gov/cgi-bin/cpicalc.pl

Louisville Urban League

A PATH FORWARD FOR LOUISVILLE

STRATEGIC PLAN FY23-FY33

READ THE FULL PLAN

Scan the code above or visit tinyurl.com/pathplan23

Read more about *A PATH FORWARD* at apathforward4lou.org

Acknowledgements

A Path Forward for Louisville was conceived of and written in the summer of 2020, a time of tremendous trauma around the nation and certainly in Louisville, Kentucky. That historic document demanded change for Black people around the integrated pillars of Jobs, Black Business, Justice, Education, Health, and Housing. This subsequent plan focuses on three of the six prioritized areas - Education, Housing, and Black Business. This plan meaningfully advances the overall body of work that the Louisville Urban League and the Path Signers are pursuing.

The writing of *A Path Forward* and this related document would not have been possible without the contributions of so many in Louisville. We ask that history remember all those involved. Particular thanks are owed to Sadiqa Reynolds, President & CEO of the Louisville Urban League. Sadiqa provided visionary leadership amid some of the most trying times in recent Louisville history. During her tenure, the League organically emerged as the backbone agency for *A Path Forward.* With a century of service, an unwavering commitment to civil rights, deep technical competence, and a track record of listening and responding to community, the Louisville Urban League stands ready to execute in this new role.

A special thank you to Blue Meridian Partners. To the nation, Blue Meridian is a partnership of results-oriented philanthropists seeking to transform the life trajectories of our nation's young people and families in poverty by investing in strategies that work. To our team in Louisville, Blue Meridian is a group of philanthropists who saw us, saw our work, and responded. Thank you for your investments in Louisville and in the creation of this plan. Together, we are charting *A Path Forward.*

Louisville Urban League

Anthony Leachman	Christina Shadle	Rhonda M. Mitchell
Anita McGruder	Lisa Thompson	Ramzi Sabree
Betty Fox	Lyndon Pryor, Principal Advisor	Sadiqa Reynolds, Principal Advisor
Chabela Sanchez	Nichole Leachman	Sarah Trainor Graves

Signers of *A Path Forward for Louisville*

100 Black Men Of Louisville, Gary N. Eley
15,000 Degrees, Alice Houston
15,000 Degrees, Audwin Helton
15,000 Degrees, Dana Jackson
40 & One Company, Johnetta Roberts
ADL Cleveland, James Pasch
African Methodist Episcopal Zion Church, Erich Shumake
Alpha Lambda Chapter, Alpha Phi Alpha Fraternity, Inc., Ken Ellis
AMPED, Dave W. Christopher Sr.
Antioch Baptist Church, Pastor Eric T. French, Sr.
artThrust, Toya Northington
Bates Memorial Baptist Church, F. Bruce Williams

Beargrass Missionary Baptist Church, Rev. Matthew E. Smyzer, Jr.
Beta Alpha Xi Zeta Chapter, Zeta Phi Beta Sorority Inc., Shervita West
Broadway Baptist Church, Rev. Kevin Gardner-Sinclair
Burnett Avenue Baptist Church, Dr. Corrie Shull
Canaan Christian Church, Dr. Walter Malone Jr.
Center for Neighborhoods, Mellone Long
Central Presbyterian Church, Rev. Dr. Ann Deibert
Christ Church Cathedral, Matthew Bradley
Church of the Promise, Mistee Spry Browning
Church of the Promise, Rev. Dr. Larry W. Stoess
Cities United and Russell Place of Promise, Anthony Smith

Closing the Gap Consulting, LLC,
  Dr. Yvonne D. Austin-Cornish
Congregation Adath Jeshurun,
  Rabbi Robert B. Slosberg
Data for Justice, Monica E. Unseld, Ph.D.
Education First Foundation, Ben Johnson
Emmanuel Baptist Church, Damian Thompson
EmpowerWest Louisville, Rev. Joe Phelps
Episcopal Diocese of Kentucky,
  (Rev. Cn.) Amy Real Coultas
Epsilon Beta Sigma Chapter, Phi Beta Sigma
  Fraternity Inc, Darryl Young Jr
Eta Omega Chapter, Alpha Kappa Alpha Inc.,
  Marna Miller
Eta Omega Chapter, Alpha Kappa Alpha Sorority
  Inc., Daphne L. Jones
Eta Zeta Chapter, Zeta Phi Beta Sorority, Inc.,
  Dr. Deshawn Burrell
Evolve502, Marland Cole
Exploited Children's Help Organization (ECHO),
  Sonja Grey
Friends of Nicole 50/50 Mentoring Collaborative
  Inc., Nicole Hayden
Gifted By Design Leadership and Consulting,
  LLC, Lettie Johnson
Grace Community Covenant Church,
  William Mack III
Highland Baptist Church's Anti-Racism Team,
  Rev. Lauren Jones Mayfield
Immanuel United Church of Christ,
  Rev. Rachel Small Stokes
Iota Phi Theta Fraternity, Inc., Marion Phinazee
J.O. Blanton House Board of Directors,
  Cecil M. Brookins
Jefferson County Public Schools, John Marshall
Jefferson County Public schools,
  Kenneth Marshall
Jewish Community of Louisville, Inc.,
  Sara Klein Wagner
Jewish Family & Career Services, Deb Frockt
Justice & Freedom Coalition, Timothy Findley Jr.
Keepers of the Torch, W. Westerfield Tolbert
Kingdom Fellowship, Timothy Findley Jr.
Leavell Counseling, LLC, Tomeika S. Leavell
Louisville Alumnae Chapter, Delta Sigma Theta
  Sorority, Inc., Tina M. Johnson, President
Louisville Alumni Chapter, Kappa Alpha Psi
  Fraternity, Inc., Eric Stout
Louisville Central Community Center,
  Kevin Fields

Louisville Urban League,
  Benjamin K. Richmond, Ret.
Louisville Urban League,
  Sadiqa N. Reynolds, Esq.
Louisville Urban League Guild,
  Dr. Yvonne D. Austin-Cornish
Louisville Urban League Young Professionals,
  Dr. Billie Castle
Making Changes Together, LLC,
  Ebony O'Rea, MSSW
Minority Mental Health Project,
  Damon Cobble, LMFT, CCTSF
Molo Village CDC/St. Peters United Church of
  Christ, Dr. Jamesetta Ferguson
NAACP, Kentucky State Conference, Marcus Ray
National Council of Jewish Women,
New Horizon Baptist Church, Ja'mel Armstrong
No More Red Dots, Inc, Dr. Eddie L. Woods
Pi Lambda Omega Chapter, Alpha Kappa Alpha
  Sorority Inc., Christie McCravy
Pi Lambda Omega Chapter, Alpha Kappa Alpha
  Sorority Inc., Jan Brown Thompson
Pi Sigma Chapter, Sigma Gamma Rho Sorority,
  Inc., Monya Logan
Play Cousins Collective, Kristen Williams
Promise Housing LLC, Rev. Ryan Stoess
Racial Healing Project, Rashaad Abdur-Rahman
REBOUND, Inc., Kevin L. Dunlap
River City Drum Corp., Jamila Young
River City Drum Corp., Jerome Baker
Shawnee Neighborhood Association,
  Verna' Goatley
Simmons College of Kentucky, Jecorey Arthur
Sowing Seeds with Faith, DaMarrion Fleming
St. George's Scholar Institute, Arthur Cox
St. Matthew's Episcopal Church, Kelly Kirby
St. Stephen Church, Rev. Dr. Kevin W. Cosby
The Bail Project-Louisville,
  Shameka Parrish-Wright
Theta Omega Chapter, Omega Psi Phi Fraternity
  Inc., Dee Muldrow
United Church of Christ, Rev. Ann Houlette
Vice President of the Alumni NPHC,
  Monica Flowers
Yearlings Club Inc., Sedgewick Parker
Arika Marshall-Embry
Carla Wallace
Rabbi Gaylia R. Rooks
Rabbi Joe Rooks Rapport
Rev. Samantha Jewell

Members of the Strategic Plan Working Group

Alyssa Ager-Booi, Louisville Urban League
Cynthia Brown, Louisville Urban League
Tanika Bryant, Buy Black Lou
LuTisha Buckner, Russell: A Place of Promise
Dave Christopher, Sr., AMPED
Marland Cole, Evolve502
Latascha Craig, Louisville Urban League
Charles Davis, Evolve502
Rosalind Donald, Louisville Urban League
Dena Dossett, Jefferson County Public Schools
Kevin Dunlap, REBOUND, Inc.
SteVon Edwards, Schenault Solutions
Asha French, Ph. D, Louisville Urban League
Michael Gardner, REBOUND, Inc.
Ayisha Hayes Taylor, Louisville Urban League
Brittany Hill-Whitehead, AMPED
Cathy Hinko, Ret., Metropolitan Housing Corporation
Vanessa Koenigsmark, LHOME

Nichole Leachman, Louisville Urban League
Rhonda Mitchell, Louisville Urban League
Glenda Nelson, Louisville Urban League
Kia Nishida, Louisville Urban League
Dave Oetken, Small Business Development Center
Lyndon Pryor, Louisville Urban League
Sadiqa Reynolds, Louisville Urban League
Johnetta Roberts, The 40 & 1 Company
Jennifer Rubenstein, Louisville Independent Business Alliance
Ramzi Sabree, Louisville Urban League
Chabela Sanchez, Louisville Urban League
Christina Shadle, Louisville Urban League
Keith Talley, LHOME
Lisa Thompson, Louisville Urban League
Jamar Wheeler, Ph.D., Kiaspo
Theresa Zawacki, Russell: A Place of Promise

5

Executive Summary

In the wake of Breonna Taylor's and David McAtee's murders in 2020, Black leaders and community members in Louisville came together in a collective movement for justice and equity for Black Louisville, standing in opposition to the brutality perpetrated by the Louisville Metro Police Department and, more broadly, centuries of systemic disinvestment in the Black community. Through grassroots efforts and with the Louisville Urban League serving as a convener, the community mobilized to create *A Path Forward for Louisville,* a blueprint for change that aims to repair the damage done to the Black community after decades of racist policies and neglect. The Path Forward focuses on the integrated pillars of Jobs, Black Business, Justice, Education, Health, and Housing. The plan presented herein focuses on three of the six areas - Education, Housing, and Black Businesses. Within these focal areas, this plan articulates a bold vision and practical strategy for change over the next 10 years, while focusing in deeper detail on the near-term (3-5 years) specific outcomes and activities we will hold ourselves accountable to.

Our vision is to: *"Facilitate the creation of a thriving Black community in Louisville, in which Black residents have equitable access to economic opportunity and wealth-building no matter where they reside. Creating economic opportunities for Black residents and acting on a vision for equity in our community will ultimately enable our city to reach its full potential and increase the quality of life for all residents."*

We believe that an explicit focus on the Black community must be central to this work. The United States has never fully reconciled its deeply racialized past. Centuries of disenfranchisement have manifested across every imaginable indicator of prosperity in this country. The Black-white wealth gap today is a continuation of decades-long trends in wealth inequality driven by both overt racism as well as more subtle, and perhaps even more insidious policies. Despite a lack of direct data on Black wealth locally, data on persistent gaps between Black and white Louisville residents on key indicators of wealth (e.g., homeownership, business ownership, education, income) are even wider than what is seen nationally, indicating a deeper crisis in Louisville. Systems that are failing Black residents are failing everyone. By centering the lives and the experiences of Black Louisville, our work will also have the curb cut effect of addressing persistent inequities that affect all.

Our plan is to achieve equity for Black Louisville in three prioritized areas, which are all inextricably linked to intergenerational wealth accumulation and economic mobility. These areas are:

- **Increasing post-secondary education attainment:** Our goal is to more than double the percentage of young adults in Louisville attaining a college degree within the next decade. The opportunity for action is two-fold. In the near term, we must act immediately and stop the academic crisis for our students by ensuring they have access to high quality, evidence-based supports to get back on track academically. We will do this through high dosage academic tutoring in quality out of school opportunities. Once proof of concept is achieved, we aim to shift the responsibility for delivering and sustaining these interventions back onto the public system. We are investing in building our capacity to mobilize our community and advocate for the systems change necessary to reshape a broken educational system so that we can close the K-12 opportunity gap and so that Black students can thrive in their own schools.

- **Increasing homeownership and housing stability.** Within the next ten years, we will catalyze development of at least 15,000 affordable housing units and help 5,000 more Black households purchase homes. By concurrently increasing the supply of affordable housing and expanding access to capital and financial and pre-purchase education, we will spur economic revitalization in historically Black neighborhoods. This will generate long lasting wealth for our city's Black residents and lay groundwork for further market-driven investment. We have set specific targets

6

over the next five years that translate to bringing Black homeownership rates back to levels not seen since the 2008 housing crisis (40%) decimated Black wealth. We will reduce the need for affordable housing by 6% and close the racial gap on housing instability.

- **Building a strong Black businesses ecosystem.** Our vision is to create parity between Black-owned business and Black population in Louisville. In the past two years we have seen strong success from piloting an ecosystem approach to support the growth of the Black business community. This model involves close collaboration between community stakeholders such as TA providers, banks and capital providers, public government, and others. In the near term we aim to further prove the effectiveness and scalability of our approach by creating 500 stable and strong Black owned businesses by 2027. This would more than double the number of Black owned businesses that currently exist with at least one employee/contractor. By demonstrating an effective replicable concept, we will crowd in other stakeholders and significant public and private capital to bring forth a robust business ecosystem that enables Black business to thrive. We will close the racial representation gap in Louisville's business community and create a thriving Black centered market that enables owners and their employees to build intergenerational wealth.

Our work to date has enabled community stakeholders to collectively engage in new ways, bringing new solutions and innovations to the table, united around a common vision for a thriving, economically vibrant and just Louisville. Through this work, we plan to radically shift the opportunity divide in Louisville and create a city where Black residents have the resources, financial, and social capital to thrive in their own communities.

This effort is set apart by the caliber of the organizations and partners involved, including the Urban League, which has been a consistent voice for the city's Black community for over 100 years. For the past two years, LUL has served as the strategic leader and convener of *A Path Forward*, creating shared goals with the community, attracting additional funding, and building capacity for systems change work. As a trusted convener, resource, advocate, and anchor in the community, LUL has organically emerged as the backbone organization of *A Path Forward's* work over the next decade. Through this planning process, and their service, LUL and partners have continued to leverage their direct expertise of community needs to determine the vision for impact and key strategies for this work moving forward.

To achieve our vision, tackling centuries of systematic racism and discrimination, will require close coordination among a range of key stakeholders, including government, nonprofit advocacy and social service providers, and private funders and partners. Bringing this bold vision to life will also require significant financial investment. Over the next five years we anticipate this work costing a total of $1.1 billion. As we will detail, we have estimated that through our collective efforts and partnerships, we will be able to further leverage public funding streams as well as private dollars to support this effort, but see a critical role for philanthropy to play in catalyzing this work. We have identified an overall investment need of $258 million over the next five years, which could be seeded by philanthropic capital. Flexible philanthropic capital will allow us to meet the critical needs of our community *now* while continuing to demonstrate proof of concept and unlock further and more sustainable investments.

While we are committed to strengthening and revitalizing Louisville particularly, we believe this effort will also be a powerful model for other Black communities across the country fighting for equity. In the past two years, there has been great momentum in the U.S. to create a more just and equitable society to counter the injustices that have been elevated in the media. Healing from these injustices and repairing the historic damage that has impacted the lives of Black Americans starts in cities like

7

Louisville, where we can demonstrate what is possible even when these wounds are still fresh. But we cannot just provide a Band-Aid. To truly live into the possibilities for a thriving society, we must bring bold, comprehensive solutions and to do that at scale requires a collective investment of time and resources. We have and will continue to call upon community members, government leaders, service providers and funding partners to be the spark in the world they wish to see.

The Opportunity

A Path Forward boldly outlines a set of specific, multi-dimensional responses and investments that will tangibly impact the lives and opportunities of Black residents, and a call to action for Louisville public and private officials and leaders. Over the past two years, we have both begun to act on these priorities and to further hone a forward-looking plan, which aims to unlock additional capital for supporting our vision for Black Louisville. We have made significant progress in identifying our goals and priorities as a community as well as a credible and realistic pathway for achieving them. In collaboration with local change agents, the Louisville Urban League has crafted **a vision for a thriving Black community in Louisville, in which Black residents have equitable access to economic opportunities and wealth-building, no matter where they reside**.

This plan represents a collective effort to articulate an inspiring vision and practical strategy for change over the next 10 years, while focusing on the near-term (3-5 years) specific outcomes and activities we will hold ourselves accountable to, and which we believe must take place to achieve our broader 10-year goals. Our vision will be accomplished by achieving equity for Black Louisville in three prioritized areas, which are all inextricably linked to intergenerational wealth accumulation. These areas are:

- **Increasing post-secondary education attainment**
- **Increasing homeownership and housing stability**
- **Building a strong Black businesses ecosystem**

Each of these areas addresses an issue which reflects a system that has locked Black residents out of opportunity in the Louisville community, forgoing their ability to achieve meaningful wealth and long-term prosperity. Through our work, we plan to radically shift the opportunity divide and create a Louisville that commits to ensuring that Black residents have the resources, tools, and financial and social capital to thrive in their own communities.

The time to act is now - the window of salience for the community is rapidly closing as the 2020 traumas, which catalyzed the initial support for change, are fading deeper with each passing day. We have incredible momentum in and around the community, with stakeholders, funders, and residents energized to make a change. Our work to date has enabled community stakeholders to collectively engage in new ways, bringing new solutions and innovations to the table, united around a common vision for a thriving, economically vibrant and just Louisville. *A Path Forward* must strike while the iron is hot and capitalize on this unique moment in our city's history.

The Problem

The United States has never fully reconciled its deeply racialized past. Centuries of disenfranchisement have manifested across every imaginable indicator of prosperity in this country. The Black-white wealth gap today is a continuation of decades-long trends in wealth inequality. Today, the average Black and Hispanic or Latino household earns about half as much as the average white household and owns only about 15 to 20 percent as much net wealth.[1] Over the past 30 years, the median wealth of white households has consistently dwarfed that of Black households—ranging from a gap of $106,900 in 1992 to $185,400 in 2007 (both adjusted for inflation to 2019 dollars)[2]. Today the median white household has a net worth 10 times that of the median Black household.[3]

---

[1] Wealth Inequality and the Racial Wealth Gap, The Federal Reserve ([2021](#))

[2] Brookings - The Black-white wealth gap left Black households more vulnerable ([2020](#))

[3] Williamson, Vanessa, Closing the racial Wealth gap requires heavy, progressive, taxation of wealth, Brookings Institution ([2020](#))

Although there is no direct data on Black wealth in Louisville, local data on areas connected closely to wealth and wealth building (i.e. homeownership, business ownership, education, and income) suggests the wealth gap in Louisville is likely even wider than what is seen nationally:

Outcome area	Racial gap nationally	Racial gap in Louisville
Education	• **21%** attainment gap between Black and white adults 25-35 with a bachelor's degree or above	• **26%**
Homeownership	• **30%** homeownership gap	• **38%**
Business Ownership	• **11.9%** gap between percent of Black owned businesses and percent of Black population out of total population	• **21%**
Income	• **$29,000** median income gap	• **$27,000**

As we will describe, these data points are rooted in systemic inequities that have barred Black communities across the country from accessing economic opportunities that would enable them to build wealth.

Our Plan to Create Opportunity for Black People in Louisville

Our vision emphasizes the need to build the intergenerational wealth that has been systematically denied to Black people. Without access to wealth building, Black communities will continue to be financially insecure, educationally behind, and vulnerable to persistent inequities. In coming together as a community, we have focused on three critical levers needed to advance economic mobility for Black residents:

1) Increasing post-secondary education attainment
2) Increasing homeownership and housing stability
3) Building a strong Black businesses ecosystem

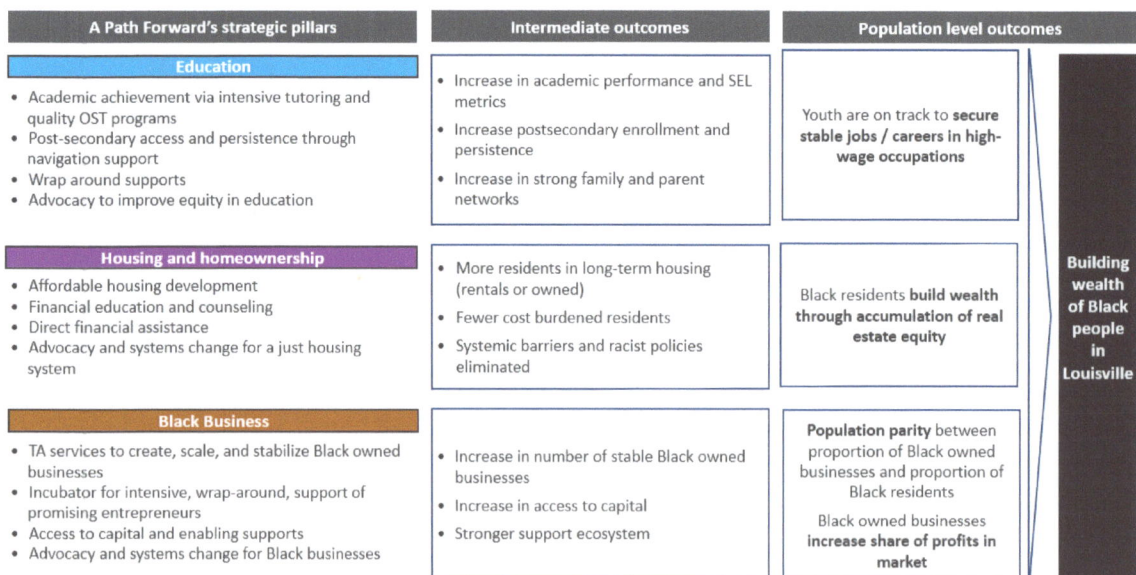

A Path Forward's strategic pillars	Intermediate outcomes	Population level outcomes	
Education • Academic achievement via intensive tutoring and quality OST programs • Post-secondary access and persistence through navigation support • Wrap around supports • Advocacy to improve equity in education	• Increase in academic performance and SEL metrics • Increase postsecondary enrollment and persistence • Increase in strong family and parent networks	Youth are on track to **secure stable jobs / careers in high-wage occupations**	**Building wealth of Black people in Louisville**
Housing and homeownership • Affordable housing development • Financial education and counseling • Direct financial assistance • Advocacy and systems change for a just housing system	• More residents in long-term housing (rentals or owned) • Fewer cost burdened residents • Systemic barriers and racist policies eliminated	Black residents **build wealth through accumulation of real estate equity**	
Black Business • TA services to create, scale, and stabilize Black owned businesses • Incubator for intensive, wrap-around, support of promising entrepreneurs • Access to capital and enabling supports • Advocacy and systems change for Black businesses	• Increase in number of stable Black owned businesses • Increase in access to capital • Stronger support ecosystem	**Population parity** between proportion of Black owned businesses and proportion of Black residents Black owned businesses **increase share of profits in market**	

We believe that focusing on these interrelated strategies will accelerate our efforts towards the ultimate vision for equity. For example, owning a home is often a critical asset and collateral that supports entrepreneurs in accessing additional capital for their business. We also know that stable housing supports educational outcomes for children. Further, post-secondary education is a critical predictor of income which can support stable housing.

Education: Increasing post-secondary education attainment

The Problem

Black students in Louisville are not achieving the academic outcomes needed to be on track for post-secondary success in college, career, and life. School district data shows that:

- Only about 20% of Black students in grades 4-9 scored at or above proficiency on the standardized math and reading test (MAP), compared with over 50% of white peers

- Only 29% of Black 11th graders scored above the ACT benchmarks and are considered likely to succeed in college courses compared to 66% of white peers

- Absenteeism and suspension rates are also disproportionately high, with approximately 30% of Black students in grades 6-9 being suspended at least once, compared to only 10% of white peers.

These outcomes coalesce to prevent Black youth from attending and succeeding in college and ultimately to minimize their opportunities for building wealth and earning a family sustaining wage. College enrollment for Black high school seniors was at only 39% this year, whereas white peers enrolled at 75%.[4]

It is important to clarify that these realities are rooted in an inherently racist system that has failed Black students over the past century. Legislation from the 1980s, referred to as the "student assignment plan," was particularly detrimental. Under the pretense of racial integration, students from Louisville's majority-Black West End were bussed to schools in historically white, wealthier neighborhoods to the east and south, yet white students could stay put and continue learning in their own home neighborhoods. This resulted in significant underinvestment for students who remained in West End schools, while also having a negative impact on Black children who had to commute across the county to learn in completely foreign environments, with little to no teacher representation. Within Jefferson County Public Schools (JCPS) today, less than 16% of teachers are Black, despite a Black student population of 37%[5]. This lack of teacher representation has been shown to have a significant impact on student achievement and performance.[6] The student assignment plan, which has negatively impacted the Black community for over 50 years, was recently revised in the summer of 2022, but the changes have not yet been implemented.

Increasingly, students and families have had to rely more heavily on supports for their children outside of the school system but access to high quality, affordable out of school time supports (OST) is limited. The onset of COVID-19 both exacerbated the need for these supports while exposing the disparities that existed between families that have the financial means to supplement their children's education and those in low-income households (disproportionately families of color) who do not. Although the pandemic affected all youth, national research corroborates that low income, and students of color,

---

[4] JCPS Data 2022
[5] Street, Eileen, Spectrum News 1 (2020)
[6] Figlio, David, The importance of a diverse teacher force, The Brookings Institution (2017)

were the most affected. Test-score gaps between students in low-poverty and high-poverty schools grew by 20% during the pandemic.[7]

Our Strategy

The ultimate outcomes we seek are to uplift social and academic achievement for Black students in order to enable our youth to get (and stay) on track to secure stable jobs and careers in high-income occupations. This will ultimately enable them to accumulate wealth and unlock better opportunities. We will accomplish this by placing our youth on a path to post-secondary education, and even more specifically, on a path to a 4-year college degree. Although we aim to support students in whatever pathway they chose to pursue beyond high school, research shows that in order to enter high-income occupations, a college education is still second to none.

Postsecondary education is an important factor in determining the lifetime earning potential of the average American, and longer-term credentials such as bachelor's degrees are associated with higher returns when compared with other postsecondary pathways[8]. The impact of a college education on potential earnings is staggering, making it a critical element in combating multidimensional poverty and building wealth. Today, 18% of Black residents ages 25-35 hold a bachelor's degree or higher, as compared to 44% for their white peers[9]. We envision spanning this gap in 10 years' time, aiming to increase this percentage to at least 50%, more than doubling the current attainment rate and putting college graduation rates back on par with the rate at which Black students are enrolling. As a direct result of improved educational opportunities and an increased proportion of college-educated Black residents, we seek to significantly shift the proportion of young adults (21-35) who earn above the median income[10]. By 2033, we aim to at least close the racial median income gap for Black adults under 35.

Our approach takes both a near and long-term outlook. In the near term, we need to act immediately and stop the bleeding, ensuring our students are able to access evidence-based supports that will enable them to get back on track and ultimately enroll and succeed in postsecondary. Over the next 5 years, we are committing to directly helping our students succeed by providing them with high-dosage academic tutoring through out of school time supports. We know that high-dosage academic tutoring and quality OST supports can be effective at improving academic achievement and social emotional learning[11], yet these services, particularly academic tutoring, are largely inaccessible to the Black community.

We also believe that by focusing on education, we have the opportunity to in the long-term influence a generation of creative, critical thinkers who will be able to meet the challenges of the present and future. In tandem, we will continue to mobilize our community and engage in the advocacy necessary to reshape the broken educational system that keeps us locked in the problems of our past.

Within the next ten years, we will work to ensure that Black students can thrive in their own schools and require increasingly less programmatic support from outside the public system. Our work will take a multidimensional approach; the strategies implemented will:

- Lift and accelerate the academic performance of students, particularly those in grades K-9

---

[7] Brookings - The pandemic has had devastating impacts on learning (2022)
[8] RAND – The Value of Education and Training After High School (2022)
[9] Greater Louisville Project – Education (2022)
[10] MIT Living Wage Calculator
[11] Covid-19 and learning loss – disparities grow and students need help (2020)

- Facilitate social-emotional development for youth in grades K-9

- Promote and enable postsecondary access and persistence

- Increase out-of-school and wraparound supports and stability for youth

- Engage in both short- and long-term systems change efforts to reshape Louisville's educational system

A Path Forward's Education Theory of Change:

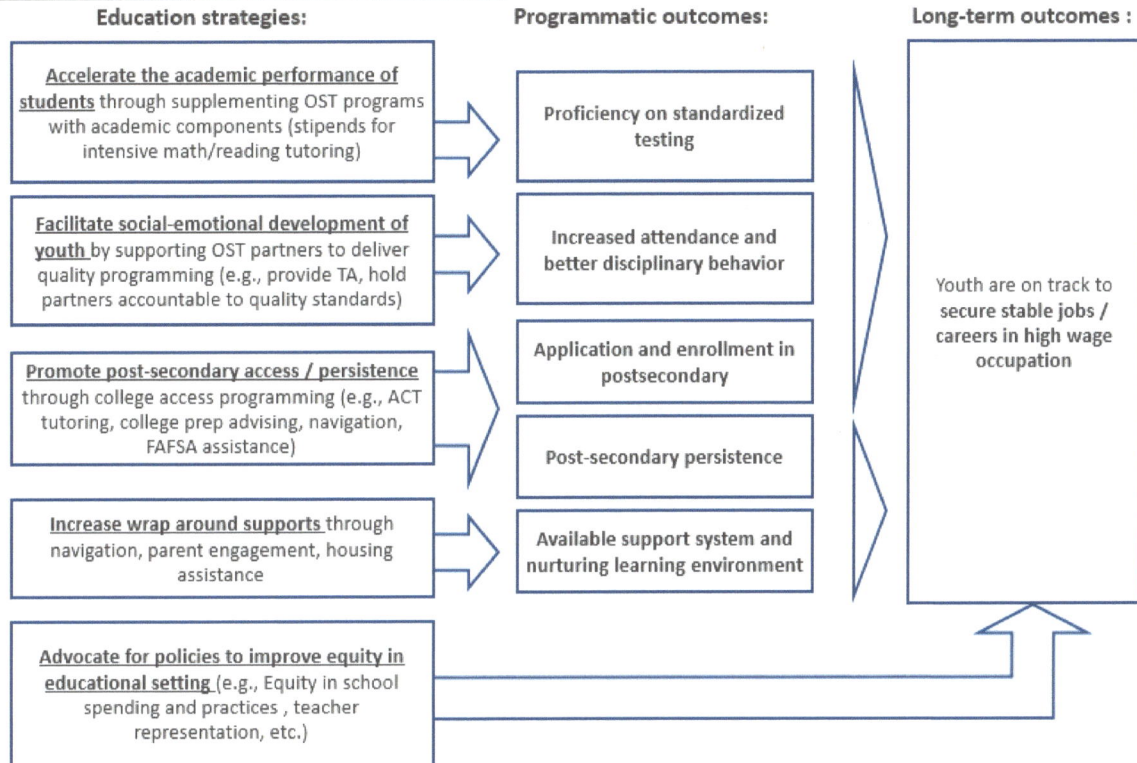

Education strategies:

- **Accelerate the academic performance of students** through supplementing OST programs with academic components (stipends for intensive math/reading tutoring)

- **Facilitate social-emotional development of youth** by supporting OST partners to deliver quality programming (e.g., provide TA, hold partners accountable to quality standards)

- **Promote post-secondary access / persistence** through college access programming (e.g., ACT tutoring, college prep advising, navigation, FAFSA assistance)

- **Increase wrap around supports** through navigation, parent engagement, housing assistance

- **Advocate for policies to improve equity in educational setting** (e.g., Equity in school spending and practices , teacher representation, etc.)

Programmatic outcomes:

- Proficiency on standardized testing
- Increased attendance and better disciplinary behavior
- Application and enrollment in postsecondary
- Post-secondary persistence
- Available support system and nurturing learning environment

Long-term outcomes :

- Youth are on track to **secure stable jobs / careers in high wage occupation**

Students will receive the support and services described below at no cost through a partnership between LUL and Evolve 502, a public-private partnership focused on growing the educational attainment of our community. By working together, we will be able to more comprehensively provide a continuum of services along the cradle to career pipeline to ensure these students are set up for success.

Accelerate the current academic performance of students:
Black students do not have access to the same quality and quantity of academic support as their wealthier, white peers, to support their academic performance. We find that 75% of students in grades K-9 are scoring below the 60th percentile (benchmark for basic proficiency) on the state's math and reading standardized testing.

A Path forward will focus on filling this gap in educational support by partnering with local Out of School Time (OST) programs in our community and bolstering LUL's own OST programming to offer additional rigorous academic components. Our efforts will target grades K-9 and aim to scale from supporting 2,500 students in year one to reaching over 4,500 students/year by year 5, representing over 20% of students underperforming on the state's standardized test. Primarily through Evolve502, K-5 students

13

will receive age-appropriate, intensive reading tutoring that includes research-based assessment and analysis and trauma-responsive literacy instruction, focused on literacy acquisition and social/emotional learning. Primarily through LUL's OST programming and partnerships with other OST providers, students in grades 4-9 will receive high-dose tutoring in math and reading using evidence-based approaches and specialized curriculum delivered by best in class providers. We will focus our most intensive academic tutoring model at this age as students will be more developmentally ready for this approach.

Facilitate social-emotional development of youth:
Attendance, disciplinary referrals, and ultimately high school graduation are also strong predictors of academic success. Black students get suspended at rates three times higher than white peers, and almost half of students can be labeled as chronically absent.[12] Louisville's complex student assignment plan, outlined previously, with its cumbersome transportation logistics, has been a major contributor to absenteeism.

To move the needle on these outcomes, *A Path Forward* will work to ensure that partner OST providers are delivering high-quality programming that is effective at moving the needle on the above metrics. Currently, *A Path Forward's* OST partners reach a total of almost 10,000 students across the community, with different types of programming at multiple levels of quality and effectiveness. By encouraging and providing hands-on support to these organizations to adhere to at least a minimum set of quality guidelines, we hope to have a significant impact on the social emotional learning of our youth.

Promote college access and persistence:
To ensure a continuum of support across life stages and transitions for individuals, *A Path Forward* will also focus on directly enabling students to access and persist in college. Programming will be delivered by both LUL and Evolve502 as well as other partners they recruit, and will be centered around multiple sub-initiatives such as:

- Improving standardized test performance: Today, over 71% of high school juniors do not meet the test's benchmark scores required for students to have a high probability of success in credit-bearing courses. Through the LUL and its partners, this sub-initiative will focus on providing high-school students grades 10-12 with access to high-quality tutoring that will enable them to reach scores high enough for college acceptance. Stipends for ACT tutoring services will be provided to students via OST partners, paralleling the tutoring partnership outlined above. We will scale these services from 450 students to over 900 students within the next 5 years.

- Providing scholarships for students to enroll in local partner colleges: Through its Promise Scholarship Program, Evolve502 will continue to enable students to attend local colleges as well as Simmons College of Kentucky, the state's oldest historically Black college, tuition free for the first 2 years of their education. All incoming seniors who desire to attend these schools will be eligible and scholars whose families earn less than $40,000 annually will be eligible for opportunity grants of $1,000 per semester (maximum $2,000 annually) to assist with costs outside of tuition and mandatory fees including books, housing, and transportation.

- Improving students' knowledge of the college navigation and application process: Focus groups with local educational stakeholders have surfaced that a major barrier preventing students from attending college is the lack of support around the complicated process they must navigate to successfully apply, get accepted, and enroll. The limited number of JCPS guidance counselors severely diminishes the capacity to provide students with these supports and Black students are not able to afford external resources to shepherd them through the college application process.

---

[12] JCPS School District Data

Our plan is to scale existent programming that consists of FAFSA assistance, application support, college tours, and general college navigation and transition assistance. We will deploy at least 6 trained coordinators across all our 22 high schools to meet regularly with youth and support them on their path to college enrollment.

- Providing support during and after transition to college: *A Path Forward's* education efforts will also include support for JCPS students who attend college. Black students have significantly lower college persistence rates than white peers, and a closer look at the degree divide shows the vast majority of students who do not complete their postsecondary education are pushed out of the system between the final two years of high school and first year of a postsecondary program[13]. To address this issue, we will partner the local colleges and universities such as Simmons College of Kentucky and Jefferson Community and Technical College, where the majority of JCPS students ultimately enroll, to make up to 15 navigators available across the college campuses. These navigators will support retention and college success through regular, intentional check-ins with students during their college tenure and provide them with guidance, emotional support, and connection to wrap around supports to help them succeed. More intensive support will be provided during transition years, but students will have access to support services throughout their college experience.

Increase wraparound supports and family stability

Research shows that for youth to perform academically they need to find themselves in a stable and supportive family environment. For many Black students in Louisville, this is often not the case, with 25% of Black households experiencing severe housing problems. *A Path Forward* will focus on two major strategies to promote stable and safe environments for students that enable academic success. Those are:

1) Promoting parent engagement strategies for all OST partners: LUL will design comprehensive communication strategies to connect with all parents and guardians whose children are engaged in programming. The primary focus will be to make adults aware of stabilizing services and resources for their families, beyond academic supports, and to make direct referrals to LUL integrated departments and partner organizations.

2) Supporting historically underserved youth in grades K-12 via trained navigators, who will provide wrap-around support and guidance to both students and families. For example, navigators will be able to identify and address housing issues for those students who live in unstable housing environments. This strategy leverages the communications infrastructure created via parent engagement.

Systems change / advocacy:

In addition to our direct programmatic work which will have a meaningful impact on student success outcomes, *A Path Forward* will also focus resources on systems change and policy efforts that attempt to dismantle many of the inequities that we outlined previously, and which have brought us here today. As mentioned, our long-term goal is the creation of an educational system that works for Black students, and we know that will require changes at the systems level to be sustainable. We believe that aggressively responding to the widening achievement gap during our first five years is critical to laying the groundwork on what interventions and partnerships are possible when we envision longer term system change. To that end, LUL has invested in expanding its policy team to ensure we are able to appropriately focus on the systems change efforts needed. Our work would include the following:

---

[13] One Goal Website – The Degree Divide (2022)

Systemic barrier	A Path Forward's System Change Efforts
Lack of teacher representation and adequate pay	• Support JCPS' efforts to spend more resources to recruit, train and retain more Black teachers and teachers of color (i.e., UofL program, HBCU recruitment). Research shows that students are held to higher standards and learn better when those who teach them look like them • Advocate for a more competitive salary for teachers in our high-need communities. This will address decades of teachers being underpaid in predominantly Black communities, and will increase the quality of instruction, decrease talent turnover, and consistently produce better student outcomes over the long term
Under resourcing of schools in majority Black neighborhoods	• Advocate for financial transparency on public funds received and spent on public education, which will help us understand how capital is being allocated and work to ensure the schools that Black students predominantly attend receive the money needed to best meet the needs of those students
Lack of wrap around and safety net support for Black students	• Push for an increase in wraparound and mental health supports to meet the immediate needs of historically underserved youth. • Advocate for universal Pre-K and increased funding for Head Start program, to ensure all children have a fair start on their educational journey • Push for the public school system to improve quality of supplemental academic support for struggling students and provide access to tutoring / help for every child that needs it

How we will measure and track our progress: To ensure we're achieving outcomes, A Path Forward will partner with the JCPS and OST providers in order to measure the progress of students against today's baseline. A data sharing agreement with the school district means we will be able to track the performance of every student served by our OST partners and through LUL's OST programming, across the outcomes and metrics listed in the table below in almost real-time. Additionally, we will also broker partnerships with local colleges to get a better understanding of the long-term impact of our collective work. A subset of the most relevant metrics we've set goals against and plan to track is found in the table below:

	Metrics to track for Black students	Today's benchmark	Goal by 2027
Academic performance	MAP testing (K-9)	25% of K-9 students score above 60th percentile	70%
	ACT testing (10-12)	29% score above benchmark[14]	70%
Social-emotional proficiency	Chronic absenteeism (grades 6-9)	45%	Less than 20%
	Suspension rates (6-9)	30% suspended at least once	Less than 10%
College going ability	College enrollment and attendance	39%	75%
	College persistence	74% attend year 2	90%

---

[14] ACT benchmark means a score of 20 in reading, 18 in English, and 19 in math

Housing: Increasing homeownership and housing stability

The Problem

The Metropolitan Housing Coalition found that more than 15,000, or 25% of Black households are experiencing severe housing problems.[15] In addition, only half as many (37%) Black Louisville residents own their homes, compared to white peers (75%); this is important given the relationship between homeownership and wealth accumulation. Housing, and in particular home ownership, is one of the most important mechanisms families can leverage to build wealth intergenerationally. Research shows homeownership as the primary contributor to wealth building -- according to the U.S. Census Bureau researchers, equity in a home accounts for 34% of the average household's net worth.[16]

These outcomes have their roots in systemic discriminatory practices that have disproportionately impacted Black residents. It has been well-documented in Louisville that homeownership disparities are driven by "redlining", a process where the federal government developed color-coded maps as tools used to assess creditworthiness and steer investment (or disinvestment) across all major metropolitan areas in the United States.[17] As a result, mortgage lenders designated low-income, immigrant and communities of color as "high risk" and as such, these communities were less likely to be extended financing towards a potential home purchase. These discriminatory practices of financial institutions have resulted in Black residents facing reduced access to affordable lending, ownership and ultimately greater housing instability.

In addition to historic redlining which today is outlawed (although it generated significant lasting harm for decades), there are many zoning policies still in place in Louisville that contribute to the city's housing issues as they pertain to race. For example, the seemingly benign practice of single-family residential zoning, was actually designed with the racist prerogative of preventing the "spread of Black slums", and today 75% of land in Louisville remains zoned for single family homes, thus excluding many low-income and Black residents from these areas.[18]

These historical trends are exacerbated by the growing cost of real estate property. For the first time in June 2022, the US median asking rate for rental housing rose above $2,000, creating a national shortfall of 3 million affordable housing units. The city of Louisville and the Louisville Affordable Housing Trust Fund commissioned a study that found that there are upwards of 31,000 affordable housing units needed in Louisville[19]. Increasing housing costs, combined with the depressed earnings for Black residents, and the pandemic, have resulted in an eviction rate that is double the national average (7th highest in the nation): Black residents of Louisville are also more likely to be evicted and be at risk for housing insecurity.[20]

---

[15]Severe housing problems definition: if a household has at least one of the following issues: lack of kitchen facilities, lack of complete plumbing, overcrowding, or severe cost burden (paying more than half of their income towards housing costs).

[16]How the government created devastating wealth disparities between White and Black families, Jefferson County (2020)

[17] In the 1950s, the establishment of the Federal Housing Administration (FHA) sought to expand government secured mortgages to working class families. In their evaluation process, federal agencies rely on race as a primary factor for mortgage approval. This barred equitable access to homeownership, reinforcing segregation and fiercely limiting the ability of Black borrowers to be approved for mortgage credit for decades.

[18] Courier Journal - Louisville examines zoning regulations for racial inequities (2021)

[19] Metropolitan Housing Coalition (2022)

[20] Ryan, Jacob;Kanik, Alexandra, Instability Grows As Louisville Eviction Rate Doubles National Average, WFPL (2018)

17

Our Strategy

To achieve our vision of promoting equity and wealth building through stable, safe and affordable housing and through homeownership, we have set both short and long-term goals. Within the next ten years, our goal is to catalyze development of at least 15,000 more affordable housing units and help 5,000 Black households purchase homes. Achieving this goal will have a transformative impact on our community and help generate an estimate of $33M in wealth for Black residents (considering equity from home appreciation at $8M, and down payment assistance to buyers at $25M).

In the near term, by 2027, we envision directly developing 3,000 more affordable units, with 2,000 units being dedicated towards renting and the remaining 1,000 towards homeownership. Success on these goals would translate to bringing Black homeownership rates to approximately 40%, back to levels seen before the 2008 housing crisis. Achieving these goals would also reduce the need for affordable housing by 6%, helping reverse the city's rapid increase in housing costs. Additionally, we aim to help shift 2,500 households from unstable living situations, where they are experiencing severe housing problems[2]. Reaching this goal would translate to a 10% decrease in the housing instability rate, from 25% to 15%, almost closing the racial gap on this outcome.

Although the direct impact of *A Path Forward* partners will be significant (i.e., increasing homeownership and stable housing rates to 40% in the near term), the vision is to catalyze broader change in the surrounding community and demonstrate a viable model that can revitalize the city. Our work will create increasingly more appealing and livable Black neighborhoods, which will spur additional outside investment over the next decades. The parallel work to increase Black business representation in our communities will also spur further investment and draw in both public and private funding. Quality of place and resident ownership as keystones of revitalization will provide housing stability that benefits renters and property managers, as well as creates generational wealth through homeownership.

We also recognize the risk of gentrification inherent in this vision. Over time, as we begin to increase the affordable housing supply and bring new development into our communities, we will create momentum for both residential and commercial developers to access the resources needed to invest additional capital into the neighborhoods we are working in. As our city improves, so will the desire of others to invest in it. We will encourage investment by experienced Black-led intermediaries who are responsive to community needs. We will invite investors who understand that market revitalization and resident engagement are keys to long term and shared prosperity. Combined with the focus on securing economic knowledge for residents, these strategies will curate positive investment and repel predatory speculation. In addition, we plan to also engage deeply in systems change and advocacy work such as reforming our zoning laws, to ensure that residents will ultimately reap the benefits of our collective labor.

Our strategies to accomplish this vision are multi-dimensional yet are all in service of unlocking homeownership opportunities. We will directly support Black residents who are, or are close to being, in a position to purchase homes within two to four years, as well as help stabilize the living situations of residents experiencing housing severe problems, to place them on a longer-term path to homeownership. To achieve this, we will:

- Increase the supply of affordable housing units through direct development and through catalyzing additional and complementary real estate development mindful to neighborhood plans

- Provide education and counseling to 1) those in the homebuying process and 2) those struggling with their current housing situations

- Provide direct financial assistance
- Engage in system change efforts through policy and advocacy initiatives to remove existing, and prevent additional, barriers to an equitable housing market (e.g., mitigate risk of gentrification, unlock access to additional public funding streams to support homeownership)

A Path Forward's Housing Theory of Change:

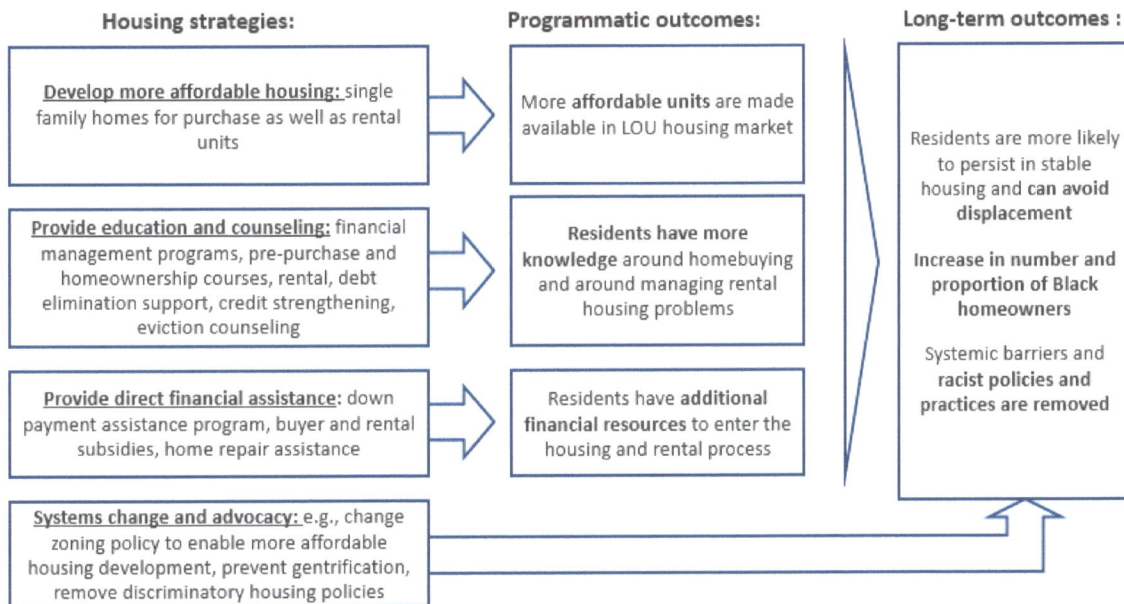

Housing strategies:	Programmatic outcomes:	Long-term outcomes :
Develop more affordable housing: single family homes for purchase as well as rental units	More **affordable units** are made available in LOU housing market	Residents are more likely to persist in stable housing and **can avoid displacement**
Provide education and counseling: financial management programs, pre-purchase and homeownership courses, rental, debt elimination support, credit strengthening, eviction counseling	**Residents have more knowledge** around homebuying and around managing rental housing problems	**Increase in number and proportion of Black homeowners**
Provide direct financial assistance: down payment assistance program, buyer and rental subsidies, home repair assistance	Residents have **additional financial resources** to enter the housing and rental process	Systemic barriers and **racist policies and practices are removed**
Systems change and advocacy: e.g., change zoning policy to enable more affordable housing development, prevent gentrification, remove discriminatory housing policies		

Increase the supply of affordable housing units by direct and catalyzed real estate development
The first component of our work is to promote stable, safe and affordable housing for residents who may not yet be qualified to own in the near term. Being in affordable and stable housing has been demonstrated to promote health and wellbeing outcomes for children.

For those households who aspire to homeownership, affordable rentals provide housing stability while enabling asset building, credit repair, and savings. In contrast, households spending 30% or more of their income on rent are less likely to prepare for homeownership.[21] This effort will be led REBOUND, a Black - led and operated, community-based development organization which has invested over $7.2 million into the community and developed close to 100 properties in West Louisville since 2020. *A Path Forward* will collaborate with 6 other major housing development organizations to create 2,000 affordable rental units in the next 5 years. Although LUL will focus on historically Black neighborhoods such as the city's West End, part of our goal is to normalize the inclusion of Black households in all neighborhoods and to destigmatize the term "renter."

The second key component of our initiative to increase affordable housing supply will be to directly facilitate homeownership opportunities for residents who are interested in owning. To achieve this, we will work to increase the supply of affordable single-family and multi-family homes available for purchase by acquiring and rehabbing vacant properties as well as by purchasing available lots for construction. The same coalition consisting of REBOUND and 6 other equity-motivated developers will work together to develop 1,000 properties intended for ownership. They will also prioritize the city's predominantly, and historically Black, neighborhoods such as the West End, as well as Smoketown,

---

[21] What it's Worth – Strengthening the Financial Future of Families Communities and the Nation (2015)

Shelby Park, and Newburg. Single-family affordable houses will be constructed for residents who are able to make a smaller initial investment, while multi-family units will be developed to help those with a larger initial budget accumulate wealth faster by potentially generating supplemental rental income from their property. REBOUND has been a local leader in this innovative development model.

<u>Provide education and counseling to 1) those in the homebuying process 2) those struggling with their current housing situation</u>

In addition to increasing the supply of affordable housing units, we will also provide educational and counseling services. Without counseling intervention, increased income is not an indicator that asset building or home ownership is easy to attain. The 2019 American Community Survey for Louisville showed that for Louisville households with an annual income between $50,001 and $60,000, 50.8% of Black households own their own homes compared to 68.3% of White households. This disparity is even more egregious at an annual income of $60,001 and $75,000 which shows Black household homeownership at a rate of 48.2% compared to the White household homeownership rate of 72.0%.

As such, aspiring Black homeowners will receive educational supports to guide them through the homebuying process via Louisville Urban League's Center for Housing and Financial Empowerment (CHFE). A key aspect of CHFE's work is to leverage public and private financial benefits for Black families while overcoming barriers to accessing banking and mortgage systems. CHFE's programs to date have been very effective, and their model has reliably worked to: 1) increase buyer success; 2) enable households to avoid foreclosure; 3) position homeowners for continued asset building, and 4) stabilize rental housing situations. Since 2016, CHFE supported the purchase of 338 homes with $44 million in affordable mortgages. CHFE counselors also rescued 226 homes from foreclosure, sustaining over $23.9 million in existing mortgage investment.

The services delivered as part of *A Path Forward* will include 1:1 advising sessions with trained counselors and access to HUD certified homeownership courses. Those struggling with their current housing situation, characterized by experiencing severe housing problems, will receive financial counseling and educational and case management support which include rental readiness services in the form of referrals to eviction legal assistance, public benefits assistance, financial management and budgeting education, credit repair, apartment referrals, and rental application support to either existing or newly developed affordable units. Our aim over the next 5 years will be to shift at least 2,500 residents who are experiencing severe housing problems into more stable housing situations, ultimately placing them on the long-term path to homeownership. We also aim to directly support 1,200 Black residents in becoming homeowners.

This opens a new channel of financial impact that will change neighborhoods by prioritizing resident ownership and generational wealth building. Additional ROI will come to the rental sector as stronger, more financially stable renting families avoid eviction and increase financial resilience. Within 10 years, outcomes and market shifts will become even more profound. This plan calls 17,000 persons to engage in financial skill building by 2023. CHFE anticipates that 20% of these people will want far more, working with counselors to budget, save, and create an action plan for housing stability. For 5,000 households, home purchase will be the ultimate goal. Reaching this goal will generate over $160 million in leveraged mortgages and will shatter old paradigms around appraisal gaps, stakeholder investment, and family legacy while confirming that Black buying power is an essential component of the regional housing market.

<u>Provide direct financial assistance</u>

Recognizing that some of the largest barriers to homeownership and stable housing are financial, and that a broken system has created massive income inequity in Louisville, our strategy will also include direct financial assistance to qualifying residents. For aspiring homeowners working with REBOUND, down payment assistance will be provided at the average amount of $25,000 per qualifying household. *A Path Forward* programming will also focus on supporting existing homeowners who are experiencing severe housing problems to stabilize their situation and ensure they are able to hold on to their properties. CHFE will lead these efforts and will provide foreclosure prevention counseling, refinancing supports, and access to publicly funded special project funding that frequently includes a counseling requirement.

Systems change and advocacy
We will work to advocate for policies that create conditions for an equitable housing market for Black residents. Our priorities include the following areas, though, we will continue to look for timely new opportunities as they arise.

- Land use policies and zoning reform, particularly as a tool used to promote segregation, and policies to prevent gentrification

- Property tax reform (e.g., moratoria for existing homeowners, increasing value of Homestead Exemption for older/disabled-headed household, renewing moratoria on tax lien sales, re-instituting the special vacant property tax to motivate occupancy)

- Rental reform (e.g., build out a landlord risk mitigation fund to encourage taking risks on tenants, Increasing the number of landlords who contribute to financial / payment histories to facilitate credit building, reform eviction practices by bolstering the Tenant Right to Counsel program)

- Explore with the local housing authority and other partners the potential of expanding the very successful Section 8 to Homeownership model to include higher-income households, thus encouraging income diversity in revitalizing neighborhoods.

- Identifying and exposing broader housing market inequities (e.g., undervalued appraisals in Black neighborhoods, predatory lending, steering that has led to over 50% of all Black homeowners living in just 22 of 198 census tracts, access to mortgages that prevent wealthier Black households from home ownership at rates enjoyed by White households, embedded credit score racial biases)

- Recalibrating financing ecosystems, including such issues as discriminatory appraisals and post-purchase predatory lending

- Encouraging funders, both private and public, to take a racial equity lens in making large capital grants on housing development

- Creating programs that redress the inequity stemming from the financial assistance that white households received while Black households were prevented by law and practice from purchasing homes

How we will measure and track our progress:
- We will work with development partners to track the number of units constructed across the city, as well as who rents or purchases them. A dashboard will be created and constantly updated by LUL, aggregating information across multiple housing developers.

- Additionally, LUL's CHFE and REBOUND will collaborate to aggregate data on educational services provided, which will center around outcomes on homeownership, and housing stabilization. Metrics that will be tracked and aggregated include:

o Housing stabilization: number and percent of residents who qualify as having severe housing problems, number and % of residents avoiding eviction, number and % of residents paying more than 30% of income on rent, number and % of residents who improve credit scores, average increase in savings/debt reduction/credit repair.

o Homeownership: number and percent of residents who go on to purchase a home after completing services, average down payment, debt/ equity over time, access to down payment assistance.

Housing stabilization	• number and percent of residents who qualify as having severe housing problems • number and % of residents avoiding eviction and foreclosure • number and % of residents paying more than 30% of income on rent • number and % of residents who improve credit scores • average increase in savings/debt reduction/credit repair.
Homeownership	• number and percent of residents who go on to purchase a home after completing services • average down payment upon purchasing • debt/ equity over time • access to down payment assistance.
Affordable housing development	Rental units: • number of rental units developed across partners • amount of debt service across each rental unit • monthly rent prices for each unit developed Single family units: • number of single-family units developed across partner • sale price for each single-family unit • demographics and income levels of purchaser • amount of down payment assistance leveraged

We will deploy these strategies over the near term to achieve our goals of developing an additional 3,000 affordable housing units and placing 1,500 residents in a stable living situation. Over the longer term, we envision significantly scaling these efforts by helping to unlock additional funds and shifting market forces in our favor.

Black Business: Building a strong Black businesses ecosystem

The Problem

Research shows that entrepreneurship is a key component of wealth building, particularly in the Black community. On average, Black business owners have 12 times more wealth than Black wage earners. However, in Louisville, historic disinvestment has significantly stalled broader community and economic development for Black neighborhoods. In the mid-20th century, commercial real estate development invaded the thriving West End neighborhood in a process known as "urban renewal", where city planners demolished existing buildings with the promise of spurring increased economic activity through new development. As a result of this redevelopment, the composition of the community drastically changed. Much was demolished, but almost nothing was rebuilt. Today much of the repurposed land is used as part of public housing projects, displacing the many Black businesses for which the city was once named "The Harlem of the South." Nearly 48% of Louisville households displaced by urban renewal were families of color, though they made up only 18 percent of the population at the time.[22] The result has had a lasting impact on the suppression of the city's Black economy.

Today, only 2.4% of employer businesses in Louisville are Black -owned, despite the city's population being 23.4% Black (a 10x gap between existing and equal business representation).[23] Due to inequities in earnings and wealth, Black businesses face persistent barriers to accessing capital as a result of discriminatory lender practices and policies. Further, many aspiring business owners rely on personal credit to launch businesses, but given the depressed Black homeownership rate, a main source of collateral is off the table for these entrepreneurs. In addition, Black business owners have not had access to the social or financial capital, coaching, and technical assistance critical to launching a sustainable business.

These inequities in Louisville have been exacerbated due to the Covid-19 pandemic during which minority-owned and small businesses were less able to navigate the cumbersome processes required to access emergency funds. National data suggests that during the pandemic, Black business owners were five times more likely to not receive any of the PPP funding they had requested, compared with White-owned businesses. Further, while 79 percent of White-owned firms received all of the PPP funding they sought, only 43 percent of Black-owned firms did[24]. As a result, nationally the number of Black businesses fell by 41% between February and April of 2020.[25]

Given these disparities, there is a clear opportunity for transformative change to the wealth and wellbeing of Black residents by strengthening the city's business ecosystem. Increasing the number of stable and successful Black owned businesses will not only help entrepreneurs and their employees generate wealth and income as individuals, but it will also inspire additional investment and improvement in Louisville by spurring needed and equity-centered commercial reinvestment and broadening the city's tax base.

Our Strategy

A Path Forward's vision is to close the racial representation gap in Louisville's business community and create a sustainable thriving economic market for Black business owners and their employees that ultimately enables them to build intergenerational wealth.

Particularly important to wealth generation are "employer businesses": businesses who have at least one employee[26]. While employer businesses only make up about 20% of locally registered businesses in Louisville, they comprise 98.2% of local business revenue. Our goal over the next 10 years will be to create and scale a robust business ecosystem in our city, which will focus on facilitating the creation, growth, and sustainability of employer Black owned businesses, while also supporting sole proprietors to earn above median income through their ventures. We envision that by 2032, the number of Black

---

[22]Gardner, Hayes, Achievement gaps show education is not a "great equalizer" in Louisville, Louisville Courier Journal (2020)

[23]Greater Louisville Project (2021);

[24] Washington Post – Racial bias affected Black -owned small businesses seeking pandemic relief (2021)

[25] Terry Ellis, Nicquel; Broaddus, Adrienne, Black leaders want targeted federal funds for Black business hi third by the pandemic (2021)

[26] Employee defined as full time, part time, as well as contractor

owned businesses in our city will be proportional to Louisville's Black population, with the resulting new tax base, increase in new jobs and new investments restoring economic revitalization.

In the nearer term, as we move towards our ultimate 10-year vision, we commit to developing a strong proof of concept for the effectiveness and scalability of our outlined strategies. We aim to create 520 stable and strong businesses in the next five years, which would more than double the number of Black owned employer businesses in Louisville.[27]

We will achieve our vision by building and scaling an ecosystem of supports to lift Black business owners in Louisville.

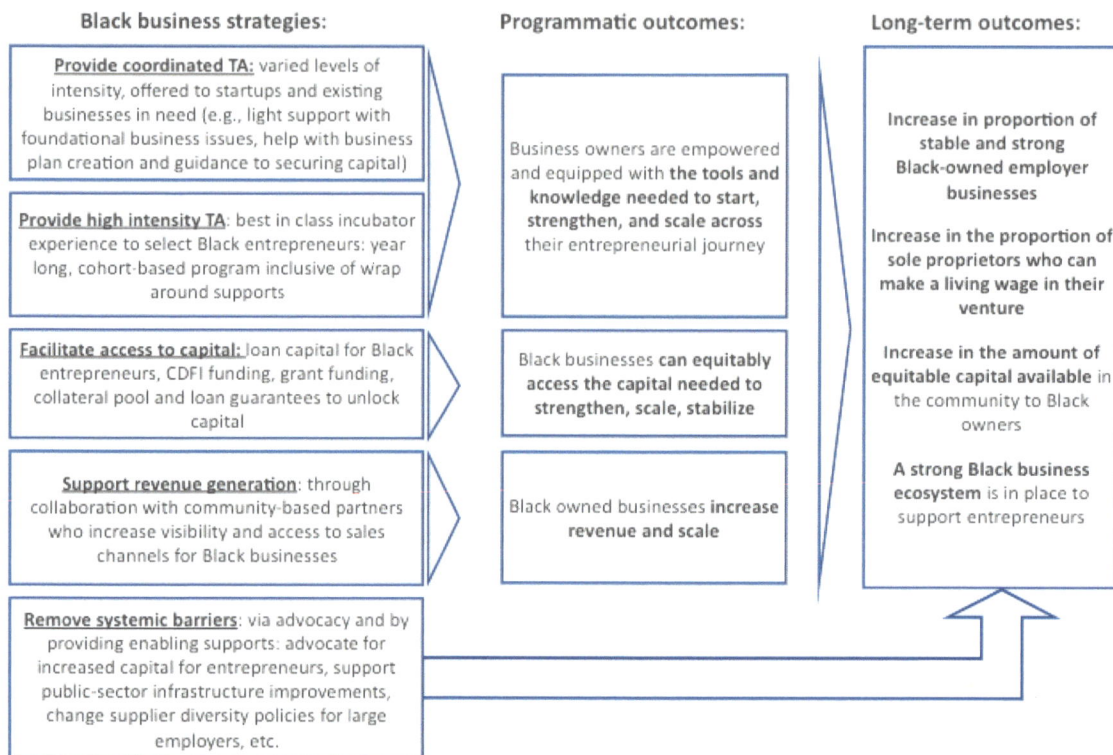

Black business strategies:

Provide coordinated TA: varied levels of intensity, offered to startups and existing businesses in need (e.g., light support with foundational business issues, help with business plan creation and guidance to securing capital)

Provide high intensity TA: best in class incubator experience to select Black entrepreneurs: year long, cohort-based program inclusive of wrap around supports

Facilitate access to capital: loan capital for Black entrepreneurs, CDFI funding, grant funding, collateral pool and loan guarantees to unlock capital

Support revenue generation: through collaboration with community-based partners who increase visibility and access to sales channels for Black businesses

Remove systemic barriers: via advocacy and by providing enabling supports: advocate for increased capital for entrepreneurs, support public-sector infrastructure improvements, change supplier diversity policies for large employers, etc.

Programmatic outcomes:

Business owners are empowered and equipped with **the tools and knowledge needed to start, strengthen, and scale across** their entrepreneurial journey

Black businesses **can equitably access the capital needed to strengthen, scale, stabilize**

Black owned businesses **increase revenue and scale**

Long-term outcomes:

Increase in proportion of stable and strong Black-owned employer businesses

Increase in the proportion of sole proprietors who can make a living wage in their venture

Increase in the amount of **equitable capital available** in the community to Black owners

A strong Black business ecosystem is in place to support entrepreneurs

We envision delivering and scaling these initiatives in a two phased approach over the next 10 years. Phase I will run over the next 5 years and center on developing a strong proof of concept for the effectiveness and scalability of the ecosystem model that we've already successfully piloted with existing funding. As described, we will demonstrate the impact of our multi-initiative, community-based model, by supporting the creation and/or stabilization of an additional 520 stable and successful Black owned businesses by 2027.

Phase II, running through years 6-10, will focus on stabilizing and scaling our model to ensure every Black-owned business and Black entrepreneur can thrive in our city on a level playing field. By the five-year mark, we will have built up a broader ecosystem of stakeholders and funding streams, (both public

---

[27] We define "stable and strong businesses" as those that remain in business for more than 12 months post receiving services, experience some level of revenue growth, and gain at least one employee defined here as full-time, part-time, as well as contracted support.

and private) that will support a significant scaling effort of our approach across the community. We envision crowding in TA providers, banks, government institutions, and private funders and investors alike. The success of our work will inspire others to come to the table. Our community-based model for change is outlined in deeper detail below:

<u>Providing Technical Assistance (TA)</u>
Coordinated technical assistance will be the driving engine and primary focus of our efforts alongside unlocking access to capital. These TA services will be provided across multiple anchor ecosystem partners, which aim to coordinate and complement each other to address the unique needs of entrepreneurs and businesses at different stages:

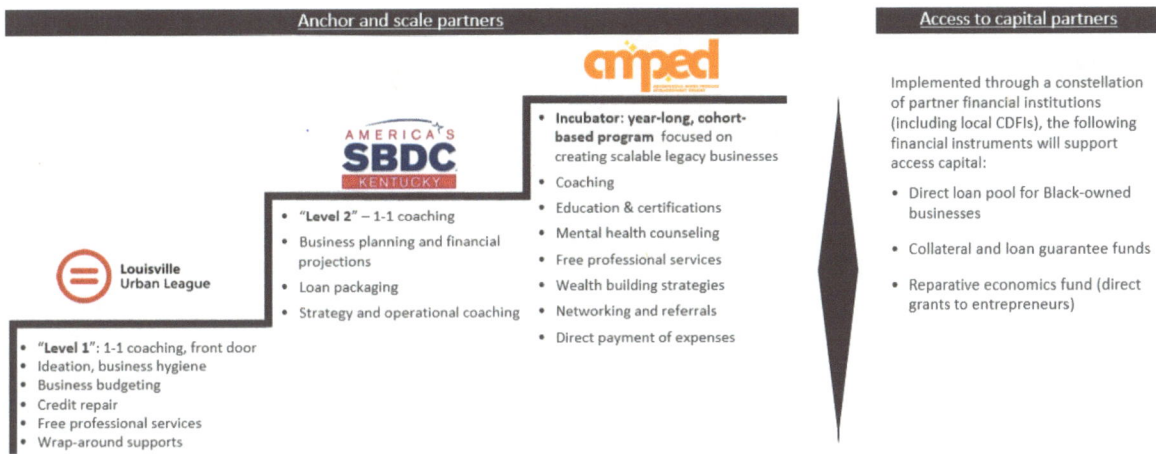

- "Level 1" support will be provided to entrepreneurs and business owners who require support with foundational business issues. Clients will include entrepreneurs who are looking to start-up, stabilize, and scale and are in an early stage of their venture. They will be connected to entry-level supports such as comprehensive 1:1 assessments and business coaching, business ideation, business hygiene assistance (e.g., registration, permits, etc.), development of initial budgets and capital needs, and credit repair. Where appropriate, entrepreneurs will also be connected with additional professional services (legal, accounting) at no cost to the participant. This suite of services can be thought of as the "front door" to the ecosystem for entrepreneurs. They will be provided through the Louisville Urban League Center for Entrepreneurship and our aim is to increase our capacity to serve at least 2,000 entrepreneurs and businesses over the next 5 years.

- "Level 2" supports focus on entrepreneurs and businesses who are more advanced in their journey and are looking for assistance with developing effective business plans as well as support with access to capital. Delivered by the Louisville Small Business Development Center, programming will include 1:1 technical assistance for aligning on strategy and translating that into fundable and effective plans. Entrepreneurs will also receive support with loan applications and developing pro-forma financial projections to better understand resource needs. Level 2 supports are envisioned to be directly complementary to Level 1 programs and we envision serving 1,500 businesses through 2027.

- The Russell Technology Business Incubator (RTBI) initiative aims to capitalize on Louisville's most promising entrepreneurs and business ideas by providing them with the intensive wrap-around supports necessary to ensure their success. The services delivered by RTBI include an intensive year-long, cohort-based program focused on creating scalable legacy businesses.

Across their participation, entrepreneurs receive in-depth business education, professional services at no cost, mental health counseling, support with wealth-building strategies, access to networking opportunities, referrals to other resources in the community, and direct payment of business expenses. We aim to serve 350 businesses over the next 5 years through this high touch, intensive intervention.

Facilitating access to capital

One of the principal barriers to Black business growth is the unequal access to start-up and growth capital that is linked to the systemic depression of the accumulation of assets in Black communities as a result of housing and development policies and discriminatory lending practices. *A Path Forward* plans to solve this by partnering with local community development financial institutions (CDFIs) and other lenders and capital providers in order to:

- Supplement and strengthen traditional lending capital: Our aim is to bring in additional loan capital into the ecosystem, which would be disbursed through multiple financial partners (e.g., CDFIs, banks, credit unions, etc.) across the community and packaged across a variety of credit products, structured for the needs of different businesses. We envision this funding will support at least an initial 500 businesses with low interest loan capital (for an average of $60k /business). This capital will stand distinct from grant dollars, will be amortized and ultimately put to work multiple times during the timeline of this work, providing significant leverage over the long term (e.g., as the loan fund is not comprised of grant money, businesses will largely repay these loans with minimal interest, which will then allow the capital to be redeployed into the community to support other Black owned businesses).

- Structure and implement enabling supports to facilitate greater access to capital: bringing funds that can help unlock access to traditional capital to Louisville's Black business ecosystem is paramount to overcoming the wealth gap and supporting business owners to access funding from traditional institutions. Many Black entrepreneurs lack the personal collateral needed to qualify for affordable credit. This forgivable capital, in the form of loan guarantees or collateral, will enable businesses to unlock traditional capital for their businesses at levels they would not have had access to previously as well as provide them with a safety net in the event of unforeseen circumstances.

- Raise concessionary capital that provides direct cash assistance to entrepreneurs: in order to support Black owned businesses scale and thrive, *A Path Forward* will also structure a fund to provide direct cash assistance to new, scaling, as well as struggling businesses in need of financial assistance. We are still in the process of piloting this approach, aligning on the criteria for eligibility and outlining an implementation plan.

- Innovate to create other flexible financial products: we plan to work closely with financial institutions within our community to structure products that feature terms and conditions which are responsive to a community who has been intentionally locked out of wealth creation opportunities

The plan for unlocking capital for Black business owners is to build on existing efforts in place in Louisville, simultaneously creating new products and enabling support, and facilitating more collaboration among financial institutions and philanthropists interested in serving Black entrepreneurs.

We have already begun to map out how to structure these funds and products with local partners, including: LHOME, LISC, Community Ventures Corporation, IFF, Park Community Credit Union, Community Foundation of Louisville, Fund Black Founders, and Liberty Bank.

Supporting revenue generation:

In addition to significantly scaling TA efforts and working to unlock capital, we will also leverage support of other partners in the community who are specifically focused on strategies to increase the visibility of and sales for Black-owned enterprises. Partner organizations will provide effective marketing and engagement strategies, sales channels, outlets that enable Black-owned businesses to increase their profiles and sell their goods and services. Potential partner entities for this work include organizations such as: Russell A Place of Promise, MELANnaire Marketplace, Buy Black Lou, and Louisville Independent Business Alliance. We will especially seek to partner with Black-led and Black-owned entities leading these efforts.

Removing systemic barriers:

We will focus on unlocking the potential of Black businesses by working to remove barriers at a systems level as well, leveraging the policy capacity that LUL is building to bolster the direct services strategies outlined above. Policy priorities for Black business include advocating for:

- Increased access to capital for Black entrepreneurs. Potential activities to engage in here include encouraging local financial institutions to increase lending and grant funding to Black entrepreneurs as well as working to increase the pool of public dollars available for entrepreneurs.

- Increased supplier diversity among corporate and government partners.

- The support and investment needed to create more Black-owned commercial and industrial real estate developments, particularly ones located in historically Black neighborhoods.

- Public sector infrastructure investments that can be beneficial to Black businesses, particularly those located in underserved neighborhoods (e.g., advocating for the creation/redevelopment of modern, commercially viable buildings, often including site acquisition, environmental remediation, and construction), improving lighting, repairing sidewalks, installing trash receptacles, improving public transportation access

How we will measure and track our progress

To understand how well we're doing and where there is room for improvement, we will track businesses served across a variety of success indicators, outlined in the table below. Each ecosystem partner will be responsible for collecting data for the entrepreneurs they provide services to, and LUL will support tracking and analyzing the data at the aggregate level to enable partners to evaluate progress and pivot in real time as needed.

Enabling stable businesses	<ul><li>% of new business start-ups served that become legally registered and incorporated</li><li>% of businesses served that expand beyond sole proprietorship (meaning add 1 or more new employee)</li><li>% increase in revenue among businesses served (at the end of client engagement)</li><li>Estimated % of entrepreneurs who feel confident about their business knowledge and ability to start/manage a successful enterprise as a result of programming</li><li>Perceived utility of TA services to businesses /entrepreneurs (e.g., customer satisfaction survey)</li></ul>

Unlocking access to capital	• Among those seeking capital, % of entrepreneurs that successfully secure capital (credit, equity, grants, etc.) and amount • % of entrepreneurs served who reach a "bankable" credit score of at least 590
Creating a strong business ecosystem	• # of culturally competent TA/ support providers in the community providing services to Black owned businesses • Total number of capital providers and corresponding overall amount of capital available to Black businesses • Amount of capital dedicated to supporting Black entrepreneurs among responding entities

LUL as a Backbone for *A Path Forward*

Our track record of success

For over 100 years, the Louisville Urban League has been a consistent voice for the city's Black community. In service of our vision to attain social and economic equality for African Americans and other marginalized communities, we have developed a set of core activities that uniquely position us to address structural racism through direct interventions and effective mobilization of key community stakeholders. Our work has enabled us to not only lead high-impact programs but also to build deep trust with residents and leaders in the West End region.

The pandemic introduced a new set of challenges and deepened long-term inequities. LUL's recent work and successes even in a pandemic demonstrate our ability to have deep impact on the Black community despite these unforeseen challenges:

- In 2021, LUL opened the state-of-the-art Norton Healthcare Sports & Learning Center in the West End of Louisville, where most of our clients reside. The 24-acre, $53 million-dollar campus, whose anchor use is indoor track and field, was built on top of what was once an uninhabitable brownfield in order to fill a void in the community and spur economic and community growth. As the developer, the League raised $43 million in 22 months for this project that was built in 18 months amid a pandemic and civil unrest. In just the inaugural indoor season, despite COVID restrictions, meets featured 9,000 athletes from more than 80 colleges, 20 foreign countries, 250 US cities and 27 US states. In addition to sporting events, the Center hosts concerts, banquets, and includes a mini-bowling alley, an interactive rock-climbing wall, and a multi-purpose space that is used for educational programming and a myriad of community events, like school board discussions, leadership training, fair housing training, mental health retreats, and walks supporting men's health and mothers' breast feeding.

- LUL has brought together key decision-makers, such as the school superintendent, the office of the Mayor, the Chamber, and the office of the Governor, to unite on policy issues affecting the Black community in Louisville in an unprecedented way. Recent policy work includes:

  - Successfully fighting to secure an executive order that enables retired teachers to return to the classroom and receive a salary while still receiving their retirement benefits. This allows for students to receive more individualized instruction from experienced teachers because of lower ratios in classrooms

  - Gathering and analyzing data on the impact of evictions on health and economic recovery to support advocacy for policy efforts such as eviction expungement, right to counsel, and just cause eviction policies

- In response to the devastation of COVID-19, LUL adjusted to support our community both by undertaking new activities, such as hosting vaccine clinics and advocating for clients during eviction court, as well as doing familiar activities at unprecedented levels, such as filling the gap for grocery shopping, rent payments, rides to the polls and much more. Examples of impact from our program delivery work include the following outcomes during the pandemic (years 2020-2021):

  - Facilitated 325 job placements, amounting to an estimated $11.1 million in new wages

  - Provided 1,837 individuals with legal services, amounting to an estimated $1.3 million saved by clients on legal / court fees

  - Assisted 1,500 people with mail-in ballots and registered 722 new voters

  - Supported 266 students and families to get access to $106,000 in earned scholarships

  - Connected 114 people with new homes, amounting to $17.8 million in new mortgages, and supported over 1,573 people in financial education and rental readiness programs

  - Conducted 6 weeks of in-person emergency assistance rental clinics to support individuals facing eviction and connect them to resources

Strong leadership has been essential to the success of LUL's historic and emerging work. To execute on our strategic plan, we have built a leadership team that brings diverse perspectives and areas of expertise. LUL's senior leadership team includes:

- Sadiqa Reynolds, Chief Executive Officer & Principal Advisor to *A Path Forward* brings a long track record of nationally recognized justice advocacy work to her role as strategic leader and executive manager of LUL. An attorney and former District Judge, Sadiqa Reynolds is the first woman to serve as President and CEO of the Louisville Urban League.

- Lyndon Pryor, Chief Engagement Officer & Principal Advisor to *A Path Forward*, manages communications for organization, helps guide the integration of services at LUL to maximize outcomes for clients, and interfaces regularly with community partners. Prior to LUL, Lyndon worked in higher education and led a nonprofit youth development organization targeting Black high school students.

- Rhonda M. Mitchell, Chief Operating Officer, brings over 10 years of operational experience in Kentucky-based nonprofits to her role in maintaining LUL's efficient and effective operational systems and processes, high service levels, and accountability across its core business functions.

- Chabela Sanchez Longoria, Chief Data & Compliance Officer, who oversees data management to ensure quality measurement and proof community impact, previously served as Director of Youth Development at the YMCA of Greater Louisville and has nearly 30 years of experience in Venezuela and Louisville.

- Anthony Leachman, CPA, Chief Financial Officer, plans, directs and coordinates LUL's financial activities. An expert in asset management, he facilitates the acquisition, general oversight and disposition of the agency's assets for the purpose of serving the mission and goals. He joined Louisville Urban League in 2017 after four years as Vice President of Finance/CFO of the Kentucky State Fair Board.

- Lisa Thompson, Chief Impact Officer, brings over 25 years of leadership experience in the nonprofit and housing sector to her role providing strategic leadership, management, and guidance on initiatives across issue areas and oversees workforce and financial empowerment expansion. She formerly served as Chief Strategy Officer of New Directions Housing Corporation, Kentucky's largest community development corporation.

- Christina Shadle, Senior Project Manager, joined LUL to assist in the development and completion of the $53 million dollar capital project—the Norton Healthcare Sports & Learning Center. Before arriving at the League, she designed and executed projects for a local research firm and worked for the local Chamber where she forged relationships between private sector companies and public sector resources.

- Nichole Leachman, Chief of LUL's Center for Housing and Financial Empowerment, holds numerous certifications, including HUD Certified Housing Counselor. Her leadership unites the talents of an 11-person team who together have over 85 years of financial services and training experience. Ms. Leachman has held similar positions at highly respected financial capacity building agencies, including The Housing Partnership, Inc. of Louisville and Indianapolis Neighborhood Housing Partnership.

- Kevin L. Dunlap is the Executive Director of REBOUND, Inc., a separate nonprofit housing development corporation created by the Louisville Urban League in 1993. He has previously served as Senior Deputy Director for Fannie Mae Kentucky Office, Relationship Manager for NeighborWorks America and Senior Housing Director for the Louisville Urban League. He is certified through the NeighborWorks Homeownership and Community Lending Program of Study, National Association of Home Builders HCCP program and certified through the National Development Council's Housing Development Finance Professional program.

Launching *A Path Forward*

In the wake of the unjust murders of Breonna Taylor and David McAtee, LUL launched *A Path Forward* in 2020 as a direct call to action[28] to address the blatant and long-standing lack of resources dedicated to economic and social justice for Black people in Louisville. Absent external resources and despite barriers presented by the pandemic, LUL uniquely mobilized more than 50 other Black leaders and Black-led nonprofits around a common set of goals for economic justice through an organic, self-organized process that leveraged LUL's existing connection to the community. When writing *A Path Forward*, LUL served as the primary strategic leader and convener to unite stakeholders around this common agenda.

For the past two years, LUL has continued to serve as the strategic leader of *A Path Forward*, working with community members to develop the core ideas, attracting initial funding to plan and build out the supporting strategies and beginning to build capacity to engage in policy and systems work. In addition, LUL has played an integral role in coordinating collective action amongst key partners and communicating with key stakeholders. As a trusted resource, advocate, and anchor in the Black Louisville community, LUL's role as a key mobilizer and convener naturally positions LUL to be the backbone organization of *A Path Forward*.

LUL's Plan as a Backbone Organization

As the backbone organization, LUL will continue to play a lead role supporting the collective goals of *A Path Forward*. Typically, a backbone organization supports a collective impact initiative via key functions that include policy and advocacy, technology, communications, stakeholder engagement, data monitoring and continuous improvement, funding, partner coordination – the infrastructure supports needed to ensure implementation success. LUL's vision for its role as backbone organization is to continue supporting partners to create measurable and demonstrable impact, serving as an example for other cities of how to move the needle on critical outcomes in the Black community.

---

[28] A Path Forward document

To live into its role as the backbone organization, LUL will build its own internal capacity. See below for a summary description of the five functions LUL will develop and see Table 2.a. in the appendix for a full description of key responsibilities:

- **Strategic oversight and program management**: Leads development and execution of the *A Path Forward*'s strategic plan across all issue areas and backbone functions

- **Fundraising:** Leads the *A Path Forward* funding model and executes on funding strategy through relationships with partners and funders

- **Data and evaluation**: Tracks data across outcomes and, in partnership with the Data Advisory Council (see below), supports continuous improvement of program delivery and public sharing of data, including a community data dashboard

- **Policy:** Manages and executes on policy agenda across core strategic pillars in order to address the underlying systems change needed to bolster the success of *A Path Forward's* programmatic strategies

- **Communications and engagement:** Develops and executes communications strategy with key stakeholders such as funders, programmatic partners, and community members

Through this planning process, LUL identified policy and data and evaluation as two areas that could benefit from near-term investment in order to progress on *A Path Forward* goals. To this end, LUL has already started to develop its policy and data and evaluation capacities, with the intention of building upon those capabilities further. Existing investment is detailed below:

- **Policy**: As an early investment into its policy work, LUL hired 4 new FTE to the policy team this year. Through this planning effort, our policy team identified that it will build on LUL's past successes and focus its efforts on three policy capabilities it feels best positioned to deliver impact: centering Black issues in the policy narrative, researching and developing policy solutions to those issues, and building strong partnerships and movements that can organize in order to see those solutions to fruition.

- **Data and evaluation**: Through this planning effort, LUL has crafted clear theories of change to guide this work, identifying the key metrics it will track for success. To support this work, LUL has contracted two data staff in order to analyze existing data and strategize data and evaluation for *A Path Forward.* In addition, LUL has been building out its Salesforce capabilities and data sharing agreements/ tools, including a pending data sharing agreement with Jefferson County Public Schools. Moving forward, LUL will coordinate partners around continuous improvement by supporting public data sharing through a community data dashboard and community-facing progress reports and lessons learned.

Stakeholder engagement

From its inception, *A Path Forward* was built on the concept of offering an open table in order to amplify the voices of the community. *A Path Forward's* founding priorities[29] were co-written with a grassroots community-driven approach alongside 50+ organizations that have developed deep expertise on the needs and desires of Black residents in Louisville based on their combined years of service to this community. LUL alone has nearly 25,000 visitors come to its doors every year for support and services. Through this planning process, LUL has continued to leverage the direct expertise of community needs and to engage community partners in determining the vision for impact and key strategies for this work moving forward.

---

[29] A Path Forward document

This collective track record of service and engagement with the community sets *A Path Forward* apart from other collective impact initiatives that might not have the same level of authentic, in-depth knowledge and relationships with the community it intends to serve. LUL and partners have committed to continuing to build upon this track record by living into the following guiding principles for stakeholder and community engagement.

- Center the voices and perspectives of Black residents in Louisville

- Lean into the expertise that comes from existing program delivery and community relationships

- Create an inclusive space and culture to receive input and feedback

- Aggregate and amplify input and perspectives from stakeholders

- Operate with candor and transparency

- Focus on, demonstrate, and be accountable for results and outcomes as informed by data

Data Advisory Council

Tactically, moving forward, LUL also sees accountability and transparency as central to their stakeholder engagement strategy. To this end, LUL will develop a Data Advisory Council (DAC) to ensure that data is being used to drive strategic decision-making, in addition to building its data capacity (see previous section, under "Backbone functions"). Through coordination between the DAC and the backbone, LUL plans to develop and manage a community data dashboard that shares key metrics with the community in order to track the efforts and outcomes of *A Path Forward* over time.

The DAC would have the following responsibilities:

- Review progress on agreed-upon indicators/targets on community dashboard and inform decision-making in partnership with the Urban League when key strategic shifts need to be made

- Hold partners accountable by tracking data against intended outcomes and setting expectations that partners follow-through on commitments to actions

- Support strong connections between the Urban League (backbone), programmatic partners, and other key stakeholders to ensure impactful coordination and efficiency

- Interact with backbone organization on strategy, community engagement, and shared measurement

- Provide input and advice on the community dashboard

Beyond the DAC, LUL will continue to engage with stakeholders through targeted conversations with community leaders, service providers, funders, and public leaders, as well through more informal conversations with community members. These conversations will range from garnering strategic alignment on specific issue areas to open forums for stakeholders and community members to share their priorities and feedback.

Financial costs and sustainability

In order to achieve the *A Path Forward* goals and tackle centuries of systematic racism that have led us to this point, this work will require significant funding (from multiple donors) and a few big bets. In recognition of what is required, we have collectively built and begun to implement a plan to address the critical needs of Louisville's Black community with the aspiration that this work can catalyze additional funding and partners while also providing a model both locally and nationally to other communities, program providers and governments on what it takes to meet these needs. These are systemic issues that will require systemic solutions and through our programmatic work and systems change advocacy, we aim to amplify the investments needed at the government and policy levels to achieve our goals.

In the near term, there is a critical role for philanthropy to play. Flexible philanthropic capital can help us scale quickly to meet the critical needs of our community *now* while continuing to demonstrate proof of concept, which we believe will unlock further resources and deepen public investments in this work. These resources will be an investment in creating significant impact in our communities that will reverberate for years to come.

The total all-in costs to execute the strategies described and to stand up the backbone are estimated to be roughly $1.1 billion over the first 5 years. Much of this cost will be driven by the development of affordable housing units, an indispensable part of our strategy. However, across our strategies, we expect to significantly leverage public and private funding at an estimated $796 million over 5 years. The net effect is **an overall investment need of ~$258 million over the next five years – which we believe can be seeded by philanthropic capital**.

The chart below shows the total costs for the work, funding and loans to be leveraged, and the **estimated gap** by category:

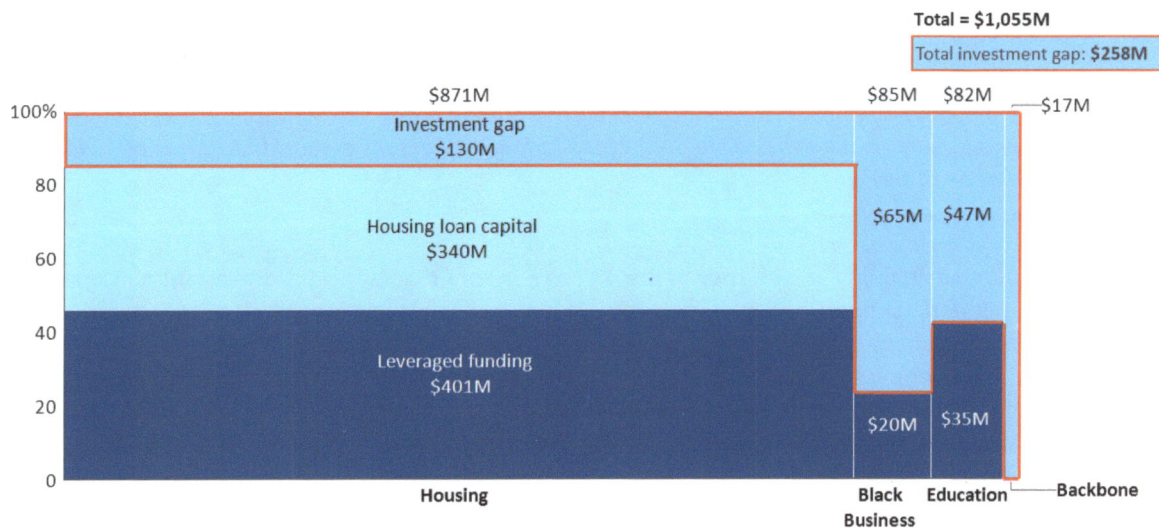

Additional details on costs and funding expected to be secured in the next five years can be found in **Appendix 1**, organized by each strategic pillar outlined above.

Here, we provide a high-level summary of costs and funding projections across the three pillars:

- **Increasing post-secondary education attainment**: The costs for the education strategy through 2027 are estimated to be $82 million. This estimate is inclusive of programming for academic tutoring and post-secondary programming, estimated to reach almost 8,000 students annually by 2027. We believe that we will be able to leverage $35 million mostly from federal ARP funding, existing private foundation grants and local funding from the JCPS school system. **The estimated 5-year funding gap in education is $47 million.**

- **Increasing homeownership and housing stability**: The costs for the housing strategy through 2027 are estimated to be $871 million, including programmatic initiatives around housing stabilization and the development of single family and rental units. We project the ability to leverage $741 million across public funding streams (e.g., federal home funds, Louisville affordable housing trust fund, low-income housing tax credits), revenue from single family sales, and loans from private lenders. This would leave us with a **5-year need for the housing and homeownership aspect of our strategy of $130 million.** We've also highlighted in the chart above an estimated $340 million of loan capital that our housing developers estimate is required for construction and which they intend to access through traditional financing products. However, we believe this could also be an innovative way for philanthropy to play a role in providing capital that could be more rapidly accessed at better rates than the market, which would have a significant impact in speeding up the implementation of this work.

- **Building a strong Black businesses ecosystem**: The costs for the Black business strategy through 2027 are estimated to be a **total of $85 million** split between this strategy's main initiatives: $41 million for providing TA to Black businesses and entrepreneurs and $44 million for unlocking access to capital for businesses. We believe that we will be able to leverage roughly $20M in public funding (e.g., ARP funding, SBA cash match program) and private donors, **leaving an estimated investment gap of $65 million**.

The costs for backbone support through 2027 are estimated to be **$16.6 million**. In total, these costs will support 15 FTE, facility infrastructure expansion in years 1 and 2 to provide space for all staff, recruitment and training costs for 8 newly hired staff, in-state travel, conferences, subscriptions to technology platforms, tools and publications, and general supplies and equipment. This will enable APF to support staff and personnel-related costs for its backbone functions: strategic oversight and program management, fundraising, data and evaluation, policy, and communications. Additionally, it includes the cost of facility occupancy and expansion in order to accommodate office space for our growing number of staff and programming needs as we scale our impact (*additional details on backbone costs by function can be found in Appendix 2*).

Sustainability

It is critical to the sustainability and efficacy of the *A Path Forward* that sufficient organizational capacity exists to scale this work. Supporting backbone costs is a key area where philanthropy will likely play a pivotal role in advancing the *A Path Forward* work as there are no public funding streams to cover these capacity costs. Yet we know that the backbone plays a critical role of coordinating stakeholders, spurring continuous improvement through outcomes measurement, systems-level policy work, and more. As such, LUL is making a significant investment in building the critical staffing needed to drive this effort.

To enable this, our team has already begun to shift the way we think about funding and sustainability and realize the importance of putting more emphasis on unrestricted capital and larger funding streams to advance our impact. We have already received some of these large unrestricted investments (e.g., $8 million from Blue Meridian Partners), and have further shown our ability to fundraise in the private sector even during challenging financial times (e.g., building the Norton Healthcare Sports & Learning Center).

As mentioned earlier, we believe this plan is an opportunity for private funders to make a big bet, as aligned to the size of the problems we seek to solve. We are looking to philanthropy to see their investments as a catalyst, to scale and grow the efforts that we have seeded to date. As we demonstrate proof of concept for this work in the next five years, we believe the impact of this work will create momentum that will attract additional funding and investors aligned with this ten-year vision for change in Louisville. None of what we do will be done without the input from the community and partners that are helping to advance Louisville in the right direction. As we progress, we will continue to share learnings within our community to bring others to the table, just as we did when we first came together to articulate what was needed for change. Philanthropists looking to invest in solutions with a clear ROI should look no further. We believe that an investment now to help accelerate the work of *A Path Forward* will have a multiplier effect for decades to come.

Variables, risks, and mitigation strategies

Resilience of partners and residents in face of a recession due to economic uncertainty. *A Path Forward's* strategic plan focuses on a community that faces multiple barriers as we have described in detail in this document and who are most impacted during times of economic downturn. We also recognize that many of the organizations that serve this community, including those we would partner with, are also often overtaxed and under-resourced and would be vulnerable should an economic recession occur. However, our ability to pivot through such economic crises, including during the most recent and ongoing COVID-19 pandemic, has given us the experience to navigate these situations. As articulated above, LUL was able to quickly shift during the pandemic to continue and provide new needed services to the community while continuing to meet our outcome targets. Through *A Path Forward*, we believe we will be better able to leverage our shared resources to help each other navigate challenging economic conditions through sharing lessons learned, providing joint TA and capacity building as needed, and collectively raising resources to support the work. In addition, should the needs of the community require it, through data-driven, collective decision-making, we plan to pivot as needed to ensure the community's priority needs are met.

Changes in policy and public funding landscape related to political and economic climate. Efforts to improve social and economic equality, such as federal tax credits and eviction protection, have seen increased bipartisan support in recent years, though they have also faced significant political setbacks. We recognize that the November 2022 election could either disrupt current legislative efforts and funding or accelerate *A Path Forward's* work and restore funding for families and renters. To mitigate this, Louisville Urban League has and will continue to invest in its policy and advocacy team, including four recent hires and two new planned hires. We are already building relationships with key partners and developing a policy strategy in order to anticipate and respond to any policy shifts, as well as proactively steering policy movements to support the availability of public resources. Our advocacy work will position *A Path Forward* to keep social and economic justice for Black people high on the agenda of government and legislative actors.

Changes in private funding streams related to housing development and philanthropic funders. *A Path Forward's* funding model anchors on our ability to mobilize key housing development funders around our plan to build units in areas that deeply need investment. Because the cost of developing houses is so high, we are relying on effectively securing development dollars and using philanthropy to fill the gap so that our tenants can affordably purchase and rent homes. To proactively influence the flow of housing development capital, we have developed relationships and shared our proof of concept with other developers. In order to mitigate the uncertainty of that funding, we have developed contingency plans in which we slow the pace of unit development per year and adjust our housing development targets accordingly. More broadly, given the uncertainty of private dollars, we plan to lean into the role that we have long occupied of prioritizing and load-balancing based on availability and flexibility of funding. Prioritization of which programs to scale across all issue areas will be driven by data on where there is greatest need and where our programs have the most evidence of impact.

Durability of changes in national narratives and norms with regards to racial equity. *A Path Forward's* path to durable policy and practice change requires complementary shifts in prevailing narratives and norms. The racial justice uprisings of 2020 created unprecedented momentum and public will to address injustice in our country. As a result, a window of opportunity for racial equity work opened, and we are aware of the risk that the window could constrict as time passes. Maintaining these narrative shifts relies on consistency and coordination across multiple actors. To mitigate these risks, APF will continue the in-depth work it has done since its inception over 100 years ago to mobilize partners and movements in order to change narratives about racial equity in Kentucky. We will continue to amplify the messaging of ourselves and our partners to help solidify and embed racial equity narratives within our community. Our plan incorporates several ways to build on this work, such as by building backbone capacity to continue to coordinate stakeholders around the Path, developing our website and social media presence, and investing in our policy and advocacy team to continue to create narrative change.

Pace and quality of operational execution, given the extent of organizational change and growth required. Implementing our plan requires significant investment in organizational capacity in order to execute and scale with quality. We recognize that effectively executing the strategies we have outlined will require increased operational capacity, which will be allocated with the Louisville Urban League as the backbone organization. As outlined in the plan, we collectively designed our backbone functions to fill the needs required to effectively manage and scale this work, identifying the most critical backbone programmatic roles to fill and developing a plan to fill these on an aggressive yet realistic timeline (Data and Evaluation Director, Policy Director, and Education Policy Lead to be recruited in the next six months). We have a strong leadership team and a supportive Board of Directors at the Louisville Urban League that are aligned on *A Path Forward's* strategic direction and ready to steer the organization through change, as well as a highly experienced and tenured staff, which will help ensure effective collaboration as we live into this plan.

Conclusion

A Path Forward outlines a blueprint for change that aims to radically shift the opportunity divide and create a Louisville that commits to ensuring that Black residents have the resources, tools, and financial and social capital to thrive in their own communities. That vision for Louisville is a community that embodies and promotes equity, justice and prosperity for all residents.

This effort is set apart by the caliber of the organizations and partners involved, including the Urban League who has been a consistent voice for the city's Black community for over 100 years. Through this planning process, LUL and partners have leveraged their direct expertise of community needs to determine the vision for impact and key strategies for this work moving forward. As a trusted convener, resource, advocate, and anchor in the community, LUL has organically emerged as the backbone organization of *A Path Forward's* work over the next decade.

Bringing *A Path Forward's* bold vision to life will require close coordination among a range of key stakeholders, including government, nonprofit advocacy and social service providers, and private funders and partners. We firmly believe the time to act is now. We have incredible momentum in and around the community, with key players energized to make a change. Philanthropy can play a critical role in seeding the catalytic part of this work helping us meet the critical needs of our community *now* while continuing to demonstrate proof of concept and unlock further and more sustainable investments to move this work forward.

Appendix 1: Financial costs and projections

1a. Additional financial context for *A Path Forward's* Strategies

Education: Increasing post-secondary education attainment

The chart below projects education programmatic costs, as well as reach, over the next 5 years:

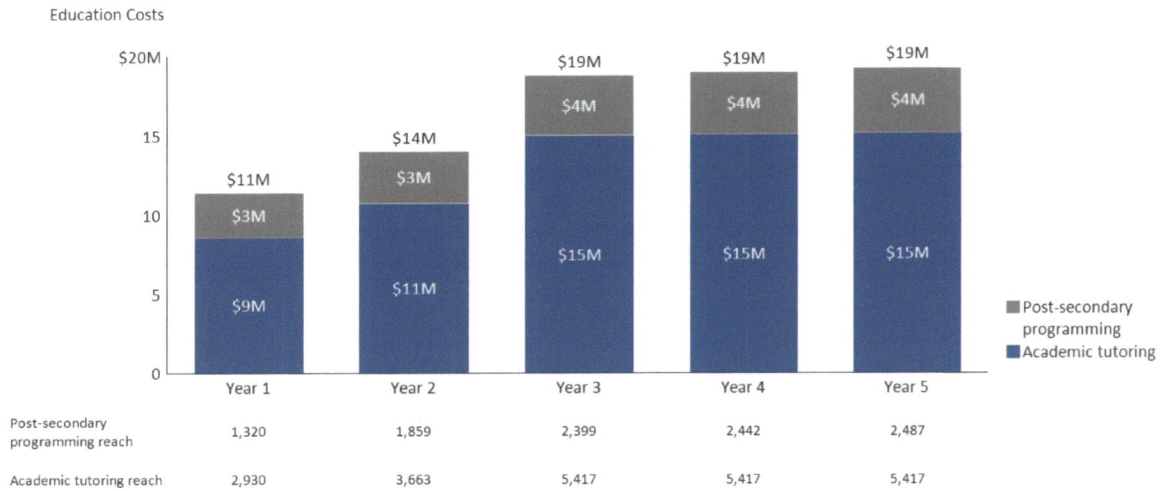

Education Costs

	Year 1	Year 2	Year 3	Year 4	Year 5
Total	$11M	$14M	$19M	$19M	$19M
Post-secondary programming	$3M	$3M	$4M	$4M	$4M
Academic tutoring	$9M	$11M	$15M	$15M	$15M
Post-secondary programming reach	1,320	1,859	2,399	2,442	2,487
Academic tutoring reach	2,930	3,663	5,417	5,417	5,417

Housing: Increasing homeownership and housing stability

The chart below projects the costs for the educational and counseling aspect of our programming (e.g., homebuying education and support with financial management and housing stabilization for renters experiencing housing problems). In the coming years, we aim to steadily increase the estimated number of residents who will purchase a home and find a stable rental situation due to CHFE services.

Estimated housing and homeownership education and counseling programming costs:

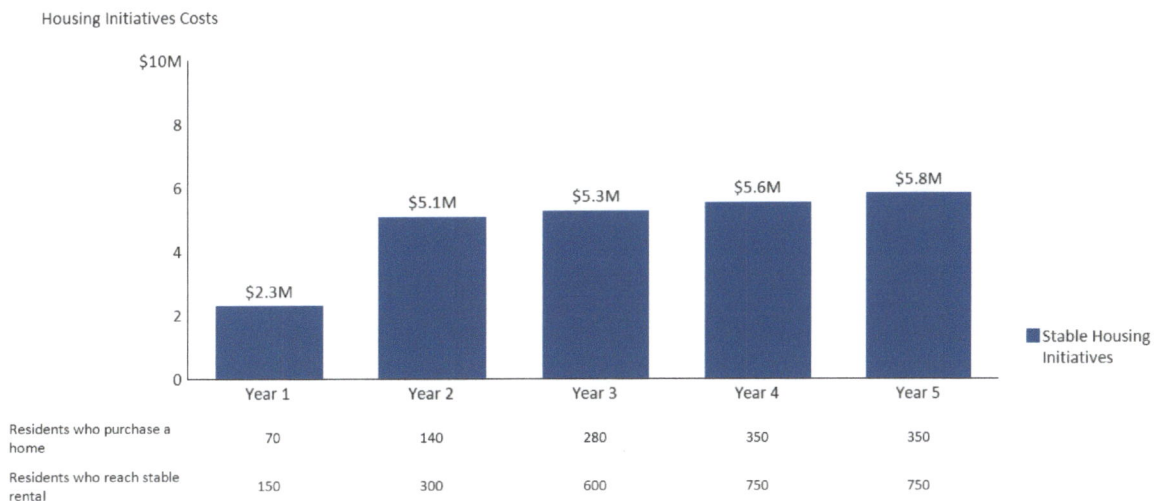

Housing Initiatives Costs

	Year 1	Year 2	Year 3	Year 4	Year 5
Stable Housing Initiatives	$2.3M	$5.1M	$5.3M	$5.6M	$5.8M
Residents who purchase a home	70	140	280	350	350
Residents who reach stable rental	150	300	600	750	750

Estimated housing Development Costs:
The chart below projects the costs associated with our efforts to increase the supply of affordable housing by developing single-family homes for sale and rental units over the next 5 years. The housing development strategy encompasses a total cost of $847 million for single family and rental housing units.

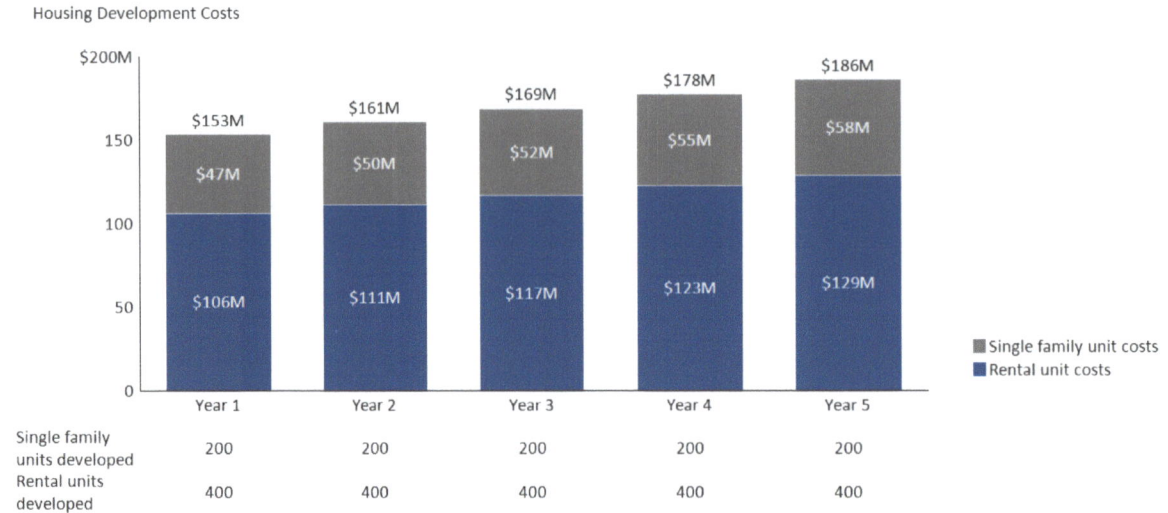

Housing Development Costs

	Year 1	Year 2	Year 3	Year 4	Year 5
Total	$153M	$161M	$169M	$178M	$186M
Single family unit costs	$47M	$50M	$52M	$55M	$58M
Rental unit costs	$106M	$111M	$117M	$123M	$129M
Single family units developed	200	200	200	200	200
Rental units developed	400	400	400	400	400

Additional context on leveraged funding for housing and homeownership initiative

For the development of single-family homes for purchase, it is our aspiration that we can continue to bring funding partners that will provide quick and flexible funding to cover these costs, while enabling us to move at the speed that the need requires. Since we expect to sell these properties at an affordable price of 40% of development costs, we will need to fill a 60% appraisal gap with both public and philanthropic dollars, to make this initiative worthwhile for housing developers. Based on the historical track record of our partners, we expect to finance 25% of single-family development costs through public dollars. This leaves 45% of development costs uncovered – a critical opportunity for high-leverage philanthropic investment totaling $12 million a year over 5 years or $60,000 per housing unit.

For our rental units, developers leverage public financing through tax credits and loans to cover building costs. At an estimated average development cost of $265,000 per rental unit, developers expect to finance 25% through public dollars and 65% through debt service (loans) to remain profitable and be incentivized to build. This leaves 10% of each rental unit's development costs uncovered, providing room for philanthropy to fill the gap of $10 million per year for 400 units and greatly leverage grant dollars.

Additionally, as we are looking to rapidly increase the scale of developing affordable rentals, we believe our mission driven developer partners will require additional incentives and support in order to scale production rapidly. Since they estimate 65% of their financing will come through private debt service, we envision an opportunity for philanthropy to correct the market and offer cheaper than market rate capital, to speed up production by unlocking affordable financing. In contrast to a grant, we envision philanthropy offering all or a portion of the $340 million in estimated debt service required to build 2000 rental units, at a more favorable interest rate than traditional financing.

Black Business: Building a strong Black businesses ecosystem

The chart below projects Black business programmatic costs, as well as business reach, over the next 5 years:

Black Business Costs

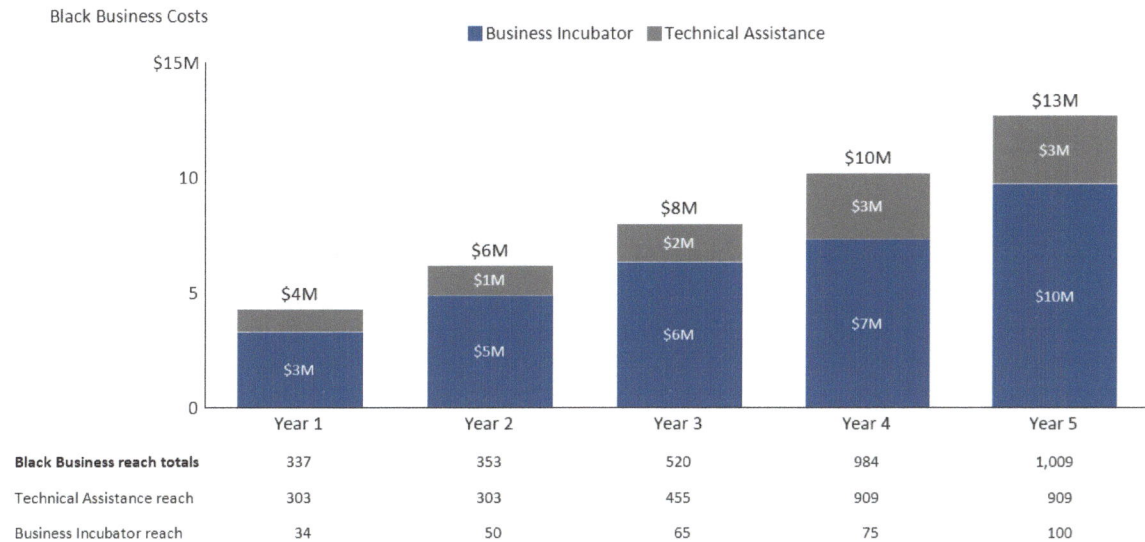

Black Business reach totals	337	353	520	984	1,009
Technical Assistance reach	303	303	455	909	909
Business Incubator reach	34	50	65	75	100

Our $85 million estimate is driven by investments in programming for a business incubator, and technical assistance for businesses/entrepreneurs. We see our first 5 years as our proof of concept, with years 6 through 10 as the years where we stabilize and scale the work. At the current moment, we have already raised the funding needed to pilot these business programs – with a combination of public and private dollars – and we see philanthropy playing the role in helping us develop our proof of concept.

Additionally, this initiative will also require $44 million over 5 years to increase access to capital for Black entrepreneurs who have historically been locked out of securing affordable funding for their ventures. This funding will be critical to provide businesses with the necessary capital needed to start, scale, and stabilize their ventures. Without being able to unlock access to capital our TA and other support services are akin to fixing but forgetting to add fuel. We envision the $44 million will support at least 500 businesses over 5 years. We estimate $4 million for administration expenses and $40 million in capital directly supporting Black entrepreneurs:

- Loan funding: Our aim is to bring an additional $30 million of loan capital into the ecosystem, which would be disbursed through multiple financial partners across the community and packaged across a variety of credit products, structured for the needs of different businesses. We envision this funding will support at least an initial 500 businesses with low interest loan capital (for an average of $60,000 per business). However, as businesses repay their loans, these funds will be re-deployed back into the Black business community, providing significant leverage to philanthropic investors.

- Enabling supports pool: $10 million over 5 years to provide qualifying entrepreneurs with access to cheaper capital and safer capital. These funds will be used as collateral to enable entrepreneurs to access cheaper capital as well as guarantees in case of default. This pool is extremely important, as in contrast to white and wealthier peers, many Black entrepreneurs lack the assets, credit scores, and wealth needed to access affordable capital to scale and sustain their ventures.

1b. Detailed cost estimates and program assumptions for each strategy

Education: Increasing post-secondary education attainment

Program	Total 5-year costs	Description of associated costs	Potential funding to leverage
OST programming and intensive academic tutoring (LUL and Evolve502)	$64.6M	• Average annual cost for **OST partner programming is ~$550 per student** (based on year 1 total of $649k for 1,180 students) • Average annual cost for **intensive academic tutoring is ~$5,400 per student** (based on year 1 total of $7.1M for 1,300 students) • Average annual cost for **ACT tutoring is ~$1,000 per student** (based on year 1 total of $450k for 450 students) • Navigator support: average costs estimated to be ~$63k per navigator (including fringe) • **Cost categories for OST programming:** Curriculum materials, tutor pay, overhead and stipends to OST partners • **Cost categories for intensive academic tutoring:** Contractual fees, overhead, travel, and barrier removal costs • **Cost categories for ACT tutoring:** Contractual fees, and overhead	• We assume we will leverage an **average of $6.9M per year** for the first 5 years (from both private and public sources – including ARP funding, foundation funding, JCPS funding and National Urban League funds)

Program	Total 5-year costs	Description of associated costs	Potential funding to leverage
Post-secondary programming (LUL and Evolve502)	$17.9M	• Average annual cost for **post-secondary college access programming (LUL's Project Ready) is ~$3,300 per student** (based on year 1 total of $395k for 120 students) • Average annual cost for **post-secondary college access programming (for Evolve502) is ~$3,100 per student** (based on year 1 total of $2.1M for 700 students) • Average annual cost for **post-secondary college retention programming (for Evolve502) is ~$558 per student** (based on year 1 total of $280k for 500 students) • **Cost categories for post-secondary access (Project Ready):** Personnel, equipment/supplies, travel and LUL indirect costs • **Cost categories for post-secondary access (Evolve502):** coordinator costs, student scholarships, program related expenses • **Cost categories for post-secondary access (Evolve502):** navigator costs, overhead, marketing, event planning	• We assume we will **leverage an average of $39k per year** for the first 5 years (from public sources – including National Urban League funds)
Total	$82.5M		

41

Housing: Increasing homeownership and housing stability

Housing activity	Total 5-year costs	Description of associated costs	Potential funding to leverage
Stable Housing Initiatives (LUL - CHFE)	$24M	• CHFE anticipates ~3,400 residents enrolling in programming over the next 5 years • Average annual cost for **all clients who enroll in the CHFE program is ~$7,100** (average cost is higher in the first couple years due to team expansion) • **Cost categories:** programming costs, overhead costs, counseling partnerships, marketing, stipends/savings incentives, travel, and training	• We assume we will **leverage an average of $959k per year** for the first 5 years (from both private and public sources – including Kentucky Housing Corporation, Louisville Metro Govt, and Fifth Third Bank)
Housing Development (REBOUND and partner developers)	$847M	• Average cost per rental unit estimated to be $265k (based on 400 rental units in year 1, total cost projected to be $106M) • Average cost per single family unit estimated to be $225k (based on 200 single family units in year 1, total cost projected to be $45M) • **Cost categories:** development costs for units, developer fees	• We assume we will **leverage an average of $60M per year in public funding** for the first 5 years (e.g., Louisville Housing Fund and housing incentives) and **leverage an average of $88M per year in private funding** (e.g., single family home sales and loans from lenders)
Total	**$871M**		

42

Black Business: Building a strong Black businesses ecosystem

Program	Total 5-year costs	Description of associated costs	Potential funding to leverage
Business Incubator (RTBI)	$31.4M	• RTBI estimates reaching a total of 324 businesses across 5 years • **Average annual cost of ~$97k per business** (based on RTBI budget of $3.3M serving 34 businesses in 2023) • **Cost categories include:** Staffing, professional service contracts, seed capital, business barrier removal funds, administrative costs (training, marketing, etc.), and AMPED indirect costs.	• We assume we will **leverage an average of $2.7M per year** for the first 5 years (from both private and public sources)
Technical Assistance (LUL)	$8.5M	• LUL estimates reaching a total of 2,280 businesses per year (35% of business referred to SBDC) • **Average annual cost of ~$4k per business** (based on LUL budget of ~$900k serving 240 business in 2023) • **Cost categories include:** Staffing, professional service contracts, business barrier removal funds, administrative costs (training, marketing, etc.), contracts with partner orgs, and LUL indirect costs.	• We assume we will **leverage an average of $960k per year** for the first 5 years (from both private and public sources)
Technical Assistance (SBDC)	$1.4M	• SBDC estimates reaching a total of 1,397 businesses per year (35% of business referred from LUL) • **Average annual cost of ~$1k per business** • **Cost categories include:** Staffing, travel, supplies/equipment/tech, subscriptions & licenses, and professional development fees	• We assume we will **leverage an average of $350k per year** for the first 5 years (from both private and public sources – including SBA cash match program)
Capital providers / financial institutions	$44M	• APF estimates that $40M of access to capital funds will be direct funding to businesses (Loan funding of $30M and $10M for an enabling support pool) • $4M of total costs will be for administrative expenses over 5 years • **Average loan per business is estimated at $60k (to support 500 stable businesses)**	
Total	**$85.3M**		

43

Appendix 2: Backbone functions

Table 2a. Backbone functions and descriptions

Function	5-year cost	Description of key responsibilities	Cost inputs
Strategic oversight and program management	$2.26M	<ul><li>Leads development and execution of strategic plans</li><li>Oversees and manages staff across all backbone functions</li><li>Coordinates efforts across issue areas (Black-owned business, housing, education)</li><li>Identifies key partners and engages key stakeholders on executing programmatic strategies, securing resources, and assessing goals</li><li>Serves as a vocal champion of the *A Path Forward's* goals and work to funders, community members, program partners, and other key stakeholders</li><li>Serves as liaison between Data Advisory Council and programmatic staff</li></ul>	Positions allocated at 15% of annual salary:<ul><li>LUL Chief Executive Officer</li><li>LUL Chief Operating Officer</li><li>LUL Chief Financial Officer</li><li>LUL Human Resources Manager</li><li>LUL Human Resources Generalist</li><li>LUL Accounting Department Staff (7)</li></ul>Positions allocated at 100% of annual salary:<ul><li>Director of Programs & Strategy</li><li>Project Manager</li></ul>Additional costs:<ul><li>In-state travel and conferences</li></ul>
Fundraising	$0.94M	<ul><li>Refines *A Path Forward's* funding model and executes on funding strategy with partner organizations</li><li>Cultivates and manages relationships with major funders and key public/ private partnerships</li><li>Identifies and taps into new funding opportunities</li><li>Serves as a fiscal agent, helping direct funding to partners as needed</li></ul>	Positions allocated at 15% of the annual salary:<ul><li>LUL Chief Development Officer</li></ul>Positions allocated at 100% of annual salary:<ul><li>Development Manager</li><li>Development Grant Manager</li></ul>

44

Function	5-year cost	Description of key responsibilities	Cost inputs

Data and evaluation	$1.69M	• Provides technical expertise for partners on collecting and tracking data, including data sharing agreements and data collection tools/ processes/ platforms
		• In partnership with the Data Advisory Council, supports a strong feedback loop amongst *A Path Forward* partners, helping to track, elevate, and make sense of key data points on defined metrics
		• Supports public sharing of data, including a community dashboard, progress reports, and lessons learned
			• Positions allocated at 100% of annual salary:
			  ○ Data & Evaluation Director
			  ○ Systems Administrator
			  ○ Data Analyst
			• Additional costs:
			  ○ Salesforce subscription
			  ○ Blackbaud subscription

Policy	$2.91M	• Manages and iterates on policy agenda across core strategic pillars
		• Oversees and manages staff across three key policy capabilities: coalition building, narrative change, and policy development
		• Builds and manages relationships with key policy partners in the local ecosystem, including policy makers
		• Helps *A Path Forward* to capitalize on state and federal policy opportunities that would advance local goals
			• Positions allocated at 100% annual salary:
			  ○ Policy Director
			  ○ Education Policy Lead
			  ○ Black Business Policy Lead
			  ○ Housing Policy Lead
			• Policy Associate
			• Policy/Communication Administrator
			• Additional costs:
			  ○ Training
			  ○ In-state travel
			  ○ Subscriptions to reports and publications
			  ○ Conferences and events

45

Function	5-year cost	Description of key responsibilities	Cost inputs
Communications and engagement	$0.69M	• Develops communications strategy with key stakeholders such as funders, programmatic partners, and community members • Ensures community members are integrated into strategic thinking and goal setting, designing forums for cross-sector convenings as appropriate to ensure community buy-in and expertise is prioritized • Plans and holds targeted community engagement activities, forums, and events for relationship building and mobilization	Position allocated at 15% of annual salary: • LUL Chief Engagement Officer Position allocated at 100% of annual salary: • Communications Manager Additional costs: • Community gatherings • APF website / digital media costs • Marketing
Support services, occupancy and HR costs	$3.5M	• Provide supports to enable personnel functions	• Support services admin costs • Occupancy costs • Supplies, equipment, and technology • Recruitment fees • Onboarding
Facility costs	$4.5M	• Facility expansion to provide office space for all employees as well as space for programming and confidential meetings with clients • Upkeep of existing space	• Costs of additional office space needed • Capital improvement costs
Total	$16.55M		

The chart below projects backbone costs over the next 5 years, broken out by cost category:

Backbone Costs

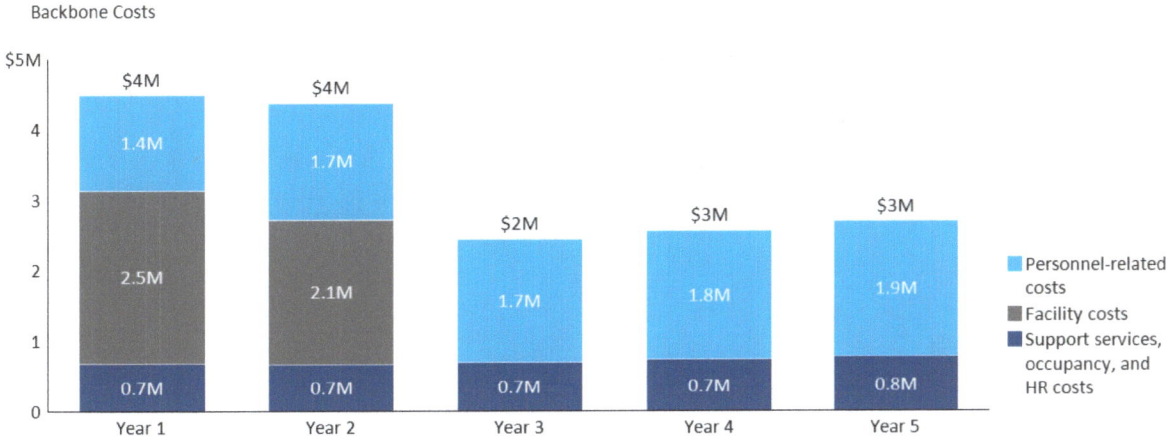

Legend:
- Personnel-related costs
- Facility costs
- Support services, occupancy, and HR costs